Companions in Wonder

Companions in Wonder

Children and Adults Exploring Nature Together

edited by Julie Dunlap and Stephen R. Kellert

To Ali —
With many thanks for
your vital help with this
volume.
Best wishes,
Julie D[...]

The MIT Press
Cambridge, Massachusetts
London, England

MIT Press books may be purchased at special quantity discounts for business or sales promotional use. For information, please email special_sales@mitpress.mit.edu or write to Special Sales Department, The MIT Press, 55 Hayward Street, Cambridge, MA 02142.

This book was set in Sabon using InDesign by Asco Typesetters. Printed and bound in the United States of America.

Library of Congress Cataloging-in-Publication Data

Companions in wonder : children and adults exploring nature together / edited by Julie Dunlap and Stephen R. Kellert.
    p. cm.
Includes bibliographical references.
ISBN 978-0-262-51690-7 (pbk. : alk. paper)
1. Environmentalism. 2. Philosophy of nature. 3. Parent and child. I. Dunlap, Julie. II. Kellert, Stephen R.
GE195.C657 2012
508—dc23   2011026384

10 9 8 7 6 5 4 3 2 1

For my parents, who opened the doors, and their grandchildren
—Julie Dunlap

For my children, their children's children, and the generations to come
—Stephen R. Kellert

Contents

father & son—
just there
the Pleiades

—Tim Singleton, 2005

Preface

This anthology celebrates an unexpected kind of nature writing—one that focuses on the relationships between people across generations as well as between people and the natural world. Only in recent years have writers begun to reflect at length on how adults and children experience the outdoors together. Since before Henry David Thoreau repaired to Walden Pond, writers have sought solitude outdoors to escape from the ills of contemporary society and to rediscover fundamental realities found only in wilder realms. Adults wander through Thoreau's woods primarily as object lessons; children appear not at all. John Muir, Henry Beston, Aldo Leopold, and others in the early twentieth century followed in Thoreau's individualist tradition, but in 1956, Rachel Carson published an essay about experiencing the seashore with her young nephew. Carson's "Help Your Child to Wonder" established the rich literary possibilities of exploring beaches, seashells, and the night sky with a small boy. This volume is the first to collect outstanding examples of this growing and increasingly significant literary genre.

Inspired by Carson's clear-eyed vision and the rich traditions of American environmental writing, our anthology explores the diverse and sometimes disparate ways that one generation shares the earth with another. In the first compilation to focus on this vast subject, we have included many distinct voices from wide-ranging geographic, ethnic, and cultural backgrounds—established and emerging authors who speak of experiencing mountains, gardens, rivers, or a handful of stones with children or in their own childhoods. They write as parents, grandparents, uncles, friends, teachers, and former children, sometimes passing back and forth in time to reflect on both the mutable and the timeless aspects of growing up. The nature they encounter is defined expansively, including wild places little touched by humans, places like wooded edges around farmland with limited or recovering human impacts or parks, backyards, and

other places essentially crafted by people for their own use and sometimes degraded by human activity. Some of the voices belong to recognized masters, such as Barry Lopez or Alison Hawthorne Deming, while
Danyelle O'Hara and Gretel Van Wieren and others are in early stages of
their writing careers. Each of the pieces was selected by the editors for its
considered reflections on adult-child relationships outdoors, its unique
perspective, and its literary qualities. These fine writers consider many of
the essential issues that face caregivers of children every day in a way that
we believe is satisfying and stimulating for further exploration, both
physical and literary.

The volume's appearance is opportune, we believe, in light of growing
awareness that outdoor experiences are not luxuries but necessities for
children. This change in attitudes is rightly credited to Richard Louv's
2005 best-selling book, *Last Child in the Woods: Saving Our Children
from Nature-Deficit Disorder.*[1] Today's parents and grandparents feel
acutely the radical shift that Louv identifies in childhood—away from
tree houses and firefly-catching and toward computer games and Twitter. Claiming that indoor childhoods are risking physical, psychological,
cognitive, and spiritual damage, Louv notes that "A widening circle of
researchers believes" that children's declining exposure to nature "has
enormous implications for human health and child development."[2] Studies showing that most conservationists spent their youths outdoors further bolster his case. For Louv, "The health of the earth is at stake as
well."[3] *Last Child in the Woods* has moved families, teachers, community
groups, nonprofit organizations, and local, state, and national governments to seek reconnection between children and green places. Individuals, groups, and agencies once thought to stand on opposing sides of every
issue are joining together to work toward a common goal of getting kids
outside. Efforts to close what Louv calls "the increasing divide between
the young and the natural world" are personal and political, multi-
cultural and international, but most of all urgent.[4]

The movement may have a harmonious exterior, but it conceals a cultural revolution. Soldiers in the struggle include lawyers fighting for children's rights to climb trees and urban planners battling for walking paths
to schools, parks, and jobs. Educators, entrepreneurs, politicians, and
physicians have been called to deploy their expertise. But the most
emphatic troops seem to be parents, grandparents, and other close caregivers of children. In September 2009, over three hundred U.S. organizations and businesses cosponsored the annual Take a Child Outside Week.
The U.S. Fish and Wildlife Service's Let's Go Outside initiative welcomes

families throughout the year to national wildlife refuges for canoeing, bird walks, fishing derbies, and other kid-friendly activities. The National Wildlife Federation's Be Out There campaign organizes an annual backyard family campout, promotes a daily home Green Hour, and hosts a Green Hour Web page subtitled "The parents' place for nature, play, & learning." The ever-expanding shelf of parenting advice books now includes *The Green Hour: A Daily Dose of Nature for Happier, Healthier, Smarter Kids* and *I Love Dirt!: 52 Activities to Help You and Your Kids Discover the Wonders of Nature*. Web sites, Facebook pages, and blogs offer safety tips, maps to neighborhood playgrounds, local park activity calendars, and inspirational quotes for families introducing their youngest members to the outdoor environment.

At the epicenter of the movement, the Children & Nature Network's Web site hosts a lengthening list of family nature clubs, with enticing names like Wildthings, Family Forest Explorers, Kids Unplugged, Caterpillar Club, and Nature Nuts. A downloadable toolkit helps more groups get started. This do-it-yourself, parent-led approach excites movement leaders who strive for rapid and significant cultural change, unhampered by funding shortages or the glacial pace of community redesign. "You don't have to wait for a 'green play' prescription from your doctor," says Cheryl Charles, president of the Children & Nature Network. "You can start today with family and friends by opening the door to go outside to explore the wealth of natural adventures right in your own backyard, neighborhood and community."[5]

Solid data back the value of nature experiences for children throughout their development, and pioneering research and theory in the field are presented in a complementary volume, Peter Kahn and Stephen Kellert's *Children and Nature: Psychological, Sociocultural, and Evolutionary Investigations*.[6] But few studies have yet to examine how, when, and where parents and other adults can help make child-nature connections. This complex, diverse, and dynamic topic will take decades to investigate in a methodical way. Given the pace of the movement and the urgency of the need, it seems vital to present alternative sources of insight into intergenerational environmental relationships.

One fertile source is environmental literature, beginning with the writings of Rachel Carson. Long before Louv, Carson called on people who love and care for children to lead, lure, or carry them to the woods and shores. "A child's world is fresh and new and beautiful," Carson wrote in 1956, "full of wonder and excitement."[7] Daily, intimate, sensory experience is essential to keep that wonder bright for a lifetime, Carson asserted, and the early companionship of a responsive adult is the best way to make it happen. "By suggestion and example," she told parents, "I believe children can be helped to hear the many voices about them. Take time to listen and talk about the voices of the earth and what they mean—the majestic voice of thunder, the winds, the sound of surf or flowing streams."[8] Carson's classic essay is the wellspring of the child-nature movement and the fundamental inspiration for this anthology.

This single work does not attempt to be comprehensive. The introduction discusses major themes in Carson's seminal "sense of wonder" writings as they relate to the selected essays and briefly summarizes recent research to place the selections in an empirical context. The research discussed, like the essays, focuses primarily on observations in the United States in the belief that an international approach would raise cultural, geographic, religious, and linguistic issues deserving future anthologies of their own. This volume does not include poetry selections or, despite the legacy of solitary contemplation in nature writing, memoirs of youths enjoyed outdoors alone. Both of these subjects offer deep wells of insight into children's relationships with nature but are beyond our present scope. Likewise, other volumes will need to consider adults' explorations with classrooms, clubs, troops, or other organized groups of children, for this one emphasizes intimate experiences with individual or small numbers of young people. As a first literary foray into the complexity of adult-child nature interactions, we felt that limiting our breadth would enhance the volume's clarity and usefulness to parents, caregivers, teachers, and others.

Our hope for these essays is that they yield action as much as inspiration. If these literary lessons are earnestly applied, no small part of that practical value will be a strengthening and healing of adults' relationships with the nonhuman world. Rachel Carson held that the muddy knees we earn exploring with children bring not only reflected joy from a young companion but rebirth of our own wonder and awe. Outdoors together, you and a child can share the palpability of tracks in the sand—the mystery of who made them and why the creature has gone away. In that regenerating circle of responsiveness lie answers to many of the environmental crises we now confront.

The philosopher Kathleen Dean Moore sees Carson's sense of wonder as a moral virtue that compels us to honor and celebrate the earth. As Moore asserts, "The same impulse that says, this is wonderful, is the impulse that says, this must continue."[9] Even as a walk in the woods can be an antidote for a child's nature deficit disorder, sharing that walk between generations is a prescription against deforestation, dwindling bio-diversity, climate change, and other ills afflicting our planet. It is not yet moribund, despite an escalating barrage of alarms, and Carson would have shared our yearning for a vibrant recovery. Leading a child to nature seems an elemental step. Rachel Carson wrote, "Wonder and humility are wholesome emotions, and they do not exist side by side with a lust for destruction."[10] As these essays convey, each in a surprising and singular way, by cultivating a child's wonder, you are cultivating a future of hope.

Notes

1. Richard Louv, *Last Child in the Woods: Saving Our Children from Nature-Deficit Disorder* (Chapel Hill, NC: Algonquin Books, 2008).

2. Ibid., 43.

3. Ibid., 3.

4. Ibid., 2.

5. Cheryl Charles, Richard Louv, Amy Pertschuk, Avery Cleary, and Sara St. Antoine, *Nature Clubs for Families Tool Kit: Do It Yourself! Do It Now!* (Santa Fe: Children & Nature Network, 2009), 4.

6. Peter H. Kahn Jr. and Stephen R. Kellert, eds., *Children and Nature: Psychological, Sociocultural, and Evolutionary Investigations* (Cambridge: MIT Press, 2002).

7. Rachel Carson, *The Sense of Wonder* (New York: HarperCollins, 1998), 54.

8. Ibid., 84.

9. Kathleen Dean Moore, "The Truth of the Barnacles: Rachel Carson and the Moral Significance of Wonder," in Lisa Sideris and Kathleen Dean Moore, eds., *Rachel Carson: Legacy and Challenge* (Albany: State University of New York Press, 2008), 275.

10. Rachel Carson, "Design for Nature Writing," in Linda Lear, ed., *Lost Woods: The Discovered Writings of Rachel Carson* (Boston: Beacon Press, 1998), 98.

Motheroot

Creation often
needs two hearts
one to root
and one to flower
One to sustain
in time of drought
and hold fast
against winds of pain
the fragile bloom
that in the glory
of its hour
affirms a heart
unsung, unseen.

—Marilou Awiakta, *Selu* (1993)

Acknowledgments

Like many walks in the woods, this book has been enriched by sharing the path with others. To everyone who has made the collection possible, we express our sincere and enduring appreciation.

The anthology would not exist without the generosity of writers and publishers who gave permission to publish or reprint their works. Two contributors deserve special thanks for their long support of the project: Rick Van Noy offered vital advice for shaping the original proposal, and Susan Cohen gave invaluable encouragement, ideas, and practical guidance through the complex process of permission collecting. Lauret Savoy also earned our gratitude through her creative suggestions of other potential contributors. Thanks to all of the writers and publishers involved for supporting the book's goal of encouraging outdoor experiences between children and adults.

Expert assistance also came to us from many sources. Linda Lear's scholarship is behind our understanding of Rachel Carson's life and writings, and Cheryl Charles's and Alicia Senauer Loge's broad knowledge of child-nature research underpins our synopsis of the current state of the field. Both Cheryl and Ali read drafts of the research summary and recommended improvements; the remaining errors of omission and commission are ours. The most recent studies can always be found where we gratefully sought them, on the Children & Nature Network's resource-rich Web site—the online nexus of the movement to reconnect children and the natural world.

The aesthetic judgments of several writers also shaped the volume. Susan Thornton Hobby kindly shared her sensitive opinions about poetry, and Marybeth Lorbiecki discussed possible prose selections often and with great insight. Two fine writers, Gail Parker and Paula Novash, are owed our deepest debt for unstintingly sharing their time and talents to criticize various parts of the manuscript. Thank you, Paula and Gail.

At the MIT Press, Clay Morgan expressed enthusiasm for the project from our first interchanges, and Laura Callen patiently answered innumerable questions that arose during the long process of manuscript preparation. In addition, we appreciate others at the Press who made possible the smooth transition from proposal to published book: Deborah Cantor-Adams, Rosemary Winfield, Marcy Ross, Sharon Deacon Warne, Molly Ballou Seamans, Jim Mitchell, and David Weininger.

Several people lent early encouragement for the project, some so long ago that they may not remember—but we do. They include Mary Braun, Jeffrey S. Cramer, Lynda DeWitt, Lisa Dixon, Barbara Kingsolver, Mark Madison, Gary Paul Nabhan, Katherine Paterson, Marianne Pettis, Sara St. Antoine, Kaylynn Sullivan TwoTrees, and Susan Zwinger.

Personal thanks from Julie Dunlap are lovingly directed to her late parents, who packed five kids into a station wagon for trips to Yellowstone National Park and the Rockies, and to her favorite outdoor companions—her wonderful husband and children. Thank you, Michael, Nathan, Hannah, Sarah, and Eli for tolerating the distractions and disarray resulting from this endeavor. I can never repay your patience, but I can join you outside again at last.

Steve Kellert would like to thank his children and grandchildren, who have given him an excuse to get outdoors and keep the kid alive in him again and again.

And thank you to everyone, everywhere, who takes a child outside today—and tomorrow.

A child said, *What is the grass?* fetching it to me with full hands; How could I answer the child? . . . I do not know what it is any more than he.

—Walt Whitman, *Leaves of Grass* (1855)

Introduction

The Sense of Wonder

One of the most haunting images in environmental literature is the opening fable in Rachel Carson's *Silent Spring*. In an unnamed village "in the heart of America," pesticides have stilled the lowing of cattle at daybreak, the afternoon droning of bees, even the splashes of fish in the streams. Carson wrote, "On the mornings that had once throbbed with the dawn chorus of robins, catbirds, doves, jays, wrens, and scores of other bird voices there was now no sound; only silence lay over the fields and woods and marsh."[1] Her tragic tale of poisoned hopes in a once harmonious natural and human community is compounded by a bitter irony. "The people," Carson writes, "had done it themselves."[2]

Carson's allegory of an unseasonable hush prefaced a 1962 book that sparked public outrage over toxic chemical pollution and galvanized the modern environmental movement. But her blighted town suffers another silence rarely noted—the absence of children's voices. A few youths in the story have been stricken and died after playing outside; the rest must be locked indoors, saved from the corrupted environment by being separated from it. Carson's concern for children's health imbues *Silent Spring* in discussions of birth defects, childhood cancers, and chromosomal damage from DDT and other persistent synthetic chemicals. In addressing the subject of children, the author opened herself to sexist attacks; one critic dismissed her scientific claims by saying, "I thought she was a spinster. What's she so worried about genetics for?"[3] But Carson refused to stand mute when faced with a moral imperative to speak out for the future.

In fact, she was envisioning a book about children's relationships with nature in the late 1950s when research on hazardous pesticides overthrew her plans. The imagined work would have been an expansion of a

1956 essay, "Help Your Child to Wonder," published in *Woman's Home Companion*. In the magazine piece, Carson recounts outings with her two-year-old great-nephew, Roger, to the shores and woods near her cottage in Maine. One autumn night, she carries the blanket-wrapped toddler into a storm so that he can feel rain on his face and hear thunderous waves pound the rocky shore. The two laugh together in the dark, sharing "the same spine-tingling response to the vast, roaring ocean and the wild night around us."[4] Already in 1956, Carson recognized that children, often living in cities and reared by busy parents with the increasing assistance of television, spent much of their time indoors. By delivering Roger to the turbulent beach, his aunt shared with him a joy in wild nature she knew was denied to other boys and girls.

The "Wonder" essay is replete with such mild adventures, as Rachel leads Roger into the garden in search of insect songsters or joins him chasing ghost crabs across the sand. Parents are offered a few practical tips on initiating their own explorations, such as investing in a hand lens to reveal miniature worlds within forest moss or a drop of pond water. "With your child," Carson advises, "look at objects you take for granted as commonplace or uninteresting."[5] But the purpose of such close observation is greater than "a pleasant way to pass the golden hours of childhood."[6] Rather, it is to awaken the child's senses, expand her definition of self and community, and open his heart—to develop a receptivity to nature that Rachel Carson deems the "sense of wonder." The capacity to wonder is so elemental to Carson that she professed an oft-quoted wish: "If I had the influence with the good fairy who is supposed to preside over the christening of all children I should ask that her gift to each child in the world be a sense of wonder so indestructible that it would last throughout life, as an unfailing antidote against the boredom and disenchantments of later years, the sterile preoccupation with things that are artificial, the alienation from the sources of our strength."[7]

What did Rachel Carson mean by *wonder*? The Latin word *mirari*, meaning "to wonder at," is the root for both *admiration* and *miracle*. Socrates called wonder the moment of knowing that one does not know.[8] Descartes likened wonder to surprise and called it the first of all passions, most often experienced in youth when unexpected, first-time encounters occur more frequently.[9] Surprise, admiration, curiosity, awe, delight, reverence, humility, loneliness, and joy are all emotions encompassed in Carson's conception of wonder. Nature evokes these feelings in her, says Kathleen Dean Moore, through "its sudden beauty, its intricate interrelations, its power, its contingency, the 'ingenuity' of its design, the stunning fact of it, and—most important—its ultimate mystery."[10] Significantly, and in contrast to Descartes and others, Carson's wonder response did not depend on rarity. She had no need to wait for a total solar eclipse or an endangered plover to land on her shore. Rather, Carson relished wonders discovered in everyday nature, responding to and seeking out new ways of perceiving a crab's claw, a bank of clouds, or a child's hand in her own. Moore says wonder to Carson was a capacity as well as an emotion, an ability to view the world like a child, as eternally fresh and indelibly surprising. "A person with a sense of wonder," says Moore, "will lift a rotten log to see what might burrow in the dampness, will listen to the fall of rain and the subtle rustle of Sitka spruce, so hard to tell apart, will go out early in the morning or late at night, not searching for something, but open to everything, exposed to the raw wind of what we can never understand."[11] Although Descartes held that wonder declines with age, Carson imagined Roger carrying it with him as she had, a source of strength and joy for a lifetime.

Durable wonder is possible, Carson asserted, as evidenced by naturalists she knew who retained "fires of wonder and amazement" to their final days.[12] But Carson also knew, from personal experience and from observing others, that economic pressures, professional disappointments, ill health, and family conflicts can drain the wonder from our quotidian existence. "Sterile preoccupations" leave too many adults deaf to the wood thrushes in their backyards and shut inside while Rachel and Roger lie on a headland gazing at the stars.

Carson attributed her own enduring bond with wildlife, plants, and the nonhuman environment to her mother.[13] Maria Carson, a dedicated schoolteacher before marriage, ushered her three children outdoors daily, exploring the family's sixty-four-acre farm in Springdale, Pennsylvania. To supplement her knowledge of native plants and creatures, Maria relied on home teaching guides based on Anna Comstock's *Handbook of Nature Study*.[14] Comstock was a leader in the early twentieth-century nature-study movement, an educational effort aimed at closing the widening gap between the children of an industrializing society and the rural landscape. To revive the abating connections, nature-study educators presented parents with simple activities, stories, and poetry that led children back to the spiders, frogs, wildflowers, and other living things around them even in towns and cities. Comstock, and Maria Carson as her adherent, worked to instill a love of nature's beauties through direct, sensory experiences rather than the dry inculcation of facts. Maria's gentle, inspiring lessons in the farm meadows and along the Allegheny River never left Rachel's imagination, animating her interactions with Roger four decades later.

Remembering her mother's influence and hopeful of her own, Carson proffers similar methods in "Help Your Child to Wonder" to a new generation of parents and teachers. In contrast with the objective science education of her day, Carson advocates emotional experience as a key to stimulating the learning impulse. Especially with young children, she says, "It is not half so important to *know* as to *feel*."[15] Barriers to nature experience can be overcome through creativity, she believed, and she urges urban parents, who perhaps lack funds to travel to the country, to listen with children as wind rushes past buildings, to find a park and watch the seasons progress, and to "ponder the mystery of a growing seed, even if it be only one planted in a pot of earth in the kitchen window."[16] To those reluctant to teach natural history because of limited expertise, she suggests ways to stir a child's senses—smell the mudflats at low tide, listen for birds migrating in the moonlight, touch rain-soaked moss with your fingertips. "If a child is to keep alive his inborn sense of wonder," Carson distills her message, "he needs the companionship of at least one adult who can share it, rediscovering with him the joy, excitement and mystery of the world we live in."[17]

The warm reception of her magazine piece convinced Carson to expand her ideas into a book. She sketched notes for her agent, complete with chapter headings for "The Sky," "The Sea," "The Changing Year," and "The Miracle of Life," remarking that the "material comes to my door without my half trying."[18] But *Silent Spring* and metastatic breast cancer intervened. She battled the chemical industry and suffered radiation treatments, yet still yearned to write about children and adults exploring outdoors together. "I want very much to do the Wonder book," she wrote to a friend in 1963, "that would be Heaven to achieve."[19] Rachel's death a few months later ended that dream, but the original essay was published posthumously in 1965 as a book with photographic illustrations entitled *The Sense of Wonder*.

A brief *New York Times* review hailed the new book as "an eloquent plea for parents to rekindle in their own lives a feeling for the joys and mysteries of nature and to help children use all of their senses as avenues of delight and discovery."[20] Although it never sparked a controversy like *Silent Spring*, through the years *The Sense of Wonder* quietly became a classic. A national push for enhanced math, science, and technology education in the 1960s preoccupied school systems, but at the same time innovative nature educators and parents began adopting Carson's philosophy and methods. Inspired by the sense of wonder concept, Joseph Cornell and others pursued a new nature-study movement that flourished in the 1970s. Cornell's *Sharing Nature with Children*, packed with sensory and emotional activities and games, became a perennial bestseller, widely translated and used in schools, summer camps, scout meetings, and homes around the world. Ideas in a flurry of late twentieth-century books can be traced to Carson. Books such as David Elkind's *The Hurried Child* (1981) and Richard Louv's *Childhood's Future* (1993) decried societal pressures that were undermining traditional childhood. The idea that adults can and should help children discover, enjoy, contemplate, and value nature has spread so widely that the "sense of wonder" phrase now appears in books ranging from vacation guides to spiritual treatises and in YouTube videos, reviews of Wii games, and monikers of garage bands. "The phrase 'sense of wonder,'" notes Robert Michael Pyle, "may be as famous as the term *silent spring*, but relatively few know that they came from the same source."[21] Though never elaborated as Carson wished, her essay on sharing the outdoors with children resonates yet more deeply today as evidence mounts of young people's disengagement from the natural world.

Measuring Wonder

About the same time that Rachel Carson was chasing crabs in Maine with little Roger, young Richard Louv was climbing trees in his grandmother's Missouri backyard. Richard and Roger are baby boomers, part of a surge of births between 1946 and 1965 and a group Louv calls "the last generation of Americans to share an intimate, familial attachment to the land and water."[22] In his pivotal book, *Last Child in the Woods*, Louv notes that millions of families after World War II abandoned cities, farms, and rural villages for sprawling, often parkless suburbs and exurbs. During boomers' childhoods, enough open space persisted so that children like Richard could watch development encroach from the windows of their tree forts. Even urban children, says Louv, retained access to unpaved spaces through family members who owned or rented farms, fishing holes, or summer cabins. But as boomers grew up and started their own families, vacant lots filled in and rural grandparents passed away. More and more children lost their last close links to nature.

No one quantified how much time baby boomers spent outdoors as children building tree houses, collecting seashells, or admiring the Milky Way. As Louv points out, social scientists (like the rest of the populace) assumed that playing outside was a permanent fixture of childhood. More recently, researchers have found some evidence of declining outdoor contact by comparing time diaries of today's children with similar records kept in the past.[23] Similarly, retrospective interviews with U.S. mothers by Rhonda Clements suggest that today's parents remember playing outdoors more and indoors less than their children do, although inaccurate recall may bias such results.[24] Another tantalizing study, an autobiography analysis by Pamela Wridt, indicates that children in New York City shifted from street and park play to indoor settings between the 1940s and early 2000s. It should be noted, however, that Wridt looked only at one working-class neighborhood.[25] In fact, robust data are lacking on how much time today's children spend outdoors as well as on how their parents behaved. The shortage of reliable research led to the 2007 initiation of the National Kids Survey, an ongoing project aimed at building a national baseline of data about children's time and activities outdoors.[26]

Until more time data are available, other studies offer insights into children's opportunities for outdoor experiences. Several studies indicate that families are spending less recreational or practical time outside. For example, Oliver Pergams and Patricia Zaradic's work shows that visitation to U.S. national parks declined 20% between 1988 and 2003, and camping, fishing, and hunting are also decreasingly popular.[27] A Centers for Disease Control and Prevention survey found that 22.6% of children ages nine to thirteen did not participate in any free-time physical activity, and other research shows that biking and walking to school have declined 26% in thirty years.[28] Opportunities for outdoor play are also often limited at school, as indicated by a U.S. Department of Education study showing that 7% to 13% of elementary schools lacked scheduled recess.[29] Schools with impoverished populations were more likely than other schools to keep children inside.

One possible indirect indicator of reduced outdoor experience is children's knowledge about the local environment. Eight-year-olds in a United Kingdom study could identify more Pokémon characters than common wildlife species, while white, Hispanic, and Native American children in an Arizona study possessed little knowledge of indigenous wildlife or foods.[30] Gary Paul Nabhan and Sara St. Antoine, authors of the Arizona study, see television and other electronic media as a major cause of the nature knowledge decline. "Now that the global electronic media dominate their knowledge of nature," say Nabhan and St. Antoine, "these children are losing the kind of local awareness that television doc-umentaries cannot supply."[31] Children's exposure to television, comput-ers, video games, and other electronic media has increased dramatically, as shown in a 2010 study by the Kaiser Family Foundation.[32] Among U.S. eight- to eighteen-year-olds, media use grew from an already sobering six hours and twenty minutes daily in 2004 to a startling seven hours and thirty-eight minutes daily in 2009. Youths over age eleven consumed the most media, blacks and Hispanics consumed on average more than whites, and boys used more than girls. Such findings in the United States and other nations have led some to dub today's children the first indoor generation.[33]

Implications of this radical change in childhood led to the provocative subtitle of Louv's book, *Last Child in the Woods: Saving Our Children from Nature-Deficit Disorder*. The author explains that the phenomenon is not a medical diagnosis "but a way of viewing the problem, and de-scribes the human costs of alienation from nature, among them: dimin-ished use of the senses, attention difficulties, and higher rates of physical and emotional illnesses. The disorder can be detected in individuals, fam-ilies, and communities."[34] Evidence of negative health and other effects is predominantly correlational but mounting to support Louv's alarm. Much public attention has focused on Centers for Disease Control and Prevention studies that tie the national obesity and childhood diabetes epidemics to children's increasingly sedentary, indoor lifestyles.[35] Hours of television viewing in particular have been correlated with body fat increases for preschoolers to early adolescents.[36] Risks to physical and mental health from inactivity in childhood have led the American Acad-emy of Pediatrics to recommend sixty minutes of physical activity daily, but many children of all ages do not reach desired levels.[37]

Conversely, benefits from outdoor contact are supported by a growing number of studies with varying methodologies. Children's body mass in-dexes in an Indiana study were inversely proportional to the amount of vegetation in each child's neighborhood, while children diagnosed with attention deficit disorder exhibited fewer symptoms after outdoor activi-ties in green settings.[38] A report by the Children & Nature Network iden-tifies numerous benefits of nature experiences at home and school including improved motor coordination, curiosity, self-discipline, conflict resolution skills, test scores, and even some vision protection.[39] Louv highlights emotional, spiritual, and imaginative benefits of nature when remembering his own childhood, when tree climbing left him "lost in wonderment."[40] Restoring such profound connections to today's children motivated him to write a book Robert Michael Pyle calls "as important as any since *Silent Spring*."[41]

In fact, argues Stephen Kellert, nature contact influences emotional, cognitive, social, and spiritual development throughout childhood.[42] His large-sample surveys of diverse populations throughout childhood show that children from ages three to six prefer contact with familiar creatures and natural settings. However, with "varied, recurrent, and direct" nature experiences, teenagers can eventually achieve understanding of complex concepts such as ecosystems and of moral responsibilities such as environmental stewardship. Middle childhood, from ages six to twelve, appears to be an especially critical period when nature play develops the capacities for creativity, problem solving, and emotional and intellectual development. Kellert's findings buttress the influential biophilia hypothesis, expounded by Harvard biologist Edward O. Wilson, Kellert, and others, which holds that humans have a biology-based affinity with other life forms.[43] Humans evolved as part of the natural world, say theorists, and remain ineluctably attuned to the environment despite societal pressures to the contrary. "What seems evident," says Kellert, "is that direct experience of nature plays a significant, vital, and perhaps irreplaceable role in affective, cognitive, and evaluative development."[44]

Studies also suggest that much as kids need nature, nature needs kids. One U.S. survey found that hiking, camping, and playing in the woods before age eleven had a significant positive effect on attitudes and behaviors in adulthood such as recycling, pro-environment voting, and participation in Earth Day.[45] Likewise, a study in Great Britain found that childhood outdoor activities led to more visits to and positive attitudes toward natural spaces.[46] In a particularly insightful study, Louise Chawla interviewed environmentalists in Kentucky and Norway to understand their sources of commitment to issues such as wildlife and habitat protection, air and water quality, and land-use planning.[47] Almost 90% of Kentuckians credited wild and semiwild places where they played as children, and 65% of Norwegians referred to outdoor activities such as skiing, hiking, or wild berry picking. Such findings that environmental commitments in adulthood may originate in youthful outdoor experiences threaten the environmental movement when coupled with evidence of nature-deficient childhoods. Says Louv, "If environmental groups wish to pass on the heritage of their movement and the ongoing care of the earth, they cannot ignore children's need to explore, to get their hands dirty and their feet wet."[48]

Chawla's environmentalist subjects also cited a second major childhood source for their later commitments—adult companionship outdoors. Eighty percent of Kentuckians and over 70% of Norwegian interviewees mentioned significant adults, usually a parent but sometimes another relative. Often adult mentors directed attention to particular aspects of nature. As Chawla puts it, "By the direction and quality of their attention, they communicate nature's value and promote the child's interest in this world too."[49] Memories resonated decades later of walks in the woods with a father who spoke of replanting as "renewing the earth" or of standing in a corn field as a father wept over soil erosion.[50] Mentoring adults took the time to admire insects while fishing with a child, to introduce favorite flowers while gardening, or to lead a family trip to the country. Just as Carson accepted Roger's damp clothes after their outings, these adults tolerated "scratches, muddy knees, wet shoes, and pockets full of pebbles" while conveying the message that inconveniences, challenges, and even risks outdoors are worthwhile.[51] Chawla emphasizes that the quality of the adult-child relationship is vital to the outdoor experience. She says, "The very fact that a parent or grandparent chose to take the child with them to a place where they themselves found fascination and pleasure, to share what engaged them there, suggests not only care for the natural world, but equally, care for the child."[52]

A few other studies have examined the roles of adults in enhancing child-nature connections. When Wisconsin teens were asked why they joined environmental action clubs, they credited experiences in nearby nature and with teachers and environmental club advisers more often than with relatives.[53] However, rural and urban children in New Mexico studied by Victoria Derr revealed that parents, grandparents, and other relatives were vitally important in the development of their senses of place.[54] For example, extended family and deep community roots gave one girl stability despite poverty and crime in her Santa Fe barrio. Similarly, memories of local stories and plant knowledge from his grandmother helped a boy cope with her loss. Says Derr, "When a child experienced nature, culture, and family as an interwoven entity, his or her connections and attachment were indeed strong and meaningful."[55]

The effect of storytelling on elementary students' attachment to place was examined by Clifford Blizzard and Ruby Schuster.[56] Comparing groups who heard different types of stories about a small woodland with students who explored on their own, the researchers found that natural history stories stimulated exploration, talking, and writing about the site more than human history tales. These results, say the authors, correspond with ethnographic and other evidence of storytelling's power in traditional cultures to impart information, establish place bonds, and stimulate listeners' imaginations. In addition, evidence of positive influence by unknown storytellers on children's response to a woodland hints at the potential for still more significant effects of stories learned from teachers, family, and other close caregivers.

As evidence accrues of the value of outdoor experiences, including those facilitated by caregivers, why do many parents and others still keep kids inside? Carson presciently recognized several barriers to nature exploration—such as children's routines, family budgets, distance from open space—but other impediments would astonish her. Clements's study of mothers found that 85% blamed computer games and other electronics for keeping kids indoors, even though 93% saw outdoor play as benefiting physical development.[57] Potential impediments range from lawsuits to urban design, but Louv contends that the steepest hurdle is fear.[58] Carson's mother let her roam free across their farm, but today's worried parents seem to drive their children almost everywhere and allow free roaming only on the World Wide Web.[59] Rationales for ever-constricting home territories include concerns about traffic and local gangs, but the greatest anxiety may be fear of strangers or what Louv calls the "bogeyman syndrome."[60] Incessant news coverage, he argues, has convinced parents that we face an epidemic of kidnappers and sexual predators, despite statistics showing a steady or declining incidence of violent crimes against children. Given the difficulty of banishing societal stranger anxiety, Louv suggests a variety of coping mechanisms, including furnishing children with cell phones and teaching them self-confidence. Often, he suggests, parents, grandparents, or neighbors can provide trusted adult supervision when children head outdoors.

A particular brand of fear is the focus of David Sobel's *Beyond Ecophobia: Reclaiming the Heart in Nature Education*.[61] Sobel warns that well-intentioned parents and teachers are frightening children away from nature, inducing ecophobia through a barrage of grim reports on acid rain, oil spills, species extinctions, and global warming. Earth Week lessons urging kindergarteners to "Save the Planet" from their fellow humans yield despondency, not action. Young children lack the cognitive and emotional maturity, says Sobel, to cope with complex and potentially tragic environmental issues. Instead, he argues, "Stories, songs, moving like animals, celebrating seasons, and fostering Rachel Carson's 'sense of wonder' should be primary activities during this age."[62] Ecophobia is exacerbated, he argues, when children have little contact with nearby nature. Without grounding in the delights of catching fireflies or scattering milkweed seeds, the environment becomes a distant and often distressing abstraction. Says Sobel, "Lacking direct experience with nature, children begin to associate it with fear and apocalypse, not joy and wonder."[63] Protecting children from ecophobia-inducing messages, along with sending kids outdoors, may be crucial steps in resolving the nature-deficit phenomenon.

Even some who value outdoor childhood activities cannot seem to make them happen. Louv says simply, "Time is the key."[64] What child has time for skipping stones on a pond when there are piano lessons, soccer practice, and homework to finish before bed? Parents are equally time-constrained, often working extra hours to earn money for tutors and team fees. When commuting time to extracurricular activities is added to the equation, families feel overwhelmed by scheduled activities. The hectic pace is often justified as essential to children's eventual academic and economic success. The resulting students may be primed for the Ivy League but, like a fourth grader interviewed by Louv, feel guilty for glancing out windows during study time. Yet these same children devote hours to computers, Nintendos, and other electronics. Children in the Kaiser Family Foundation study, by using more than one device at a time, crammed ten hours and forty-five minutes worth of media content into their average seven hours and thirty-eight minutes of use per day.[65] Richard Louv calls electronics thieves of time; their overuse reflects the skewed priorities of adults shaping young lives. By rejecting excessive gadgetry and extracurricular activities, caregivers can open children's lives to vital outdoor experiences. Louv asserts, "It takes time—loose, unstructured dreamtime—to experience nature in a meaningful way."[66]

Breaking down barriers of time, ecophobia, and stranger anxiety appear to be crucial steps that adults can take to get children outside again. Yet evidence is not clear on the optimal approach once adults and children are under the sky together. The literature cannot yet answer fundamental questions about what activities and experiences children of different ages, genders, ethnicities, or geographic backgrounds should pursue. Notably, the field of emotion research has little to say about how to affect or even measure the complex emotions (such as wonder, awe, and reverence) that can be inspired by nature.[67] But as Kellert points out, "The natural world provokes pleasure and enthusiasm but also a sense of uncertainty, danger, and at times terror. From the perspective of maturation and growth, all these and other emotions associated with the child's experience of nature serve as powerful motivators and stimuli for learning and development."[68] Edith Cobb's influential book, *The Ecology of Imagination in Childhood*, contends that children possess a heightened emotional responsiveness to the natural world.[69] Based on analyses of three hundred autobiographies, Cobb speculates, "The child's sense of wonder, displayed as surprise and joy, is aroused as a response to the mystery of some external stimulus [i.e., nature] that promises 'more to come' or, better still, 'more to do'—the power of perceptual participation in the known and unknown."[70] Although Cobb's methods have been criticized, many share her conviction of the emotional power of natural experience.[71] If facts are the seeds of children's knowledge and understanding, says Carson, then emotions are the fertile soil they need to grow. Engaging children emotionally outdoors appears to be one key to reconnecting them to the natural world.

Carson also intuited the crucial role played by direct sensory experiences throughout development in creating memorable nature experiences. As Kellert puts it, there is something about nature that "attracts, stimulates, and retains the child's attention" and cannot be replaced by television, computer games, films, or other vicarious experiences.[72] Even such popular family activities as zoo and aquarium visitation, which Kellert calls indirect nature contact, may be too artificial, passive, and fleeting to have much influence on emotional, cognitive, or spiritual development. He predicts that more lasting, positive effects come from experiences in outdoor adventure programs, nature travel, local nature parks, and backyards. Even a degraded urban nature setting can offer rich play benefits for children who experience it directly, as shown in studies by Robin Moore.[73] According to Kellert, the most effective types of direct experience depend on the developmental phase of childhood, with children younger than six benefiting from contact with familiar animals and natural spaces. Children between six and twelve thrive when venturing further afield, investigating wild animals and habitats and often creating tree forts and other outdoor shelters to explore their autonomy. In adolescence, says Kellert, children seek out challenging and risky experiences in unfamiliar and even wilderness settings. A Kellert and Derr study of adolescents in outdoor adventure programs indicates the potential significance of such experiences for teens. A large majority of participants reported improved autonomy, decision-making skills, and interpersonal skills, and most also indicated greater appreciation for nature and involvement in outdoor activities.[74] Kellert recognizes that symbolic nature experiences, such as listening to stories or reading books, can also stimulate children's emotional and imaginative connections with animals and natural places. But more than any imagined creature or land-scape, he believes, everyday direct experiences lead to connections with the nonhuman world—what Carson calls "the rush of remembered delight"—that endure in children's memories and shape their futures.[75]

Yet in facilitating regular nature contact for children, adults must take care not to become barriers to connections themselves. In *The Great Outdoors: Restoring Children's Right to Play Outside*, education researcher Mary Rivkin cites freedom as a basic value of outdoor play:[76] "Not only is there typically more space out-of-doors, there is less in that space to bump into, break, or lose parts of. One's body is no longer under need of tight control—its capabilities to shout, sing, leap, roll, stretch, and fling are unleashed."[77] There is freedom, too, in "being out of the owned space of schools and houses. The sky, the clouds, the rain, the wind are for everyone."[78] Several studies show that children develop less aggressive, more egalitarian peer relationships under conditions Rivkin labels the "democracy of outdoor play." Other research demonstrates that children's discovery and inventiveness during play depends on the number and variety of play elements or "loose parts" in the play environment. Unlike the finite world of even the best-stocked playroom, outdoor loose parts include everything from the deepest hole kids can dig to the Pleiades. Rivkin and other educators believe that nature's virtually limitless possibilities are fundamental reasons why outdoor play enhances creativity, problem solving, social interactions, and other aspects of learning and development. How does the presence of an adult change a free, unstructured outdoor experience? Can adults resist straightening up messy parts, establishing rules, and controlling attention and behavior outside? In what ways can adults maximize the possibilities outdoors, including emotional and sensory interactions, while still keeping children safe? Findings such as Chawla's that environmentalists cherish memories of their childhood mentors indicate that not all adults stifle children in natural settings. But much more research is needed to determine how adults can balance their caretaker roles of protecting and directing with children's needs for freedom and spontaneity outdoors.

Despite broad gaps and shortcomings in research to date, burgeoning numbers of individuals, organizations, and government agencies are pushing for immediate efforts to reconnect children and nature. Parents and grandparents are deluged with advice on how to begin from teachers, Web sites, parenting magazines, nature centers, self-help books, and the national news. Individuals, organizations, and government agencies are already implementing programs and ideas about restoring children's relationships with nature. Many crucial research questions remain: Are there developmental thresholds in the quantity and quality of children's experiences in nature? How do diminished exposures to various elements of nature affect future environmental attitudes, behaviors, and values? Is solitude an irreplaceable experience for establishing connections with natural places and creatures? What settings and what experiences are most significant in creating lasting connections? How do barriers to connection compare between children from different ethnic and cultural backgrounds? Can emotions such as awe, attachment to place, and wonder be adequately measured? Much more research is needed to begin to understand the complex process of reconnecting children with the outdoors.

Yet waiting for answers to these and many other questions is incompatible with the urgent needs of growing children. As with the global warming crisis, there is already enough evidence to help guide our actions. Restoring children—as individuals and as a generation—from the disorders of nature disconnection cannot be put off until science reaches consensus on all issues. As Richard Louv puts it, "We have such a brief opportunity to pass on to our children our love for this Earth, and to tell our stories."[79] Parents, guardians, and others who care about the future can find young companions and head outdoors.

Reflections on Wonder

Rearing children has always been more about art than science, and those aiming to rear nature-connected children can turn to music, film, photography, and other artistic media for ideas and inspiration. Since the nineteenth century, the art of writing about the nonhuman world has been a rich literary tradition and a driving force in the environmental movement. George Perkins Marsh's *Man and Nature* helped convince the New York State legislature to preserve much of the Adirondack forest, and John Muir's ecstatic descriptions of the Range of Light stirred public support for Yosemite National Park. In the twentieth century, Aldo Leopold's depiction of "a fierce green fire" in a dying wolf's eyes shifted perceptions of wilderness from adversary to inheritance, ultimately leading to the 1964 Wilderness Act, while Rachel Carson's *Silent Spring* led to the establishment of the Environmental Protection Agency and to the questioning by millions of people of their roles, individually and collectively, in the degradation of the earth. Carson called on other nature writers in a 1952 speech to do still more to awaken all who remain unmoved by the planet's wonders. "If they are indifferent," Carson writes, "it is only because they have not been properly introduced to it—and perhaps that is in some measure our fault."[80]

However artful and provocative, traditional nature writing at first appears of little relevance to adults who accompany children outdoors. For two centuries, nature essays focused on individual observers contemplating pristine land- and seascapes. Most celebrated the solitary observer's escape from human society as much as his immersion in the woods or waves. Thoreau in his cabin at Walden Pond, Beston's outermost Cape Cod house, and Abbey's *Desert Solitaire* are just a few examples of this pervasive approach. These authors occasionally encounter and respond to other adults sauntering by, but a child's raucous presence would feel like a clanking, smoking machine in their wilderness idylls. As Rick Van Noy points out about such literary icons, "they are a monastic bunch (except for Abbey), eloquent on the need for wild places but silent on the subject of raising children."[81]

Yet some elements within the genre are compatible with reflections on intergenerational relationships outdoors. Relevant traditional themes identified by *The Norton Book of Nature Writing* include exploration, search for home and connection in nature, and, perhaps surprisingly, play.[82] Just as Rachel Carson and Roger pretend that spruce seedlings in their woods were squirrel Christmas trees, Thoreau imagines himself a hound pursuing a fox across the snow, and Emerson invents an ice harp with stones on frozen Walden Pond. Finding community is an increasingly prominent theme, argues Bill McKibben, as environmental writing has flourished in recent decades.[83] McKibben attributes the evolution in approach to authors outraged by pollution, deforestation, and other defilements fueled by a culture of hyperindividualism. Says McKibben, "Fighting the ideology that was laying waste to so much of the planet demanded going beyond individualism."[84] McKibben lauds Aldo Leopold's "gentle insistence that we needed an ethic large enough to encompass everything, including the land," as an exemplar of community-focused nature writing.[85] Although children are not specified in Leopold's "community of interdependent parts," surely there is room for them in a land ethic that encompasses soils, water, plants, wildlife, and human adults.[86]

A Sand County Almanac credits father Carl Leopold for young Aldo's first lessons in responsible partridge hunting, but the father-son relationship is a minor element in that 1949 book.[87] Similar hints and allusions about intergenerational influences have appeared more recently in passages and chapters in increasing numbers of memoirs, such as Robert

Michael Pyle's *The Thunder Tree*, and single-author essay collections, as in Barbara Kingsolver's *Small Wonder*.[88] The first literary volume to focus on adults exploring nature with children (aside from Carson's) was *The Geography of Childhood*, a 1995 book of alternating essays by Gary Paul Nabhan and Stephen Trimble. "The geography and natural history of childhood begins in family, at home," say the authors, at that time each the father of two small children.[89] Most children today, Nabhan and Trimble lament, not only lack intimate nature contact but seem to prefer artificial, indoor activities. By observing their children, reflecting on their own childhoods, and speaking with parents from southwestern ranching and Native American cultures, the authors gain insights into how adults can instill a "sense of wildness" in the young. "As parents," says Trimble, "our job is to pay attention, to create possibilities—to be careful matchmakers between our children and the Earth."[90]

Trimble believes that by camping together in the desert, witnessing Pueblo harvest dances, and waiting as a family for moonrise he has given his preschool-aged children a good start. Yet he asks, "Beyond these beginnings, what will my children's need for answers to mysteries lead them to believe?"[91] Nabhan adds other questions: Why do some children bond with nature while others find it frightening?[92] With most children living in cities and suburbs, how can parents help them find or create wild places to explore?[93] How best can caregivers nurture a "sense of wildness" or "sense of place"? Nabhan and Trimble's thought-provoking volume stimulated interest in adult-child relationships outdoors before Louv's *Last Child in the Woods* appeared in 2005. In 2008, their work was followed by Rick Van Noy's perceptive *A Natural Sense of Wonder: Connecting Kids with Nature through the Seasons*. That book is Van Noy's attempt to discover with his son and daughter "how to get them *out* so that, paradoxically, they develop a healthy *in*."[94] These discerning fathers and a growing number of other writers are beginning to address the myriad questions raised when children and adults head outside together.

Public responsiveness to *Last Child in the Woods* and subsequent campaigns has intensified the need for a literary anthology of geographically, culturally, ethnically, and gender-diverse perspectives on these vital issues. Collecting the contributions for this volume has been a long and unsystematic process. In *The Norton Book of Nature Writing*, Robert Finch and John Elder note that "the terrain of nature writing is a vast and only partially mapped one."[95] We have been wanderers in that poorly charted territory, easily identifying a few pieces on literary promontories such as *Orion* magazine. But more works were found only because others kindly pointed the way. A few have been cached for years, while others are recently discovered. About one third are original to this volume.

Guided by the outstanding collection, *The Colors of Nature: Culture, Identity, and the Natural World*, we invited voices of those who have been underrepresented in environmental literature, including African Americans, Native Americans, and many demographic categories outside white males.[96] Geographically, the collection ranges from Washington, D.C., to the Pacific Northwest woods, and from a preschooler's suburban garden to a teen's Rocky Mountain slope. Despite our efforts, selections have been limited by many factors, including unavailable permissions, accidental oversights, and our own tastes and interests. An underrepresentation of urban-focused pieces, notwithstanding attempts to find and solicit appropriate works, suggests a particular area for future elaboration. The selected pieces, by established and emerging writers, cross many boundaries in time and space while contemplating multifarious relationships between children and parents, grandparents, uncles, aunts, teachers, and friends. As they explore the basic question of how children and adults explore nature together, the authors address several recurrent themes of particular import:

- *Sharing of place.* Rachel Carson mourned that children's limited outdoor experiences undermine their connections to wild places like her beloved Maine coastline, and cultivating a sense of place is a dominant theme in environmental writing. Several essays in this collection reflect on the origins of the author's connection to a landscape or on efforts to establish a similar relationship with a child. In making those links, authors consider the roles played by rituals, animals, humor, smells, and, especially, food (from huckleberries to ice cream cones) in attachment. Stories play especially powerful parts in understanding of place, and for writers such as Rick Bass and Stephen Trimble, family tales about generations sharing a bountiful land-based history leads to a legacy of connection. But for Danyelle O'Hara, David Mas Masumoto, and others, inherited stories of racism, economic oppression, and dispossession become barriers to attachment. Their insights suggest that belonging to a place depends on experience, memory, imagination, and, sometimes, acts of will.

- *Redefining relationships.* *The Sense of Wonder* documents Carson's devotion to her great-nephew and to encouraging in him a lifelong love of nature. Many essays explore conventional parent-child relationships in unconventional ways, while others meditate on relationships between children and grandparents, uncles, aunts, teachers, and friends. Nonbiologically related elders, says Robert Michael Pyle, have not just the ability but the responsibility to transmit natural knowledge and wisdom to the young. Again, stories passed down through generations play significant roles, transmitting to Enrique Salmon, for example, the Rarámuri belief that kinship should be extended to the plant world. Sometimes, parent-child roles are reversed, as when Stephen Lyon's twelve-year-old daughter demonstrates her resilience in the face of their separation. Or as Richard Louv puts it, "Your child can say something to you, just one small thing, and suddenly the universe expands." Whatever the adult-child relationship at hand, each piece progresses toward an understanding of how adults attempt, however tentatively, to give children a resilient security of human and non-human connections.

- *Extinction of experience.* Carson noted that loving parents often keep children indoors rather than risk dangers or inconveniences such as darkness, rain, or dirt. Similarly, authors in our collection meditate on what happens when adults expose children to risky, inaccessible, and ecophobia-inducing activities, places, and creatures. Michael Shay faces questions about why he lets his eight-year-old son with attention-deficit disorder climb steep granite rocks, and Brenda Peterson considers how storytelling about wild predators can empower a teen scarred by urban violence. Several authors express a need to release children from electronic fetters and share experiences of a wilder world. "I so wanted him to be a child of stars and dirt," says Janisse Ray of her son, "not jiggering images of aliens and laser guns." And Sandra Steingraber reflects on how to talk to her children about global warming, which threatens to extinguish one of the most basic natural experiences— reliable seasonal change.

- *Mystery and imagination.* A much-celebrated passage of Carson's essay describes a search with Roger for an elusive insect she calls the "fairy bell ringer." Again and again, our selections also recognize that nature's mysteries, whether real or imagined, captivate young minds. Some writers embrace the awesome realities of biodiversity, such as Kathleen Dean Moore, whose mother exclaimed, "*Imagine* living in the same world as the scissor-tailed flycatcher." Similarly, Chiori Santiago celebrates the mystery of her mother's gift for seeing beauty in small, commonplace objects in the midst of chaos. The theme has a darker side as well. A grandfather's mystical belief in his farm soil's beneficence yielded a toxic legacy for writer Margo Tamez, and a family's religious views of animals led nine-year-old Brenda Peterson to doubt her own faith. But other writers, such as Stephen Kellert, reimagine a brighter world where children connect more intimately, creatively, and equitably with their natural surroundings.

- *Healing together.* Spiritual renewal and inner healing are fundamental values in many of Carson's writings. Like Carson, who found strength in the regularity of tides, a teen runaway in Susan Cohen's essay seeks comfort at the shore after her father's death. Children in Michael Branch's and others' essays help their elders heal from mistakes by revealing unexpected strength and wisdom of their own. Stories play a vital role here too, as expressed by Alison Deming, who writes, "And so it is that family stories become grafted onto our own individual ones, giving us a sense of continuity and consolation in times of loss." Healing a rift is the purpose of Scott Russell Sanders's Rocky Mountain hike with his seventeen-year-old son. Along the way, Sanders discovers that anger has dimmed his perceptions, just as fear of the future has robbed his son of nature attachment. Sanders must find an answer to his son's accusation: "You make me feel the planet's dying and people are to blame and nothing can be done about it." Essays by Sanders and others reveal that lack of hope may be the steepest barrier of all between children and nature.

Cultivating hope is the essential aim of all these literary excursions, as the authors and editors share Richard Louv's goal of "healing the broken bond between our youth and nature."[97] These literary works inevitably raise more questions than they answer and leave many stones unturned. But when read with care, they will stimulate thoughts and conversations about our most essential relationships—with our children, our earth, and our future.

Notes

1. Rachel Carson, *Silent Spring* (Boston: Houghton Mifflin, 1962), 1.

2. Ibid., 3.

3. Douglas Walton, *Ad Hominem Arguments* (Tuscaloosa: University of Alabama Press, 1998), xi.

4. Rachel Carson, *The Sense of Wonder* (New York: HarperCollins, 1998), 15.

5. Ibid., 76.

6. Ibid., 100.

7. Ibid., 54.

8. Philip Fisher, *Wonder, the Rainbow, and the Aesthetics of Rare Experience* (Cambridge: Harvard University Press, 1998), 10–11.

9. Ibid.

10. Kathleen Dean Moore, "The Truth of Barnacles: Rachel Carson and the Moral Significance of Wonder," in Lisa Sideris and Kathleen Dean Moore, eds., *Rachel Carson: Legacy and Challenge* (Albany: State University of New York Press, 2008), 269.

11. Ibid., 271.

12. Carson, *Sense of Wonder*, 106.

13. Linda Lear, *Rachel Carson: Witness for Nature* (New York: Henry Holt, 1997), 14.

14. Anna Comstock, *The Handbook of Nature Study* (Ithaca, NY: Cornell University Press, 1967).

15. Carson, *Sense of Wonder*, 56.

16. Ibid., 66.

17. Ibid., 55.

18. Rick Van Noy, *A Natural Sense of Wonder* (Athens: University of Georgia Press, 2008), 130–131.

19. Rachel Carson to Dorothy Freeman, November 1963, in Martha Freeman, ed., *Always Rachel: The Letters of Rachel Carson and Dorothy Freeman, 1952–1964* (Boston: Beacon Press, 1995), 490.

20. "The Sense of Wonder," *New York Times Book Review*, November 28, 1965, 76.

21. Robert Michael Pyle, "Always a Naturalist," in Peter Matthiessen, ed., *Courage for the Earth* (Boston: Houghton Mifflin, 2007), 179.

22. Richard Louv, *Last Child in the Woods: Saving Our Children from Nature-Deficit Disorder* (Chapel Hill, NC: Algonquin Books, 2008).

23. S. L. Hofferth, "Changes in American Children's Time: 1997–2003," *International Journal of Time Use Research* 6(1) (2009): 26–47; F. Thomas Juster, Hiromi Ono, and Frank P. Stafford, *Changing Times of American Youth: 1981–2003* (Ann Arbor: University of Michigan Institute for Social Research, 2004).

24. Rhonda Clements, "An Investigation of the State of Outdoor Play," *Contemporary Issues in Early Childhood* 5(1) (2004): 68–80.

25. Pamela Wridt, "An Historical Analysis of Young People's Use of Public Space, Parks and Playgrounds in New York City," *Children, Youth and Environments* 14(1) (2004): 86–106.

26. H. Ken Cordell, Carter Betz, and Gary Green, *National Kids Survey*, Internet Research Information Series (2009), available online at http://warnell.forestry. uga.edu/nrrt/nsre/IrisReports.html.

27. O. R. W. Pergams and Patricia Zaradic, "Is Love of Nature in the U.S. Becoming Love of Electronic Media?," *Journal of Environmental Management* 80(4) (2006): 387–393; O. R. W. Pergams, and Patricia Zaradic, "Evidence for a Fundamental and Pervasive Shift away from Nature-based Recreation," *Proceedings of the National Academy of Sciences of the United States of America* 105(7) (2008): 2295–2300.

28. U.S. Centers for Disease Control and Prevention, "Physical Activity Levels among Children Aged Nine to Thirteen Years: United States," *Morbidity and Mortality Weekly Report* 52(33) (2003): 785–788; U.S. Centers for Disease Control and Prevention, *Kids Walk-to-School: Then and Now—Barriers and Solutions* (Atlanta: Department of Health and Human Services, 2006).

29. B. Parsad and L. Lewis, "Calories in, Calories out: Food and Exercise in Public Elementary Schools, 2005" (Washington, DC: U.S. Department of Education, National Center for Education Statistics, 2006).

30. A. Balmford, L. Clegg, T. Coulson, and J. Taylor, "Why Conservationists Should Heed Pokémon," *Science* 295(5564) (2005): 2367–2367; Gary Paul Nabhan and Sara St. Antoine, "The Loss of Floral and Faunal Story: The Extinction of Experience," in Stephen R. Kellert and Edward O. Wilson, eds., *The Biophilia Hypothesis* (Washington, DC: Island Press, 1993), 229–250.

31. Ibid., 241.

32. Victoria Rideout, Ulla Foehr, and Donald Roberts, *Generation M2: Media in the Lives of Eight- to Eighteen-Year-Olds: Full Report* (Menlo Park, CA: Kaiser Family Foundation, 2010).

33. Samantha Cleaver, "Classrooms Are Going Green," *Instructor* 117(3) (2007): 20–24.

34. Louv, *Last Child in the Woods*, 36.

35. Cheryl Charles, Richard Louv, Lee Bodner, Bill Guns, and Dean Stahl, *Children & Nature 2009: A Report on the Movement to Reconnect Children to the Natural World* (Santa Fe: Children & Nature Network, 2009), 20; C. L. Ogden, M. D. Carroll, L. R. Curtin, M. A. McDowell, C. J. Tabak, and K. M. Flegal, "Prevalence of Overweight and Obesity in the United States, 1999–2004," *JAMA: Journal of the American Medical Association* 295(13) (2006): 1549–1555.

36. M. H. Proctor, L. Moore, D. Gao, L. Cupples, M. Bradlee, M. Hood, and R. Ellison, "Television Viewing and Change in Body Fat from Preschool to Early Adolescence: The Framingham Children's Study," *International Journal Obesity Related Metabolic Disorders* 27 (2003): 827–833.

37. T. Hinkley, D. Crawford, J. Salmon, A. Okely, and K. Hesketh, "Preschool Children and Physical Activity: A Review of Correlates," *American Journal of Preventive Medicine* 34(5) (2008): 435–441; P. R. Nader, R. H. Bradley, R. M. Houts, S. L. McRitchie, and M. O'Brien, "Moderate-to-Vigorous Physical

Activity from Ages Nine to Fifteen Years," *JAMA: Journal of the American Medical Association* 300(3) (2008): 295–305.

38. J. F. Bell, J. S. Wilson, and G. C. Liu, "Neighborhood Greenness and Two-Year Changes in Body Mass Index of Children and Youth," *American Journal of Preventive Medicine* 35(6) (2008): 547–553; Andrea Faber Taylor, Frances E. Kuo, and William C. Sullivan, "Coping with ADD: The Surprising Connection to Green Play Settings," *Environment and Behavior* 33(1) (2001): 54–77.

39. Charles et al., *Children & Nature 2009*.

40. Louv, *Last Child in the Woods*, 9.

41. Pyle, "Always a Naturalist," 178.

42. Stephen R. Kellert, *Building for Life: Designing and Understanding the Human-Nature Connection* (Washington, DC: Island Press, 2005).

43. Edward O. Wilson, "Biophilia and the Conservation Ethic," in Stephen R. Kellert and Edward O. Wilson, eds., *The Biophilia Hypothesis* (Washington, DC: Island Press, 1993), 31–41.

44. Kellert, *Building for Life*, 139.

45. N. M. Wells and K. S. Lekies, "Nature and the Life Course: Pathways from Childhood Nature Experiences to Adult Environmentalism," *Children, Youth and Environments* 16(1) (2006): 1–24.

46. C. W. Thompson, P. Aspinall, and A. Montarzino, "The Childhood Factor: Adult Visits to Green Places and the Significance of Childhood Experience," *Environment and Behavior* 40(1) (2008): 111–143.

47. Louise Chawla, "Learning to Love the Natural World Enough to Protect It," *Barn* (2) (2006): 57–78.

48. Louv, *Last Child in the Woods*, 147.

49. Chawla, "Learning to Love the Natural World," 71.

50. Ibid., 73.

51. Ibid., 68.

52. Ibid., 74.

53. D. Sivek, "Environmental Sensitivity among Wisconsin High School Students," *Environmental Education Research* 8(2) (2002): 155–170.

54. V. Derr, "Children's Sense of Place in Northern New Mexico," *Journal of Environmental Psychology* 22(1–2) (2002): 125–137.

55. Ibid., 135.

56. Clifford R. Blizzard and Rudy M. Schuster, "Fostering Children's Connections to Natural Places through Cultural and Natural History Storytelling," *Children, Youth and Environments* 17(4) (2007): 171–206.

57. Clements, "An Investigation of the State of Outdoor Play."

58. Louv, *Last Child in the Woods*, 123; A. Carver, A. Timperio, and D. Crawford, "Playing It Safe: The Influence of Neighbourhood Safety on Children's Physical Activity—A Review," *Health & Place* 14(2) (2008): 217–227.

59. Lear, *Rachel Carson*, 16; J. Veitch, S. Bagley, K. Ball, and J. Salmon, "Where Do Children Usually Play? A Qualitative Study of Parents' Perceptions of Influences on Children's Active Free Play," *Health & Place* 12(4) (2006): 383–393.

60. Louv, *Last Child in the Woods*, 123.

61. David Sobel, *Beyond Ecophobia: Reclaiming the Heart in Nature Education* (Great Barrington, MA: Orion Society, 1996).

62. Ibid., 13.

63. Sobel, quoted in Louv, *Last Child in the Woods*, 134.

64. Louv, *Last Child in the Woods*, 175.

65. Rideout et al., *Generation M2*, 2.

66. Louv, *Last Child in the Woods*, 117.

67. Dacher Keltner and Jonathan Haidt, "Approaching Awe, a Moral, Spiritual, and Aesthetic Emotion," *Cognition and Emotion* 17(2) (2003): 297–314.

68. Stephen R. Kellert, "Experiencing Nature: Affective, Cognitive, and Evaluative Development in Children," in Peter H. Kahn Jr. and Stephen R. Kellert, eds., *Children and Nature: Psychological, Sociocultural, and Evolutionary Investigations* (Cambridge: MIT Press, 2002), 117–151.

69. Edith Cobb, *The Ecology of Imagination in Childhood* (New York: Columbia University Press, 1977).

70. Ibid., 28.

71. Louv, *Last Child in the Woods*, 93–95.

72. Kellert, "Experiencing Nature," 139.

73. Robin Moore, *Childhood's Domain: Play and Space in Child Development* (London: Croom Helm, 1986).

74. Stephen R. Kellert and Victoria Derr, *National Study of Outdoor Wilderness Experience* (New Haven: Yale University School of Forestry and Environmental Studies, 1998).

75. Carson, *Sense of Wonder*, 83.

76. Mary Rivkin, *The Great Outdoors: Restoring Children's Right to Play Outside* (Washington, DC: National Association for the Education of Young People, 1995).

77. Ibid., 11.

78. Ibid., 12.

79. Louv, *Last Child in the Woods*, 316.

80. Rachel Carson, "Design for Nature Writing," in Linda Lear, ed., *Lost Woods: The Discovered Writing of Rachel Carson* (Boston: Beacon Press, 1952), 95.

81. Van Noy, *Natural Sense of Wonder*, 15.

82. Robert Finch and John Elder, eds., *The Norton Book of Nature Writing* (New York: Norton, 1990), 21.

83. Bill McKibben, ed., *American Earth: Environmental Writing Since Thoreau* (New York: Library of American, 2008), xxvii.

84. Ibid.

85. Ibid.

86. Aldo Leopold, *A Sand County Almanac and Sketches from Here and There* (New York: Oxford, 1949), 203.

87. Ibid., 121.

88. Robert Michael Pyle, *The Thunder Tree* (Guilford, CT: Lyons Press, 1998); Barbara Kingsolver, *Small Wonder* (New York: HarperCollins, 2002).

89. Gary Paul Nabhan and Stephen Trimble, *The Geography of Childhood: Why Children Need Wild Places* (Boston: Beacon Press, 1994), xiii.

90. Ibid., 172.

91. Ibid., 171.

92. Ibid., 136.

93. Ibid., 9.

94. Van Noy, *Natural Sense of Wonder*, xv.

95. Finch and Elder, *Norton Book of Nature Writing*, 17.

96. Alison H. Deming and Lauret E. Savoy, *The Colors of Nature: Culture, Identity, and the Natural World* (Minneapolis: Milkweed Editions, 2002).

97. Louv, *Last Child in the Woods*, 3.

1

The Farm

Rick Bass

It was still the end of winter at our home in northern Montana, but down in south Texas in April, at my father's farm, it was full-bore spring. It was a joy for me to realize that Lowry, just turned three, would now have the colors and sights of this place lodged in at least her subconscious, and that Mary Katherine, just turned six, was old enough to begin doing some serious remembering.

Some children, of course, hold on to odd-shaped bits and pieces of memory from a much earlier age, but around the age of six and seven, nearly everything can be retained—or at least that was how it worked for me when I was a child.

It was like a kind of freedom—a kind of second welcoming her into the world. Now when I am an old man I will be able to say to her, "Remember when . . ." and she will remember.

We had flown to Austin, rented a car, visited my brother, and then driven down into the brush country and toward the live oaks and dunes that lie in braided twists some fifty miles inland: to the farm. As we drove, Elizabeth and I talked and watched the late-day sunlight stretch across the green fields; the girls slept, tired from their travels, in the back seat. Angels. So much joy do they bring me that sometimes I wonder if, since my mother is not here to love and know them, I'll carry also her share of that joy, having inherited it prematurely. For a fact, this joy seems too large. I think that maybe that is what is happening sometimes, at certain moments. I glance at them and love them fully and deeply, but then a second wave or wash comes in over that one, as if she is watching them over my shoulder, and I feel it again.

It used to give me a bittersweet feeling, but now I'm not sure what the word for it is. Gratitude, sometimes: to the girls, of course, but also to my mother.

They woke when we stopped to open the gate. We drove through and closed the gate behind us, and because we could not wait, we parked the car there and decided to walk instead of drive the rest of the way to the farmhouse. We walked in the late-day light, the last light, down the winding white sandy road, beneath the moss-hung limbs of the enormous live oaks—trees that were five and six hundred years old. It's so strange, the way there will be certain stretches of time, certain moments, when for a little while it will feel exactly as if I am walking in her every footstep, as if I am her in that moment, set back in time—and enjoying that moment as I know she must have enjoyed it, or one like it, thirty or forty years ago. And I wonder, is it just this way for me, or do others experience such feelings, such moments?

Buttercups, winecups, and black-eyed Susans—before we had taken ten steps, Lowry and Mary Katherine both had picked double-fistful bouquets and had braided flowers in their hair. Another ten steps took us across the culvert that ran beneath the road. There was water standing in the culvert and in receding little oxbows on either side of the road, and as we approached, ten thousand little frogs went splashing into that muddy water. "Frog alert, frog alert!" we cried, and ran down to mud's edge to try to catch one, but there were too many, springing zigzag in too many directions; you couldn't focus, and couldn't chase just one, because their paths were crisscrossing so. There were so many frogs in the air at any one time that occasionally they would have midair collisions; they were ricocheting off each other. The mud around the shoreline of their fast-disappearing pond glistened, so fast was the water evaporating, and the mud was heiroglyphed with the handprints of what might have been armies of raccoons, though also it could have been the maddened pacings of one very unsuccessful raccoon.

We finally caught one of the little frogs, and examined it: the gray-brown back that was so much the color of the mud, and the pearl-white underbelly. I wondered why, when frogs sunned themselves, they didn't stretch out and lie on their backs, the way humans do at the beach. I guess they would get eaten. I guess if a frog had a mud-brown belly it could lie on its back, camouflaged to the birds above, and still be able to listen for the approach of terrestrial predators, but I guess also there's no real evolutionary advantage to a frog being able to warm its belly in the sun. Though for that matter, the same could be said of us.

Into the farmhouse she loved so much—she had lived in it, and loved it, for only a few years before she fell ill, but had loved it so fully in that time that I still cannot step into it without feeling that remnant love-of-place. And it is thin substitute for her absence, but with the exception of my own blood in my veins, and memories, it is all there is, and I am grateful for it, place.

Elizabeth wanted to go for a run in the last wedge of light—after the long Montana winter we were nearly delirious with the gift of these longer days—and so she laced up her running shoes and went on back up the road at a trot. Mary Katherine wanted to go fishing in the stock tank, so we rigged up a line and went off toward the pond, following the winding sand road and walking beneath those old trees.

We stood on the levee and cast out at the ring of flat water. Turtle heads appeared in the center of the lake, tipped like little sticks, to observe us. In the clear water of the shallows we could see the giant Chinese grass carp, thirty pounds each and seemingly as large as horses striding just beneath the surface, cruising; my parents had put them there when they first built the pond as a means of keeping algae from overtaking the pond. The carp are hybrids, so they can't reproduce, though it's rumored they can live to be a hundred years old—and because the carp are strictly vegetarians, there was no chance of them striking at our spinnerbait. It was strange, though, watching the giant fish circle the pond so slowly, their dorsal fins sometimes cresting the surface like sharks, and knowing that we were fishing for something else, something deeper in the pond—fishing for fish-beneath-fish.

On the far side of the pond, a big fish leapt—not a carp, but a bass. We cast to it for a while in the gathering dusk, but I was hoping that we wouldn't catch it. It's good for the girls to learn that you don't get something every time you go out, or right away.

A water moccasin swam past, its beautifully ugly wedge of head so alarming to our instincts that it seemed almost to cause a mild form of hypnosis—as did the eerie, elegant S-wake of its thick body moving across the surface. Floating on the pond were four-leaf clovers that my parents had planted—a special variety in which every one of them had four leaves—and we stopped fishing for a moment and picked some for friends.

Across the field, across the rise, we could see the cattle trotting in front of the blood-red sun, running from something, and in that wavering red light, and across the copper-fading visage of the pasture, it looked like some scene from Africa, some vast herd of wildebeests. The cattle passed from view, and then a few moments later we saw the silhouette of Elizabeth jogging along the crest of the rise—she was what had spooked the cattle—and across the distance we watched her run in that Mars-red light, the sun behind her, as seven years ago I had sat by this same pond with my mother and watched Elizabeth and my father ride horses across the face of that sun.

We resumed casting. A mockingbird flew up and landed in the little weesatche tree next to us, not five hundred yards away, and as the sun's fireball sank (as if into an ocean), the mockingbird began singing the most beautiful song: some intricate melody that, in the blueing of dusk and then the true darkness, was one of the most beautiful songs—a serenade—I'd ever heard.

"Sing back to him," I told Lowry, and so she did; she sang her alphabet song there in the darkness, her "A-B-C's—next time you can sing with me," etc.

Finally it was true dark—the mockingbird was still singing—and we headed back toward the house. We saw a shuffling little object, a humped little creature, shambling down the sand road in front of us, and I cried, "Armadillo! Chase him!"

We set out after him in full sprint, and were almost even with him—he was running in zags and weaves through the trees—when I noticed the white stripe running down his back and was able barely in time to shout, "Skunk! Get back!"

Perhaps it was the four-leaf clovers. The skunk went his way, and we went ours. I had the strangest thought, in my relief, however. I found myself wondering how—had we been sprayed—the girls would have thought of me afterward, growing up. What if they grew up to be story-tellers? What kind of mirth would they have with that—recounting, for the rest of their adult days, the time their father told them to chase and catch a skunk?

How lucky they were, by fluke chance, to remain in normalcy and to escape unsprayed, untraumatized; and how lucky I was, by the matter of a few feet, to not have such identity fastened to me by my children with the permanence of myth.

I remembered the time when I was about Mary Katherine's age, when my cousin Randy was sprayed by a skunk. It was right around Christmas. We were all gathered up at Grandma and Granddaddy Bass's in Fort Worth—my parents, brothers, and myself; Aunt Lee, Uncle Jimmy, and my cousins Rick, Randy, and Russell. I had already gone to bed—I think it was Christmas Eve—but Randy, being a few years older, was allowed to go down to the creek to check his troutlines and his Havahart trap one more time.

I had just nodded off to sleep when I awoke to the impression that all the doors in the house had been blown wide open by some awful force. All of the adults had just let out a collective roar—a primal group groan—and then there were gasps and more groans and my uncle's voice, angry and above all others, "Randy, get out of the house!"

Then the smell hit me. Even in the back room, it was stout. I hadn't known that an odor could be that powerful. It seemed that it could levitate the house. It certainly levitated the people in the house.

When I went out to ask what all was going on, I seem to recall a furious, sputtering inarticulation on the part of the grown-ups, until finally— or this is how I remember it—they shouted, in unison and choreographed with much arm waving, "Randy!"—as if that said it all.

Thirty-plus years later the girls and I let the skunk travel on his way, and we went ours, still sweet-smelling. We could see the glow of the farmhouse through the woods and were striking toward it, holding hands and walking carefully in the darkness to avoid stepping on any skunks, when I saw a firefly blink once, then twice, in the distance, and I shouted with happiness.

The girls had never seen fireflies before. I am not sure they had even known such creatures existed.

For the next hour we chased them through the meadow, trying to catch just one. It seemed a harder task than I remembered from my own childhood—I remembered filling entire lantern-bottles with them—and I figured that it might be because it was still early in the spring and they were not yet blinking with full authority or intensity. We'd see only an individual blinking, and always at some great distance. We'd break into a run, hoping to arrive there before the blink faded, but they were always a little too far away, and their luminescence lasted only a few seconds. We would leap at that last instant, toward the always-ascending (they heard us coming) fading glow of gold—leaping with cupped hands and blind faith toward some imagined, calculated place ahead of us where we believed their flight path would take them—and opening our hands cautiously then, in the silver moonlight, to see if, like a miracle—like plucking a star from the sky—we had succeeded in blind-snaring one.

As beautiful as the on-again, off-again drifting missives of the fireflies was the seamlessness with which Mary Katherine accepted unquestioningly the marvel of such an existence, such a phenomenon. As if secure almost to the point of nonchalance, or at least pure or unexamined wonder, that yes, of course, this was the way all silver-moon nights were meant to be passed, running and laughing and leaping with great earnestness for drifting, blinking low-stars against a background of fixed, higher stars.

Eventually we caught one. And one was enough. We went through the time-honored ritual of putting it in a glass jar and punching air holes in the top. We took it inside the house: turned off all the lights. That simple, phenomenal, marvelous miracle—so easy to behold—as old familiar things left us, replaced by a newness in the world. The heck with electricity, or flashlights. Yes. This is the world my daughters deserve. This is the right world for them.

Later that night, after a supper cooked out on the grill, and after the girls were asleep (dreaming, I hope, of leaping), Elizabeth and I went for a long walk in the moonlight. The brightest, most severe platinum light I have ever seen. Revealing more, in the glare of that intense silver-blue light—highlighting certain things—than would the normal broad light of day.

It didn't feel as if we'd been together nearly twenty years. Or rather, part of it did: the good part.

Such strange brilliance.

The next day we all went fishing. It was windy, and Elizabeth's straw sunhat blew off and landed right side up on the pond. We watched it sail quickly, without sinking, all the way across the little lake. Mary Katherine ran around to the other side of the lake and was there to fish it out with a stick when it arrived. She ran it back to Elizabeth, who put it back on and tied it tighter this time.

The joy of children catching fish: there's nothing like it. Most of the few fish we were catching were too little, and we kept throwing them back. Low's pink skin, her bright blonde hair, in that beautiful spring sun. A hundred feet of snow, it seemed, back home, where we live now, though this was once my home, south Texas, and it's a wonderful feeling to be able to come back to a place that you have left and to feel that place welcome you back and to feel your affection for it undiminished across time.

Mary Katherine kept wanting to keep some fish for dinner that night. We finally caught one that was eating size, and as I put the fish on the stringer, I said, "It's your unlucky day, my little friend." And for the rest of the day, whenever we'd catch one, Mary Katherine (while hopping up and down and clapping her hands if I'd caught it, or simply hopping

up and down if she'd caught it) would say "Oh, please let it be his unlucky day, oh please!"

That night, after our fish fry, I took her into town for an ice cream cone;
Lowry had already fallen asleep. I get so used to doing things with them
together, the two girls, that I have to remember this: to always be there to
spend some time alone with each of them. The special quality or nature
of that as unique, as sacred, as the unique quality of sunlight early in the
spring, seen dappled through a new-green canopy of emerging leaves, or
in the late fall, when the light lies down soft and long again after the
harsh bright summer.

It was dusk again, and nighthawks were huddled along the edges of
the white sand roads as we drove slowly, twisting and turning, beneath
the arched limbs of more old live oaks. Fireflies were out in the meadows
again and we rode with the windows down to feel the cool night air. The
radio was playing very quietly—a jazz special, with the music of Sonny
Rollins and Louie Armstrong—and I knew by the way Mary Katherine
rode silently, happily, that she had never heard such music before.

We got into the little town of Yorktown a few minutes before closing
time. We went into the coolness of the air-conditioned Dairy Queen and
I waited while Mary Katherine pondered her selection, deciding finally
on a chocolate dip cone.

She ate on it the whole way home—back through the starry night, back
through the fireflies, back to the rest of our waiting, sleeping family—just
riding and listening, all the while, to that strange, happy, lulling music
from so long ago.

I have never felt more like a father: never more in love with the world.

2

My Child's First Garden

Michael P. Branch

Next year, our daughter, Hannah Virginia, will go to kinder*garten*—a *children's garden* where, we hope, she will grow and grow. In advance of kindergarten, though, I wanted Hannah to have a garden of her own at home. I wanted to share with her a sustainable practice of labor, meditation, and production that has been essential to my life and that I hoped would become important in her life too. I wanted her to experience the miracle of a seed germinating, have the satisfaction of seeing things she planted with her own little hands grow to flower and fruit. I wanted not so much to watch Hannah's garden grow as to watch her watch it grow. To quote Ken Kesey, I wanted to help her "plant a garden in which strange plants grow and mysteries bloom." And even if some of the strange plants in Kesey's garden were illegal, as I suspect they were, his admonition to cultivate mysteries speaks directly to the higher law that governs true gardening. The garden is not only the place where we grow food but also the place where we plant hopes and nurture ideas, where many plans grow from each thought that is sown. The garden is also a metaphor for what is peaceful, harmonious, and productive in our lives, and even our language reveals how deeply our imaginations are rooted in the garden. We celebrate ideas that are *seminal* because so much can grow from the *seed* of a single thought. When we deeply question our culture's values, we are considered *radical* because we attempt to address problems at their *root*. We work hard to bring our projects to *fruition*, for nothing is sweeter than the *fruit* of our own labor. The garden is the imaginatively fertile ground where we harvest metaphors along with squash and beans.

Without realizing it at the time, in planning Hannah's first garden I had conflated parenting and gardening in my mind. After all, both are practices of love, attention, and creativity that result in healthy growth. Both require vigilance, nurturing, and care, and both result in progressive development that leads to sustaining harvests. Gardening and parenting are disciplines of sustainability, acts of faith in the future that must be renewed through daily practice. Of course, this is the same sort of thinking employed by people who believe they are ready to have children because they managed to own a dog. Be that as it may, a gardener's universe is all sweetness and light, and the gardener's mind, like his garden, must remain an inviolable space that is impervious to the world's heartless logic. I had been a good gardener, and now I intended to use a garden to be a good father.

Even in my glowing optimism, I knew that my child's first garden might present a challenge. We live at 6,000 feet in the Great Basin Desert, at the foot of the Sierra Nevada, on an exposed hill, amid conditions no gardener would relish—short growing season, extreme aridity, severe temperature fluctuations, desiccating winds, ravenous critters of every stripe. This is a place where even our human neighbors sometimes dry up, burn down, and blow away, which hardly bodes well for a green pepper. Still, to a true gardener the unplanted garden is ever a canvas before paint, an idea not yet gone wrong, a sweet dream from which we have yet to awaken. As with any good idea, the trouble with a garden begins only when we attempt to realize what we have imagined.

As I spent the last nights of winter by the woodstove, sipping bourbon and strategizing to ensure the success of my child's first garden, I realized that the pressure was on. What if the garden I promised this sweet four-year-old girl didn't prosper? Given the metaphorical and philosophical significance of the garden, what larger, darker conclusions might she draw about her small place in the hard world if her own garden failed to come to fruition? I had to get this one right, and so I planned and planned. First, I would site Hannah's garden on the lee side of our big hill, where the hot wind would be more forgiving, and I'd stake and cage everything that grew upright to provide reinforcement against the scorching afternoon wind known locally as the "Washoe Zephyr." I would also go to the trouble of constructing a large garden box out of railroad ties; this way I could backfill the raised bed with the primo double mix soil I call "black gold," while also discouraging the cottontails and, especially, the big jackrabbits that can graze a bed to its roots in the time it takes to fetch a beer. To be safe, I'd wrap the whole garden in impervious wire fence. And in the interest of ensuring my daughter's success as a neophyte gardener, I would set aside my environmentalist scruples and declare her plot a xeric-free zone where she could water to her heart's content. Finally, I would swallow my gardener's pride and grow only hardy, reliable plants, those that are fast-growing, difficult to kill, and, if possible, spicy enough to be unpalatable to rodents. As winter waned, I came to think of my child's first garden as "the radish plot," as radishes have long been the mascot vegetable for amateur gardeners—fast, easy, cheap, unfailing, and plenty spicy. In a world of waiting and suffering, the lowly radish signifies certain success and short-term gratification.

When spring came, which it does mighty late at 6,000 feet, I built the garden just as I had designed it. Reminding myself of Kipling's admonition that "gardens are not made by sitting in the shade," I worked all day in the glaring desert sun, transforming a bare plot of weedy hardpan into my child's first garden. After the chainsaw, mattock, shovel, rake, spading fork, and field hammer were put up, I grabbed a trowel and hand cultivator and called Hannah out to plant her garden. It was a momentous occasion, and I insisted that my wife, Eryn, photograph this moment for posterity. I still treasure those pictures. In one, Hannah is deep-setting her first tomato plant with all her might; in another, she is broadcasting radish seed from her little, green-gloved hand; in a third, she is smiling broadly from behind the frame I built to trellis her beans. Throughout this photo op, though, Eryn's face wore a look of bemusement that suggested pleasure tinged with concern.

"Hey, what's the matter?" I asked Eryn, as I stepped away from the garden, leaving Hannah to water in her new plants. "Isn't this great?"

"I don't know, Bubba. She's pretty into this. Are you sure this is going to work?"

I shot a glance over my shoulder at Hannah in her garden and then turned back to Eryn with a look of wounded pride. "Come on, I've been gardening my whole life. Besides, I've got this nailed. Look at what we're growing," I said, lowering my voice to a whisper. "I've stooped to radishes, for crying out loud. Honey, this is foolproof."

Only a fool believes that anything in this broken world is foolproof, and so the proliferation of things called foolproof is proof only that the world has fools and plenty. But the troubles in Hannah's garden didn't start immediately. There was a golden, two-week honeymoon during which seeds germinated, plants grew, and we gathered around the heavily armored plot to witness our little garden prevailing, even against daunting desert odds. We had planted tomatoes, squash, beans, sweet and hot peppers, collards, basil, and, of course, plenty of radishes. It was an unambitious, low-risk, starter plot—a prosperous, shining little garden upon a hill that would make the desert bloom and fructify according to promises of old.

We showered our plants with well water and attention and screened them with burlap to protect them from the hot wind. My fence kept out the cottontails and jacks, just as I had hoped. As our plants grew, we also took more pictures, proudly documenting for posterity the triumph of a little girl's first efforts as a gardener.

Despite Bobby Burns's conviction that "the best laid schemes o' mice an' men gang aft a-gley," around our place the mice have aft done extremely well, while it is only my own schemes that have gang very, very damned a-gley. One aspect of my garden fortress scheme that was not well laid was my failure to foresee that slack spots along the base of my hardware cloth barricade would be virtual highways to a field mouse, which has no difficulty squeezing through a gap less than a half-inch in diameter. So the "wee, sleekit, cow'rin, tim'rous beastie" got some seeds, as did the chisel-toothed kangaroo rats (*Dipodomys microps*) that abound here, foraging nocturnally for just such simple treasures as radish seeds. But this was sustainable damage, and I explained to Hannah that, really, we were just being nice by "sharing" with our nonhuman neighbors. As an added form of insurance, however, I secretly overseeded her plot, and I tightened the fence carefully in hopes of mending the breaches. Within hours of fixing the fence, though, I discovered a mixed flock of bushtits, chickadees, and sparrows tearing up the seedbeds and so rushed to string in a half dozen aluminum pie tins, which whipped in the zephyr and made racket enough to keep out the hungry birds.

The next morning, Hannah and I were happy to find the seedbeds undisturbed, but just as I began to relax into a feeling of satisfaction, I noticed that the squash plants had been shorn to the ground. After the time-consuming process of unwrapping various layers of fence, I was at last able to get close enough to the plants to examine them with a magnifying glass. Judging from the size of the lacerated stems and the clean, sharp angle of their cut, I was certain that packrats had been the culprits. I knew all too well that the bushy-tailed packrats (*Neotoma cinerea*), which occupy this land in impressive numbers, are fantastic climbers, but I had hoped that the wire fence would deter them despite their ability to scramble up sheer cliffs.

Hope is the coin of the gardener's realm, but it is a devalued currency, worth increasingly less as it is traded against the incessantly rising tender of the gardener's despair. It was several days before I made it to town to get plastic bird netting—which I now needed to keep out not birds but packrats—and by then I was forced to buy replacement seed and bedding plants for the garden, which had already been substantially ravaged by the birds, mice, kangaroo rats, and packrats. Indeed, the salad bar that was once my child's first garden was now so heavily frequented by rodents that the local great horned owl calculated his economies of scale and took up a hunting perch on the peak of our roof. While the final stages of the garden's destruction proceeded apace despite the owl's nightly vigil, I now had the additional chore of cleaning from the sidewalk many overlapping bursts of snow-white owl crap, which were so voluminous as to make it inconceivable they could have been dropped by anything daintier than a pterodactyl.

During this time, Hannah and I continued to water what was left of her garden, and she had a great time playing in the mud—even as I was constantly humiliated by having to explain to her mother why I, the seasoned gardener, was finding it so difficult to grow a few radishes. The ripe fruit of my gardener's pride began to wither on the blasted vine of my child's first garden, and while I was relieved that Hannah seemed unfazed by what Eryn had begun to call "The Vegpocalypse," I had no way of knowing how long this grace period might continue. Grace, like good gardening weather, is welcome it when it comes, but you're in deep, uncomposted manure if you come to count on it. At some point, I reckoned, this garden must *produce*.

Returning from town one day, despondent but with plenty of bird netting and beer, I once again unwrapped the various layers of artillery separating the little garden from the cruel world, and we started over. I dug out the rootballs of the clearcut squash and removed the hard stems of the limbless tomatoes, while Hannah gathered the scattered leaves of the savaged sweet peppers. We retilled and replanted Hannah's first garden from end to end, and while she was in great spirits the entire time—even telling me that she wished we could replant the garden "every single day"—I was plenty surly about it. Given the brevity of our growing season, I knew that the precious time already lost might compromise the success of this second attempt. When our replanting was done, Hannah went in to wash up while I spent another hour reinforcing my defense systems, concluding with the double layer of plastic netting that I draped over the top of the fortress and snapped down with yellow bungee cords. Then I called Hannah, sat down in my old aluminum lawn chair with her in my lap, and stared at my child's second first garden as if it were my mortal enemy.

I stared, I say, and yet I could see nothing that we had planted. With all the railroad ties, posts, trellises, stakes, tomato cages, hardware cloth fences, burlap wind breaks, shimmering pie tins, and panels of bird netting, it was now virtually impossible to see any living thing through the overlapping walls of the garden. I could in fact see no garden at all, but only a hideous monument to my determination to establish a barrier where my brute neighbors would have none. My child's second first garden looked like a miniature factory or prison or maybe the tangled bones of a steel barn after it meets the tornado's funnel. It was challenging to water, impossible to weed, difficult even to see. What the hell kind of garden was that, especially for a child? "Something there is that doesn't love a wall, that wants it down," wrote Robert Frost in "Mending Wall." I had instead abided by the maxim Frost's neighbor endorses in the poem: "Good fences make good neighbors." If the furry and feathered would just stay on their side of the fence, all would be well. It was a simple concept, and I was exasperated by the lengths I was being driven to in order to make sure my kid could pull a radish before her fifth birthday.

Discouraged as I was, as a gardener I had been toughened by disappointment as well as by wind and sun. Even The Vegpocalypse, I reasoned, wasn't worse than some other gardening catastrophes I had endured, and as I sat meditating on my failure, I was reminded of the heartening words of Thomas Jefferson, one of our most philosophical gardeners. In the garden, wrote Mr. Jefferson, "the failure of one thing is repaired by the success of another." Perhaps, as T.J. suggested, there would be some hidden consolation to compensate for my current losses. Just at that moment, however, something tragic and unexpected happened—something that fatally radicalized my approach to gardening in the high desert. As I sat in my bent lawn chair, with Hannah in my lap and one half of my ass poking down through the ripped canvas seat, two tiny, white-tailed antelope ground squirrels skittered across the rocky patch of dirt that is our "yard," raced beneath us, and ran over my right foot in their gleeful sprint to get to our newly replanted garden. There they disappeared momentarily behind the railroad ties forming the garden box before popping up in the garden itself, wasting no time in starting to crop our squash.

All of this happened in a matter of seconds, of course, but in that moment I felt the sting of failure curl over me in a slow-breaking wave of despair. My gardener's hubris—that profound, unsubstantiated delusion of superiority without which no gardener could long endure his trials—had bitten me on the half of my ass that was exposed to the cruel world. In allowing myself to believe that the replanted and rearmored garden was impenetrable, I had foolishly ignored one of the basic principles of fatherhood, a principle so fundamental that it belongs with such core insights as "If it smells bad, it is bad" or "When your kid tells you to cover your eyes, do it with one hand, and cover your nuts with the other." *Humility* is the alpha and omega of both parenting and gardening. I had failed to be humble, and in failing to be humble I was now humbled by failure, albeit a failure I was experiencing as anger. In mute frustration, I now reckoned that my daughter's happiness—her future as a gardener, the optimism of her worldview, perhaps her entire philosophical orientation to life—was staked on the uncertain success of the little garden these white-tailed beasts were now devouring. And, damn it, they had stepped on my foot. Both the gardener and the father in me were now called to battle. As I sat with my jaw locked, watching my child's second first garden being destroyed, I could feel that I was about to cross an invisible line—that extraordinary and perhaps violent measures would be necessary. Hannah, whose response was quite different from my own, just screeched excitedly: "Daddy! Look at the cute little chipmunks in my garden!"

As the cracked stubs of what were once our plants baked in the sun—a sun whose azimuth had grown troublingly higher in recent weeks—I began a calculated assault on the "chipmunks" that had now become more numerous than flies around our place. The white-tailed antelope squirrel (*Ammospermophilus leucurus*) is in fact a remarkable creature, one whose adaptations to the grueling excesses of the desert environment can only have been shaped by a zillion evolutionary near misses, each one resulting in a crunchy snack for a hawk or coyote. Until you've been in the desert awhile, the antelope squirrel really does look like a chipmunk, though the differences are many and extraordinary. For starters, optimal habitat for the antelope squirrel is sparse juniper, sagebrush steppe, and desert scrub, and it would never be seen in the alpine forest. The white-tailed antelope—the species of *Ammospermophilus* most widely distributed throughout the arid West and the one that was chowing down on my child's second first garden—sports a narrow, white stripe from shoulder to rump, has white cheeks, and carries none of those unsightly chipmunk stripes on its face. Antelopes have thin, coarse fur that is light brown with a gray or, as in my local population, reddish tint. The infallible means to distinguish them from chipmunks, though, is by their amazing ability to run with their tail pulled up over their bodies, a feat your average chipmunk could only dream of attempting. The underside of that raised tail flashes as white as the rump of a pronghorn in flight, an unmistakable visual correspondence that is the source of the antelope squirrel's odd name. And the antelope lives up to the name "squirrel" perfectly. The word *squirrel* comes from the Vulgar Latin *scuriolus*, which is a variant of the Latin *sciurus*, which comes from the Greek *skiouros*, which gives this family its name, *Sciuridae*, and which is almost certainly the source of the word *scurry*. Antelope squirrels are so small—four ounces or so—that you could mail one across the country for about a buck, but they scurry with such inconceivable swiftness that they make sprinting chipmunks look like they are shuffling from couch to cupboard to get a bag of Cheetos during halftime. Once running, the antelope squirrel, unlike its namesake the pronghorn, never stops or looks back, instead flying across the earth like a white-flagged shot that vanishes into the ground at hyperspeed.

Unlike chipmunks and even other kinds of ground squirrels, the antelope is active throughout the year, which frees it from the need to hoard food in preparation for hibernation. It is not particularly territorial and in fact will huddle with others of its kind to conserve heat during the winter, so you can't count on them to off each other the way an aggressive, territorial rodent like a packrat might. They excavate tunnels with multiple entrances, have several burrows in their large home range, construct separate tunnels for food caches and quick escapes, and often appropriate the burrow systems of kangaroo rats, all of which makes them virtually impossible to locate once underground. Somewhere in one of those many tunnels, the antelope will make a nest six inches in diameter, which it has likely lined with the golden hair that is cast off when Eryn brushes Hannah's hair outside on sunny mornings. You can't easily starve an antelope squirrel, as they are generalist omnivores that will eat almost anything, from seeds, plants, roots, grasses, and fruits to insects, lizards, and carrion, even including the flesh of fellow rodents. Virtually invulnerable to dehydration, they need no free water to survive, instead deriving all their hydration from the plants and bugs they eat. Their kidneys are so highly efficient in saving water by reducing nitrogenous waste that if we were as well designed, we could go several years on a single roll of toilet paper. Antelopes around here usually mate in late February and are born around Hannah's birthday in early April—a reproductive cycle that is precisely calibrated to the emergence of leafy annual plants here in the high desert.

What is most amazing about the antelope squirrel is its astonishing ability to keep itself cool in the brutal desert heat. Unlike the nocturnal foragers whose lifestyle seems more compatible with this scorching environment, the antelope is diurnal, cruising around above ground even on the hottest days. It has a number of tricks that make this marvelous feat possible. Its water-conservation strategies help, of course, as do its habit of keeping its back to the sun and shading its body with its tail and its ability to climb into bushes to catch a breeze. Most important, the antelope doesn't cool itself evaporatively, as humans and most other mammals do, so it isn't water stressed by cooling. For this little squirrel, keeping cool is literally no sweat. Instead, it is so well adapted to the desert environment that it can allow its body temperature to rise to an incredible 110 degrees Fahrenheit. When it begins to overheat, it returns to its burrow, splays its legs, drops its sparsely furred belly against the earth, and lets the ground pull the heat right out of its body—after which it pops up again and resumes razing our garden. If they are well hydrated when they get hot, they will also use the neat trick of rubbing saliva on their face to cool themselves, a behavior that makes me suspect that our one-year-old daughter, Caroline, may in fact be a ground squirrel.

The antelope squirrel's adaptive strategies are so many and so effective as to give it a daunting home-field advantage, and as a beer-guzzling mammalian biped with an oversized but virtually useless cerebral cortex, I do not feel myself a very worthy opponent. Still, there was the garden to be saved, and so, like anyone desperate for love or money, I turned to the Internet for solutions to my problem. The testimonials online were numerous and disconsolate, and it quickly became clear that of the many unappealing strategies for antelope squirrel control, only live trapping seemed likely to succeed. After driving to town to buy several small traps, another case of beer, and a large jar of crunchy peanut butter (which I labeled "NOT FOR KIDS"), I began my attempt to catch the cute little antelope squirrels. Following some misadventures in which I trapped a pinyon jay, a kangaroo rat, a scorpion, and my own fingers (twice), I did at last discover that the wee squirrels like Uncle Crunkle's Old Fashioned Peanut Butter at least as well as they like squash stems. During the next two weeks, as I became a more experienced trapper, I nabbed sixteen antelopes—all of which I released on public lands far from my child's garden, as some studies claim that this six-inch-long creature can find its way home from several miles away.

Having more or less succeeded in my efforts to remove the antelope tribe from the neighborhood of our garden (there was one smug little urchin I never did catch), I raked together what was left of my gardener's self-respect and helped Hannah put on her gardening boots and gloves. We completely replanted her plot yet again, which was perfectly fine with her, even as I feared that the seasonal window would shut on her plants before they came to fruition. I was now sufficiently desperate that I hatched a plan to photograph Hannah next to the plants as they grew, later interpolating these shots of her third first garden with the earlier ones of her planting the actual first garden so as to create the appearance of success where in fact there had been two complete failures. The fact that I had sprung for larger, more developed bedding plants this time would help support the illusion. When I suggested to Eryn that some Photoshopping might also help out where evidence of The Double Vegpocalypse was inadvertently revealed (for example, I had carelessly planted a pepper where a tomato had been), she smilingly dismissed my idea as only the most extreme of "the many clear signs" that my obsession with my child's first garden had driven me to desperation. Undeterred by her diagnosis, I insisted that the plan would work and so took a raft of pictures of my child's third first garden, which really did look quite nice. Hannah and I then put up our tools, got out the old lawn chair, and sat together admiring our neat little garden as Venus arced toward the mountains.

The next morning I awoke before daybreak with a deeply unsettled feeling. I had experienced a disturbingly vivid dream in which I stood in Hannah's garden, leaning at a slight angle but with arms straight out like a scarecrow, immobilized by a strange paralysis as rodents of every kind crawled up and down my body, even clinging to my beard with their claws as they grinned directly into my eyes. In the dream, I was in a state of heightened sensory awareness, and I could not only smell the dank fur but feel the tiny whiskers and even the quivering breath of the mice, voles, moles, pocket gophers, kangaroo rats, packrats, and antelope squirrels as they clambered over me. When I awoke, I was just beginning to lose sight as one especially cute antelope squirrel nibbled on my exposed, unblinking eyeball.

Trying to chase away my bad night with java that I made a good bit stronger than usual, I stood at the slider door, sipping from my cup and awaiting sunrise over my child's third first garden. At last the ascending Venus dimmed, the sky brightened, and the little plot was bathed in a golden, effulgent light. There it was, suddenly, in all its shining glory, the little garden for my little girl, and somehow all my struggles now seemed entirely rewarded. Here was the garden I had envisioned, the garden that would grow with Hannah, teaching her to nurture the flower and fruit that binds us to the nonhuman world. Here she would learn the ethic of care that is the highest mark of a moral person, and here she would practice techniques of sustainability that would give her healthy food to eat and a harvest basket overflowing with metaphors to live by.

As I admired the garden and contemplated my inspiring success with earth-centered parenting, one of the tomato plants disappeared. I quickly scurried back and forth in front of the slider to make sure of what I was seeing and then yanked open the door and sprinted to the garden, leaning over the various fences and pressing my face against the nylon bird netting to get a closer view. In the soil directly beneath the center of one tomato cage, which was still rocking slightly, there was a hole where the plant had stood only a moment before.

In that moment I did not cry out, like Job, to the unjust heavens to demand explanation for why I was being punished for a crime I did not commit. I did not observe the natural historical evidence before me in search of a scientific understanding of the depredation nature had here wrought. I did not engage in the inimitable brand of breathtaking, blue-streaking profanity for which I have been reviled by some and celebrated by others. Instead, I felt something deep inside me begin to uncoil, some mainspring in the engine of my tolerance for my fellow creatures irreversibly unwinding, the psychic rivets of my environmentalist identity popping off as the spring unwound.

I have only a hazy recollection of what happened next, but Eryn, whom I trust implicitly, reports that she awoke to see me walking through the house very slowly, "like a zombie," wearing only lime green boxer shorts decorated with orange ladybugs, blaze orange sound-protection muffs over my ears, and carrying a shotgun. I vaguely recall the muffled sound of Hannah shouting, "Daddy has a firestick!" as I passed the open door of her bedroom, but this too remains rather foggy for me. I do, however, remember sharply how different the garden looked when sighted down the barrel to the bead, and I recall the feeling of the trigger moving beneath my finger when he popped his head out of the hole where the tomato plant had recently stood.

It is true, of course, that the shot blasted apart the fence on both sides of the garden—creating gaping holes through with other ravenous beasts would enter and finish off my child's third first garden in the days ahead. And it is true that the buckshot perforated the leaves of many plants, which hardly mattered since they were soon eaten by the animals that came in through the fence anyway. And it is true that trying to stop rodents is like trying to dig a hole in water: a bucketful of water closes in where every bucketful is lifted out, forever. And it is true that no knuckle-dragging human is a match for animals that are so brilliantly adapted to the desert environment. It is further true that the very proliferation of these rodents was my own fault—not only because the caloric easy money of the garden drew them in but also because our presence here created a charmed circle that coyotes would not enter. And it is true that gunplay in the garden is not especially consistent with the environmental ethic of care and sustainability that I had hoped the garden would teach my little girl. And it is disconcertingly true that once a pacifist nature lover blows something's head off with a shotgun, it generates in him a certain amount of cognitive dissonance, which in turn is deeply subversive of the environmentalist identity said nature lover may have spent a lifetime cultivating. But it is also indisputably true that, when pushed far enough, even a person with a firm grip on the ethical steering wheel can veer suddenly off the road of their own morality.

The wise Cicero, who wrote that "if you have a garden and a library, you have everything you need," clearly didn't know about the California ground squirrel, or he would have had a shotgun too. *Spermophilus beecheyi* is, if possible, even more remarkable than his cousin the antelope squirrel, though I did not know that at the time I disemboweled him with a firestick. Almost a foot long with a tail that can extend another nine inches, often more than two pounds in weight, and a prodigious excavator and vegetarian with a huge appetite, this beautiful monster is a real threat to agricultural enterprises on the commercial or domestic scale. One study found that a single squirrel home containing eleven animals consisted of a tunnel system extending over 700 feet, including thirty-three openings, and descending nearly thirty feet below ground. Females often mate with more than one male and sometimes do so more than once each season, and they may give birth to a dozen or more pups in each litter. Their tunnels usually protect them from predators other than rattlesnakes, and even here their defenses are daunting. Adult squirrels are actually immune to rattler venom, so when a buzzworm slithers into a tunnel system, it is not unusual for a squirrel to harass it, even kicking sand in the bully snake's face like the pugnacious little bad ass that he is. And while squirrel pups are not immune to rattler venom, female squirrels collect sloughed rattlesnake skins, chew them up, and lick the snake-scented saliva onto their pups, thus using smell to trick the rattler into thinking the baby ground squirrels are actually a fellow snake and encouraging the predator to seek elsewhere for supper. The California ground squirrel is fast, agile, intelligent, and resourceful and has vision as sharp as yours. It protects others of its kind with high-pitched alarm cries by which it communicates danger across miles of desert—a piercing, surging, metallic cry that now plays in my ear as the soundtrack to my own defeat as a gardener. Although diurnal like his cousin the antelope, the California ground squirrel goes into estivation (a period of strategic inactivity) when the weather becomes too hot and goes into true hibernation in the winter—a physiological shutdown so amazingly like suspended animation that the animal's heartbeat is reduced to a tenth of its normal rate, and it draws a breath only once every few minutes.

After I learned all this about my neighbor *Spermophilus*, it seemed fairly clear that I was overmatched. Since he didn't need to chew through or climb the wire protection around our garden, he could tunnel under from anywhere he pleased and pop up beneath a tomato plant—which, as the literature on ground squirrel crop damage shows, is among his favorite foods. But everything I read suggested that if I didn't deal with these ground squirrels immediately, they would soon overrun the place, undermining the foundation of our house with their tunnels, eating ornamental plants as well as vegetables, spreading fleas that can carry bubonic plague, and driving my truck to town to buy expensive whiskey with my credit card. They are in fact so destructive to croplands and irrigation systems that it is illegal to release a squirrel that has been live trapped, and a sense of how far folks will go to try to kill them is suggested by this discouraging remark, which I discovered somewhere in the voluminous antisquirrel literature: "truck-mounted vacuum devices that suck ground squirrels out of their burrows have not demonstrated sufficient efficacy to justify their use." Still, I made up my mind that if my child was ever to have a first garden, I would have to try everything short of burrow vacuuming.

Having already become a cold-blooded killer on that fateful morning, I at first decided, like Huck Finn, that "I would take up wickedness again" and so resolved to keep blasting away at my scurrilous neighbors. After all, once you've crossed the line and become a heartless murderer, what are a few dozen perforated corpses more or less? But Eryn talked me out of the gunplay, not so much by pointing out its incompatibility with the environmental values I aspired to inculcate in my daughter but more by reminding me that if I was going to walk around heavily armed, I wouldn't be able to drink at the same time—something I prognosticated could become imperative in the battle ahead.

I began with attempts to live-trap the big ground squirrels, as I had their smaller cousins, but they proved far too wily to be snared, and as my traps sat empty, my child's third first garden was completely wiped out. At this point I could have acknowledged that after three strikes you're out, but instead I did what my species does best: I chose foolishly to believe against all evidence that nature *doesn't* bat last, that I could still somehow win one for the humanoids by knocking it into the bleachers in the bottom of the ninth. *Spermophilus* had become my white whale. In a weak moment I ordered a case of "Wild Bill's Shure Kill Varmint Hole Fumigating Bombs" and had soon prepared a new strategy to defend my child's first garden—which, granted, was now an entirely hypothetical construct—by smoking out my subterranean opponent. The next Saturday morning I dressed for the occasion in boots, long pants, long-sleeved shirt, gloves, hat, safety goggles over my eyes, and bandana tied over my mouth. As Eryn observed, I did resemble the insane, drunken-looking "Wild Bill" who appeared on the cylinder of every single bomb. Carefully following Bill's directions, I first located what I felt certain were all the holes to the squirrels' tunnel system and then began to execute my plan. For a moment there was a wonderful rush of excitement as I sprinted hole to hole amid swirls of fuchsia smoke, dropping flaming canisters into the four burrow entrances I had located. Hannah stood at a safe distance with her Mom and clapped her hands, hopping up and down enthusiastically. Then there was an ominous hiatus during which nothing at all seemed to happen. As I stood perched over the squirrel hole nearest the house, I finally looked up to see Hannah and Eryn smiling and pointing at something that was apparently behind me. Lifting my goggles from my eyes to my grimy forehead, I turned slowly around. I wouldn't be telling the truth if I said that one, two, three, . . . *fourteen* columns of fuchsia smoke curling off into the cobalt blue desert sky wasn't a lovely sight, in an *Apocalypse Now* sort of way. Thus was it colorfully brought to my attention that the burrow system had far more escape hatches than I knew of and that this superb ventilation system had prevented my aerial gas attack from being anything more harmful than a fireworks show for Hannah, who in fact liked it so much that she made me a thank-you card out of fuchsia-colored construction paper.

Being averse to using poisons and having now given up on the trap, gun, and bomb, I had but one weapon remaining in my armory—piss. Relinquishing the treasured idea that a human could defeat these squirrels, in my desperation I resorted to an unlikely, indirect form of biological control. The ground squirrel used smell to trick the rattlesnake into believing that *Spermophilus* pups were not what they seemed. What if I could pull a stinking page from the ground squirrels' own playbook and make the scurrilous brute think I was his lethal arch predator, the coyote?

And so, having failed in my roles as Mr. McGregor, Elmer Fudd, and Wild Bill, I now prepared to transform myself into Old Man Coyote. And how is this trickster, *Canis latrans*, known unmistakably to his neighbors in the wild world? By his wicked grin and by the reek of his piss. After becoming the first person in my family to mail order a jug of coyote urine, I now possessed both the grin and the pee. And while I tried not to think about just how one would go about *getting* a statute gallon of coyote wiz, I did feel a late surge of hope that my final plan had a chance of working because I was now strategizing to go with the flow of nature, so to speak, rather than against it. If the crucible of evolution hadn't taught these squirrels to fear gardeners or smoke bombers, it had certainly taught them to dread the loping death that was Old Man Coyote.

The problem with my "desert doggie wee wee plan," as Eryn unsympathetically taught Hannah to call it, was that in order to test its results, we would have to plant my child's first garden a fourth time, even as I was now virtually certain that after the time consumed by The Triple Vegpocalypse and its attendant skirmishes, frost would kill the garden even if *Spermophilus* did not. And so Hannah and I spent the next Saturday replanting the plot from scratch, of course using the most humiliatingly large bedding plants that a child's raided college savings can buy. While I experienced the replanting as a Sisyphean labor, Hannah spontaneously preserved a Jeffersonian equanimity that demonstrated a healthy resilience that I was incapable of. She expressed her happiness that the squirrels had eaten such a healthy dinner ("Dad, vegetables make them strong too!" she said, holding up her tiny arms in an attempt at a bicep flex), and she repeated that planting the garden was so fun that she wanted to do it every day—which, as things were going, seemed a distinct possibility. Once replanted, the garden had yet again to be rearmored and in fact now looked even more unsightly, what with the additional hardware cloth patches I had wired in to cover the large holes blown out by the buckshot. None of this bothered Hannah, of course, and she "made rainbows" while watering in her new plants, after which we put up our tools and went inside to wait for late afternoon, when I would administer the last deterrent in my arsenal.

I should admit that as the day wore on, I became increasingly nervous about the outcome of my looming experiment and that I drank a fair amount of whiskey in an attempt to swallow my growing uncertainty. I had to admit that things didn't look good. My wife, who is both more sensible and more intelligent than her husband, thought the "desert doggie wee wee plan" absurd, which seemed vaguely inauspicious. I had of course failed in every other attempt, so my poor track record suggested that I was the only creature in my local environment completely ill-suited to inhabit it. And what could it signify that in my hour of greatest need I had resorted not to the dual consolations of acceptance and prayer but rather to the twin elixirs of bourbon and coyote urine? If I failed in this final attempt, I would have to admit, finally, that I was not only a humiliated gardener, an ineffectual environmental educator, and an environmentalist pariah but also a half-drunk, first-order, second-grade, third-string, fourth-first-garden-planting, gas, gun, and pee-toting five-star vigilante.

By late afternoon I was sufficiently lubricated that I should perhaps have reconsidered my plan to resume work in my child's fourth first garden, but I knew that the garden would soon be gone without some form of protection, and I still had a rather expensive Jug O' Wiz with *Spermophilus*'s name on it. I drained one last whiskey, fetched my secret weapon, and approached the garden with the jug gripped tightly in my right hand. I climbed up onto the garden's railroad tie frame and balanced myself there, slowly wrapping the fingers of my left hand around the jug's screw-top cap. I paused, taking one last, deep breath before opening the seventh seal.

I still remember how lovely that newly planted garden looked in the glow of the low-angle afternoon sun, how the light breeze rippled the leaves of the tomatoes and squash, how moist and fertile the seedbeds appeared, how neat and well tended the plot seemed. I vividly recall feeling that I was seeing the perfect garden in a perfect moment, though this transcendental epiphany was no doubt animated by the blush and tingle of the whiskey that had by then loosened all my muscles. I remember how lovely that moment felt, how hesitant I was to twist that cap and lose the wonderful feeling that little garden inspired in me. I remember, with a dreamlike sense of distance, an overflowing feeling that it had all been worth it after all—that this tender plot was truly a monument to my love for my daughter and for the earth, despite the trials it had presented. Maybe, I recall thinking, there is some cosmic plan within which this struggle has been an indispensable part of my own journey as both a father and as a gardener. And then I twisted off the lid.

Friends, there can be no word in any human language that even begins to suggest the overpowering, unspeakable stench that exploded from the jug the instant that lid came off. Nothing in human evolutionary biology could have prepared me for this reeking bomb, the first whiff of which instantly flooded my eyes with tears, filled my mouth with a choking metallic tang, and set the whiskey roiling violently in my gut. I felt as if my body had suddenly become a permeable membrane through which the worst stink in the universe was blowing at gale force, carrying off my flesh as it howled through and reducing me to a shattered pile of smoldering bones. It was, in truth, as close to spontaneous human combustion as you can get and still live to tell the tale. After all, this was not just the urine of who knows how many very angry and presumably catheterized coyotes; it was a highly concentrated *gallon* of the stuff, and it had been stored for who knows how long in this vacuum-sealed container. While it was at least hypothetically possible that a single drop of this behind Old Man Coyote's ear might get him laid, I now held at the end of my hyperextended arm a quivering vessel of the kind of stench that could make a gagging human hope to be sprayed by a polecat just to cover it up.

This all happened in a flash, as you can imagine, but in the instant that I recoiled from the revolting stink, which blasted out of the jug and attacked my face like a swarm of yellow jackets, I heard that signature metallic chirp of victory ring out from the sagebrush behind me. It was *Spermophilus*, either laughing at me or warning his kin that ten thousand coyotes had just simultaneously taken a huge leak. Spinning my contorted face away from the jug and toward that piercing cry, I suddenly felt my boot sole begin to slip on the edge of the railroad tie upon which I had perched. And it is at this moment—the only such moment in my life as a gardener, either before or since—that time seemed to slow almost to a stop, and I experienced the next second or two in that frame-by-frame fashion that the human brain reserves for only the most unthinkable of accidents. I fell for what seemed quite a long time, and I even remember seeing the pee that splashed out of the jug floating in midair, as if in the zero gravity of a space capsule. Eventually the handle of the jug released its grip on my fingers, and it too turned slowly in midair as if it would remain spinning there forever. And then, at last, came the splintering crash of my body as it landed on my child's fourth first garden, taking down fences and netting and stakes and cages as it did, and crushing the plants that by now had assumed a metaphorical significance very different from what I had originally intended. As I looked up through my bleary stink tears and through the fragments of the garden in which I now lay, I could just make out Hannah in the distance, pinching her nose with one hand and waving at me with the other. She was smiling. As always, that little girl was smiling.

I scrubbed until I had about peeled my skin off, but I still had to sleep outside that first night. In the weeks that followed, I couldn't get near enough to the superfund site that was my child's fourth first garden to initiate remediation, though we diluted the terrible pee stench by hosing the garden down from about thirty feet upwind, an ablution that Hannah and I performed twice each day in order to make it tolerable for her to play outside. Five weeks later an early frost hit, and the cold snap knocked the stench down enough that I could approach the wrecked garden to clean it up before the first snow. When I pulled away the broken fences and cages, I found that a few plants had actually survived, unmolested because the not quite empty Jug O' Doom still rested near their stems. One of these was a tomato plant, and while its tiny yellow flowers were now burned by frost, it had set some fruit, and a single tomato looked pink enough that it might ripen off the vine. I harvested the tomato, washed it well, and gave it to Hannah to put on the sill of her bedroom window. Over the next few days that tomato did ripen, and so our family gathered around the kitchen table to celebrate the ritual of the first fruits—well, fruit—of the season, even as the snow began to fall outside. Hannah took a bite, wrinkled her nose, and said "Thanks for the tomato, Daddy. I don't like it. Can we have a garden again next year?"

In gardening and in parenting we risk failure every moment of every day, and how could it be otherwise? We hope and yet we fail; we fail and yet we hope. What education would our children and our gardens provide us if they did not constantly show us our limits? A sustainable relation to both the human and the natural worlds depends not on our ability to transcend but rather on our ability to embrace these limits. Sustainability is not a game we can play to win. Like parenting and gardening, it is instead an endless string of failures, a practice of love, humility, and humor through which we just keep trying, not because our success is certain but because it certainly is not.

I have promised Hannah that we will plant her garden in the spring. And it will again be her first garden, just as every garden is a first garden, just as every day with those we love is a chance to start over, to hope and to learn, to plant something again. I hope and trust that my child's next first garden, which certainly will not be her last, will succeed just as wonderfully as it has this year.

3

Tracking Our Way

James Bruchac and Joseph Bruchac III

Ndakinna means "our land" in the Abenaki Indian language. It's the name that my son, Jim Bruchac, chose for the Education Center located in the converted barns and on the over 80 acres of New York State forests and fields that were the Dunham and then Bowman family farms in the nineteenth and early twentieth centuries. In the early 1940s, it became the home of Bruchac's Taxidermy after my father, Joseph Bruchac Jr., was given the land by the parents of his wife, Marion Dunham Bowman.

So in a way, that name of Ndakinna represents the several generations of the Bruchac family that have cared for that place and called it home—a place and its memories passed down from those ancestors who were here before us. But it is more than that. The Abenaki name reflects the fact that an American Indian understanding of place is at the heart of much of what Jim and I do. "Our land" is not so much a term of possession as it is a statement of relationship and responsibility. In that Native sense, we don't so much own the land as accept the responsibility to care for it and share it, mindful of all those who were here, those who are here now, and those who are yet to come.

Because of that awareness of the generations, much of what we do focuses on children, particularly on developing and strengthening the relationship of children to the natural world through guidance, storytelling, and hands-on experiences. One of the oldest American Indian traditions is that of teaching in nature. We have learned that young people gain strength and balance—physically, intellectually, emotionally, and spiritually—by being taken on a regular basis into the outdoors by knowledgeable and trustworthy grown-ups. This is not just a Native American idea. It used to be true of all cultures, but many seem to have lost that way in a modern world where adults and children have never been more separate and where in the so-called developed nations, both generations use their free time to escape alone into "virtual" computerized reality.

Yet when we take young people into the woods, something happens to them. Sometimes their initial reaction is uncertainty or even fear. That's understandable after two or more generations of movies in which the forest is equated with death at the hands of mutated predatory beasts or semihuman monsters whose only aim in life is to kill unwary campers. But as the old and wise Medewiwin teaching of the Anshinabe people puts it, "The more you know, the more you will trust, and the less you will fear." After only a few minutes, you can see many of the children start to relax, especially when we remind them to use their senses. Stop talking, and start listening. We were given two ears and one mouth because we are supposed to listen twice as much as we talk. Look at the earth, and see what it has to tell you. And when they begin to listen and see that every track tells a tale, they begin to change.

The term "nature-deficit disorder" has gained some currency in recent years, and it does exist. But we put it in simpler terms. Unless children and adults go out into the natural world in whatever weather, whatever season or time of day or night, we lose ourselves and we lose each other. What do we find when we go into nature? Balance. Virtually all American Indian cultures hold the belief that balance is the proper way. That balance is equated with patience, with gentleness, with peace and happiness, and with health. When you are out of balance, you are angry, jealous, greedy, unkind—and sick.

So as we follow the tracks in the forest, we are tracking our way back to our dreams.

Jim and I often share our own stories with the adults and children who come to Ndakinna because the trail that we've both followed is an example of the way turning to the land can be restorative, a map to the heart. Here is a little of what we say.

Joe   When I was a child, going with my grandfather into the small woods behind the house where he and my grandmother raised me seemed like the most natural thing in the world to do. I followed his footsteps so closely that people called me his shadow. Although my grandmother was the one with the education—the books on shelves in every room of the house a visible reminder that she was a graduate of Skidmore College—my grandfather's quieter knowledge of the animals, the plants, and the land beneath our feet was just as important to me as the stirring stories by Sir Walter Raleigh, Rudyard Kipling, and Robert Louis Stevenson that she read me from those leather-bound volumes.

It wasn't just because Grampa Bowman was Abenaki that he went into the woods on a daily basis and took me with him. Going into the forest to hunt or gather or just walk with their children was true, more or less, of most of the families—whether or not they had Indian blood—in rural Greenfield Center back in the 1940s and 1950s when I was a boy. Cutting wood for the stove, following a trout stream, tapping the maple trees in late winter, hunting (not for sport but to feed the family), gathering medicine plants, and many other woodland activities were a part of everyday life for most of the rural people I knew back then. There was no hard and fast line between us and the natural world. And I was always learning that natural world without any sense of being taught. It just happened.

Farming it, which is what most people did, was part of that learning time, too. Much of the plowing was still being done with horses, not tractors. Working with an animal is a far cry from using a machine. The feel of a horse's skin under your palms, the smell of its sweat, its hot breath on your neck as it nuzzles you in greeting (and in the hope that there's a carrot in your pocket), the way it responds to "Gee" and "Haw" and to the sound of its name—all draw you into an old and deep partnership between human and animal, one that few American children know today. I remember, too, how when we were working together in the vegetable garden out back—ground that I still plant each spring—my grandfather would often stop at the sound of a bird song, lift his head from the weeding, and say "Baltimore oriole," "cardinal," or "song sparrow." Then he'd whistle its call back to it.

Today, as my son Jim does his programs with young people—taking them into the 80-acre nature preserve that was once my great-grandparents' farm land—I think back on my own childhood and those times when my grandfather walked in the woods with me. I watch as my other son, Jesse, points out plants and animals to his four-year-old daughter and his two-year-old son, who are just beginning to experience some of those teachings. And I realize that the tracks my grandfather left are ones that our family has continued to follow.

However, it is not just about parents or grandparents experiencing nature with their own children. Such shared experiences can strengthen the bond between the generations, but it also is an antidote to the uncertainty that seems to permeate much of modern daily life, where every hour brings new images of disaster to the television screen or another self-righteous talking head telling us how to think. Turning off and putting aside all the hand-held devices and then sitting together quietly in the woods or walking a trail by a body of water is a deeply restorative experience for a parent and child to share. Fold your hands and hear the birds twitter. As my old friend and teacher Swift Eagle, a Pueblo/Apache elder, explained it to me, you can "Slow down your brain waves."

Jim   When it came to learning about nature, my brother Jesse and I were very lucky. Besides his knowledge of stories, our father also knew a lot about the forest and its animal inhabitants. Some things he learned from his Grandpa Jesse, who always had time to spend with my Dad. As they walked together in the woods, Great-Grampa Jesse would point out the tracks of animals or tell him the names of flowers and plants and how they were used as food or medicine. Jesse helped Dad catch his first trout and reminded him to say thank you to the fish for allowing him to catch it. Great-grandfather's quiet love of the forest inspired my father to seek out and share Native American traditional knowledge when he grew up.

When in the woods with his sons, Dad, as Grandpa Jesse had done with him, would point out and name the trees and plants and the occasional animal sign for Jesse and me. He might say, "Look, Jamey. This is a white pine tree. See the bundles of five needles?" or "Check out that woodchuck hole. See how round it is?"

We'd also take walks in the woods at night. That was when Dad taught us about the many sounds and smells of the night and also how to get over our fears of the darkness. He would have each of us sit in a field or the middle of woods and then leave us there.

"Be still and listen," he'd say, before disappearing into the darkness. He never went too far away, but we were all by ourselves. Instead of panicking, we remembered what he'd said about using our senses. In the night, there are many things to hear and many different scents on the wind. When you learn to focus on those things, it's easy to forget about your fears.

As I grew older, the forest was also a good place for me to go to and be by myself. In the middle of the forest, there is a big old pine tree that I still love to sit under. One time as I sat beneath that tree, a deer walked in front of me. I stayed perfectly still, and it didn't seem to see me. I spent so much time in the Bruchac forest as a kid that it became as familiar to me as your living room is to you.

When my younger brother, Jesse, was old enough, we spent time exploring nearby Adirondack Park. From climbing many of the high peaks to canoeing the numerous waterways, there was always plenty to see and learn. Every trip brought new discoveries—a pair of playful otters swimming under our canoe, beautiful mountain views, or the haunting call of the loon. Just as in our small woods, there were also plenty of tracks. I still remember seeing my first set of bear tracks. During a camping trip to the Big Moose recreation area near the town of Indian Lake, Dad pulled our canoe to shore to set up camp and pointed out that the riverbank was covered with fresh bear prints. Closing my eyes, I can still see them now. They were perfect tracks, every toe, pad, and claw showing in the wet sand. They were the kind of tracks I dream of finding when leading groups into the woods.

And as soon as we stepped out of the canoe, Dad began interpreting for us the story that those tracks told. When it came to nature or storytelling, he always had something to teach us.

Joe   But there comes a time when it is more difficult for a father or a mother to be the one who teaches such lessons. One of the oldest truths is that adolescence is when young people need to assert their independence and walk away from their parents. But it is perilous for them to do so on their own or simply with groups of their own peers. They still need guidance. In American Indian traditional cultures, that is usually when others would step in. Wise and patient uncles and aunts or unrelated and trustworthy adults would take on that necessary role as mentors and teachers. Even though these adults might be sharing the same lessons that parents might be able to teach, those lessons can seem new and more relevant when they come from someone outside the close familial circle.

Jim   My first experience like that was Pine Island, a wilderness camp in Maine on an island in a lake called Great Pond. My parents sent me there for a whole summer when I was twelve.

The winter before, I'd watched a slide show about the camp, and it seemed pretty cool. Kids who went there spent lots of time camping, swimming, hiking, and doing a host of other outdoor activities with the guidance of highly qualified counselors. Once I got there, though, it was a different story.

I felt abandoned and lost. I sent letters home with circles drawn around teardrops that fell as I wrote my words. My parents were so worried that they made a trip out to Maine to see how I was and take me home if I was too homesick.

Along with missing home, I also had a hard time making new friends. Many of the boys, even those my age, were bigger than me. Some, including two boys from Boston named Mark and Roger, loved to pick on me. They especially liked to make fun of my name: "'Jamey'? Sounds like a girl's name to me." or "Hey, Jamey. The girls' camp is on the other side of the lake."

I did my best to ignore them. It wasn't easy, especially since Roger, the bigger of the two, enjoyed hitting me. Whenever I wasn't paying attention, all of a sudden—BLAM! Hard shot to the arm.

"Hey, sissy boy. Gonna cry?" he would laugh.

"Yeah, gonna cry, little girl?" Mark would add.

Despite the fact that I'd already had two years of martial arts training, it never seemed right to strike back. It wasn't like they were really going to beat me up. But I didn't like it. At some point, something had to change, or I wasn't going to make it. My parents still have some of the letters I sent from camp complete with the tear marks I made extra sure to circle with my pen.

As the weeks went on, though, I found myself feeling less lonely. Along with making a few new friends—smaller, quiet kids like myself—we were kept very busy. Each morning, we could choose among any number of activities—sailing, canoeing, archery, marksmanship, arts and crafts, swimming, and a host of wilderness skills. Every week, we also had a chance to sign up for overnight trips, including one to Whitehead Island just off the coast of Maine. Mark's and Roger's names were not on the sign-up list, so it was one I chose.

During this trip, our small group of campers and staff stayed at an old Coast Guard rescue station complete with its own lighthouse. There was plenty of time to explore the rocky coastline. We set out lobster traps, dug for clams, and played a version of capture the flag. While walking the beach, a group of us found a large man-of-war jellyfish. There was also storytelling, although the stories were nothing like the lesson stories Dad told me. They were about homicidal campers and ghosts, and the only point to them seemed to be to scare kids. Although my Dad told scary stories, they always had a reason to be told, and you could learn something from them.

After four weeks of camp, the halfway point, my parents came to visit. Having read my letters, they had every intention of bringing me home.

"It's not so bad. I think I want to stay," I told them.

They were pleased that they had not made a huge mistake in sending me but still were concerned about the bullying. "Have you told your counselors about those boys?" Mom asked.

"Really, it's not that bad," I answered. Although it was tougher than I wanted to admit, I didn't like the idea of being a tattletale. If I told on them, I thought it might get worse. Plus, by that point, I had actually gotten pretty good at seeing Mark and Roger coming. I would take another trail or simply hide behind a building. All those years playing hide-and-go-seek games in the woods seemed to be paying off. By the time my parents arrived, I had already learned seven different ways to walk to the mess hall.

"Hey," my father said. "How about giving a martial arts demonstration while we're here?" Although I was a little uncertain about the idea, I agreed. We set it up for that afternoon.

After my Dad and I sparred and broke boards in that demonstration, I took on new status in the eyes of the other campers. From then on, Mark and Roger thought I was OK and became my friends. My parents went back home without me, and I finished the summer at Pine Island.

During those last four weeks, I learned a host of new things about the outdoors, including map and compass reading, knot tying, and turning a canoe and a rain poncho into a shelter. I learned how to load and carry a backpack properly, and I hiked over fifty miles on the Appalachian Trail, camping in tents and lean-tos all along the way.

In the end, Pine Island Camp was a great growing experience. It accustomed me to being away from home and helped me find self-confidence and self-reliance. Although it was only eight weeks of my life, the amount of personal growth gained during Pine Island Camp proved pivotal in later years.

Joe Jim's experience at summer camp taught him quite a bit, but it also pointed out something to me. The experience at summer camp is often traumatic for kids who are not properly supervised. Bullying is a huge problem and something that anyone involved in sharing wilderness experiences with young people needs to control. I also was disturbed by the way Pine Island, as well-rounded as it was, also—unintentionally, I am sure—instilled fear of nature (and other people) in kids through the kind of mad camper, vengeful killer, Friday the thirteenth stories that seem to be part of most summer camps.

As both my sons entered their teenage years and became heavily involved in contact sports, I also saw the need for another kind of teaching—not to counter but to go along with the lessons about teamwork and masculine strength that Jim and Jesse were learning from playing football, where both of them were beginning to excel. I looked for someone I knew to provide the kind of mentoring that I hoped would help him and his brother stay connected to the natural world and a gentler but no less powerful part of their own nature.

Jim   My parents, always believing my trail was my own, never openly interfered with my decisions, even when they seemed to lead me further from my roots as football and everything involved in fitting in with other teens tended to do. However, as with Pine Island Camp, at just the right moment, they provided me with opportunities to reconnect with nature. One such opportunity began in 1983 at the Six Nations Indian Museum in Onchiota, New York. My father and several Mohawk friends were invited for a weekend at the museum to work with tracker and educator John Stokes. John had been traveling around the country teaching traditional survival skills, some of which he learned while living among the Aborigines of Australia. He'd also worked with a man named Tom Brown, who ran one of the biggest wilderness survival schools in America. John was eager both to teach and to acquire even more skills, stories, and knowledge by working with various Native peoples.

Wilderness survival was the real draw. It was only a year after Sylvester Stallone's first *Rambo* movie played in the theaters. Its Green Beret antihero, with his bulging muscles and tough-guy persona, was intriguing to my football buddies and me. My father had taught Jesse and me quite a bit about the outdoors, but this Stokes guy was a "survival instructor."

"He must be kind of like Rambo," I thought to myself.

Staying the weekend on the grounds of the Six Nations Indian Museum also seemed pretty appealing to us. Jesse and I had already made several trips to the museum to meet with its director, Ray Fadden, and his son John. Along with founding the museum, Ray ran a program for young Mohawks—something like the Boy Scouts but based on Iroquois culture. Many of the graduates of that program went on to be Native educators and chiefs. The Six Nations Museum, deep in the northern Adirondacks, was a perfect setting for wilderness training, and I looked forward to meeting John Stokes.

"Look, there's John," my dad said as we pulled into the museum's parking lot. I was a little surprised to see that John seemed a bit small and that his muscles weren't half as big as Stallone's. After our first introductions, however, I could tell John was a special kind of character. Although not the biggest of men, his personality and self-confidence seemed to fill the room.

"G'day, Mate," he said in an Australian accent. "Tall bloke aren't yeh?" he added with a smile. Despite the fact I was now sixteen years old and six feet, two inches tall, I felt a little intimidated.

This was several years before the 1986 movie *Crocodile Dundee* and over a decade before Steve Irwin's cable shows, so I didn't know much at all about Australia. Nonetheless, I knew it was going to be a very interesting weekend.

From our first introduction on, it was nonstop learning. John's stories alone made me hungry for more. Like Dad's tales, John Stokes's included the themes of having respect for the natural world and giving thanks.

We learned awesome skills, including the bow drill fire. This ancient method uses friction to make fire and is not easy. In fact, although my dad picked it up on the first day, it took me the entire weekend to get a single puff of smoke.

"Before you can make fire, you must first have fire in the heart," John told me as I struggled. That idea of fire in the heart was an overriding theme that pointed to our inner strengths. The heart, respect, and the mind overpower outward brawn—a lesson that was quite different from Rambo's in-your-face toughness.

Along with firemaking, which gave me some trouble, we built shelters, used throwing sticks, and worked on our stalking and natural camouflage. We worked on our ability to be quiet, walk slowly, blend in, and be invisible. They were skills I had practiced a little in the past, but I had much more to learn.

John made all of these skills, including the ones I was already familiar with, seem cool. With a seamless flow of story and skills training, John not only helped me appreciate things I had learned as a child but left me eager to learn more. He even worked in some martial arts training, which I had all but given up since starting football. It was then that I began to see that being a little bit different isn't all bad. It could even be, as John gracefully illustrated, an advantage.

That weekend really put my feet back on the trail. It was the start of an apprenticeship with John that would last for years, as Jesse and I made trips out to the Southwest to train with him and eventually become instructors ourselves with his Tracking Project, passing on to young people the teachings we'd learned.

One of the symbols that both my son, Jim, and I use in our teaching is that of the circle. As Harold Tantaquidgeon, a Mohegan elder, passed it on to us many years ago, a circle can be divided into four quadrants, and each of those quadrants can stand for part of a person's life. The first part is childhood, and then comes adolescence. The third part is adulthood, where you may have children of your own. The fourth is the time of being an elder and a grandparent. In each of those parts of your life, you have a task to focus on and then carry on throughout your life. The first task is to listen, the second is to observe, the third is to remember, and the fourth is to share.

There's much more that can be said about that circle, enough to fill a book. We will just point to two more teachings of the circle to conclude this brief walk along the parallel trails of our two lives.

The first is that the circle may bring us back to where we began. The journey never really ends. Here in these woods that have taught us and our ancestors much and given us many gifts, winter is always followed by spring. The second is that the natural progression of that circle—toward being an elder and sharing the wisdom gained through a life of listening, observing, and remembering—brings us as teachers back to the children of the new generations who need to listen.

Olipamkaani. May your journeys be good.

4

Tidal: Subtidal

Susan A. Cohen

The geography of my childhood was shaped by water. I did not know this essential fact when I was a child; only when I looked backward and sifted through my memories could I see how I had expanded from an awareness of my own body to an awareness of a coastal ecosystem. It should not surprise me then, as it does, that my most constant relationship has not been with my family or old friends but with a place. I don't know exactly when I took that great leap from my sense of self as autonomous to a sense of connection to this specific place in the universe, but at some time during my childhood an ecological bridge must have presented itself to me, and, just as easily as smiling, I walked over it and found myself at the shore.

Mermaidia Oceanica: Queen of the Absolutely Amazing Atlantic

I am nine years old walking on the beach with my father. We have walked most of the way in silence, both deep in thought. My nine-year-old self has determined that she needs to change her name, that she needs a much more important and watery name. So while she and I splish-splash along the shoreline jumping away from sudden wave bursts that soak the rolled bottoms of my pants, I contemplate a new identity for myself. It is my birthday, you see, and now, at nine, I am certain that the world needs to notice something about me it has until now ignored.

I do not know what my quiet father is thinking as we walk east toward the lighthouse; at nine I am not terribly interested. Instead, I roam around in my thoughts for a truly great "sea" name. I list all the oceans and seas that I know—the Atlantic, of course, Pacific, Indian, and Arctic oceans. I like the sound of "Caspian Sea" and have just learned about the Bay of Bengal at school, which has a nice ring to it. My mother has repeatedly expressed her wishes to visit the Mediterranean or the Caribbean seas, also melodic and impressive words. I run further through my water lexicon, arriving at waves, surf, dune, schooner, whales, floods, and the like. The words slide back and forth for a while as I concoct my new name.

My daydreamy father appears to have forgotten that I am walking beside him, so I interrupt his thoughts with my oh-so-very important announcement: "You may now call me Mermaidia Oceanica: Queen of the Absolutely Amazing Atlantic."

Because my father is my best friend, I can test my ideas out on him, but I test much more than a new name, and he knows that. Well, he tells me, he isn't one for titles, so he thinks I really need to get rid of the "Queen" part of my new name, and then he tries out what is left, "Mermaidia Oceanica." I am thrilled. He has drawn out the syllables, and I love the way my new name sounds. I nod my head in agreement and imagine writing Mermaidia on my school papers, saying "This is Mermaidia" when I answer the telephone, and I see a swirly Mermaidia signature after the "Yours truly" of all my thank-you letters to my aunts.

"Nah," he says slipping back to his New Yorkese. "Not right for you at all. I think we should call you Shipwreckius Susanicus, or Shipwreck Sue for short."

No, no, no. I am furious with him and stomp ahead in the waves soaking my pants and new Zips sneakers.

My adult self had forgotten this moment, buried below my world of preparing for classes, attending meetings, and getting my children to their doctors' appointments on time. But recently while skimming through the *American Littoral Society Newsletter*, a photograph of a father and daughter walking along the beach at low tide triggers my memory. Subtidal currents are significantly weaker than tidal currents, much like this memory residing below the surface of the more active thoughts of my daily life. While this beach experience was not the first or the last time the force of my imagination would crash into the force of the ocean, as I search through my memories, I believe it is the first time that I tried to articulate my need to identify myself with a place. To become this tidal place.

Rachel Carson understands the edge of the sea as a place with "a dual nature, changing with the swing of the tides, belonging now to the land, now to the sea. On the ebb tide it knows the harsh extremes of the land world, being exposed to heat and cold, to wind, to rain and drying sun. On the flood tide it is a water world, returning briefly to the relative stability of the open sea." You wouldn't know it to look at us, father and daughter walking along the shore on a sunny April day, but he and I have been living within such a dual nature; we belong to this edge place that exhibits only relative stability. Today we are taking the day off from our unstable lives. Exactly one year earlier, we were both patients at North Shore Hospital, and on the morning of my eighth birthday, my father sent a dozen roses from his side of the hospital to the children's wing, with a promise that we would go to the beach as soon as the doctors set us free.

Mermaidia Oceanica Compromises

When I look back at my father from the surf, he smiles at me. Although only nine, I understand his patient, teasing, but loving smile, and so I stop my stomping along in the water and instead begin a rhythmic counting of the waves. My father taught me how to do this when he taught me how to count. On Yom Kippur each year, rather than go to temple, we would come to the ocean supposedly to throw our sins into the water, but instead, we counted the waves. What I will learn later in life is that counting the waves is its own form of meditation, but today I just begin with a whisper, "one, two, three, four," and soon he joins me, "nineteen, twenty, twenty-one."

The truth is we are both troubled, and on this shoreline walk today it takes an effort to find a moment of peace. His worries are certainly greater than mine, but we have both been ill, we are both frail, both afraid of spending more time in the hospital. And although at nine I do not understand the why of it, I do know that we both feel better when we are walking along the water's edge. It is not enough to walk the streets of our little suburban neighborhood or walk along Fifth Avenue on our way to the New York Public Library; it is only the beach that satisfies us.

At some point during the walk, I come upon a compromise. My father and I have long since stopped counting waves; we have given up looking for the perfect smooth white stone or a shell with a small hole at the top to run a string through. My father no longer quizzes me about American presidents or asks me to recite "Annabel Lee" for the zillionth time. We have grown tired of watching the bank swallows dart in and out of their dune dwellings, and we no longer care how wet we are. So yet again I test the newest version of my name on him, hoping he will see the importance of renaming myself. This time I go for Susan Aloysius Mermaidia Cohen. He cannot help it. He laughs out loud, grins the kind of grin where all of his teeth show, and then hugs me. "Okay, Mermaidia, what would you like to eat for dinner tonight?"

In *Discovering the Vernacular Landscape*, J. B. Jackson writes, "It is place, permanent position in both the social and topographical sense, that gives us our identity." When I first read this sentence, I agreed with it and moved on, but the more I think about the connection between place and identity, the more I believe Jackson's equation to be incorrect or perhaps just incomplete. As I reflect on my own experiences, I believe imagination to be the force that interprets place and ultimately settles it into our identity

Littoral Drifter

I am fifteen years old and brushing my teeth in the ladies' bathroom at Jones Beach State Park. It is the morning after my first day as a runaway. The day before, I filled my beach bag with the necessary items, counted out my cash earned from six months of babysitting, and with ease caught one bus, then another headed for the beach. In case you don't already know, June is the perfect month for a teenager to run away. With school just out of session, the world of adults sees only a sudden confusion of children everywhere, barely noticing one unattended teenager. On Long Island, the warm summer weather, easy bus transportation, and an abundance of inexpensive food make walking away from home only an impulse away. One lone teenager sleeping on a towel at the beach is invisible.

I have thought about my destination carefully as I head east from my home in mid-Nassau County to Montauk Point, traveling one beach at a time. I operate out of instinct and grief, for less than two weeks ago I was called out of my ninth-grade biology class by my sensibly shod and oh-so-very-stern biology teacher, who quietly delivered the news that my father had died and that an older cousin, waiting in the principal's office, would drive me home. Not only is this my first morning as a runaway; it is also the first morning after a night spent sleeping curled up on a towel in the curve of a sand dune, the first night I have slept easily in months, lullabied by the waves.

Jennifer Ackerman writes, "Studies of human preferences for landscapes have found that our tribe tends to favor savanna-like land—flat, grass-covered landscape studded with trees, where we had our origins and earliest home. Also promontories overlooking water. Some scientists even speculate that somewhere along the way we veered off the common primate course of evolution not just by swinging down from trees, but by going toward the sea. . . . I like this idea that our earliest home landscapes are buried deep, embedded in our minds like an anchor at great depth, that we know in some dark, birdly way where we want to go." In some awkward, teenager, birdly way, I have found my way to Jones Beach, where I will stay for a few days, washing up in the public restroom in the mornings, dreaming peacefully to the sounds of waves at night.

A bus and a train ride later, I disembark in Montauk, the Long Island Railroad's last stop. During these runaway days and nights, I begin to understand the pull of the tides. Sir Isaac Newton, the first to explain tides, writes in the second volume of the *Principia* in 1686, "it appears that the waters of the sea ought twice to rise and twice to fall every day, as well lunar as solar and that the greatest height of the waters in the open and deep seas ought to follow the appulse of the luminaries." While Newton may have unraveled the science and math behind the tides, he does not explain their aesthetic pull on humans. Tides are rhythmic, predictable, and unpredictable. The astounding power of the moon's gravitational pull to shape and reshape my coastline becomes the single most fascinating aspect of my life as a runaway. I quickly learn to be wary of the high tides and go shell seeking during the low tides. I discover, though I cannot name it, an intertidal period that leaves a band of shiny stones ribboned along the shore—and I fall in love with these transitory moments.

My beach life becomes increasingly regular: I sleep at night securely tucked into the crook of a cliff dune, walk the shoreline at the low tides, and read the one book I have dragged along (a collection of Edgar Allen Poe's works given to me by my father). Beyond the brief conversations I have to buy food, I talk to no one for two weeks. No one knows my name, no one recognizes me, and I am, for the first time in my life, identity-less to those around me. My main occupation becomes listening intently to the landscape. The tides sooth and guide me, and soon I recognize their essence—*predictable change*. I also begin to measure my life against this mutable constancy, pondering who I am and what path I will take. I catch myself spinning out imaginary and silent stories that have only one common denominator: they are all set at the edge of the sea. Shaped by this ocean, my imagination broadens and wakens from the sound and feel of the wind, the itch of the sand, and the calm of the light, and, in turn, my imagination prompts me to story this place at first with mermaids and sea captains and later with many other watery or shorebound characters. During one stormy night, I find limited protection by sleeping in a deteriorating World War II concrete army bunker, and while the tides are beautiful to watch on a peaceful day, the storm wakes me to the power and violence they can generate. I discover not only that I am drawn toward the geography of edges but am in sympathy with this margin of the world. When I finally decide to catch a train back home to interior suburban Long Island, it is not because I have been lonely or frightened living wild on the beach but because I have been taught by the landscape about the basic ebb-and-flow rhythm of life and I know it is time for me to return to my mother's house.

Accepting a New Name

I am twenty-three, sitting on the jetty behind the Montauk lighthouse, and if I sit on the right rock, it appears that the waves break perpendicularly to the shore. I have come here, as I often do, to let my thoughts drift freely, to count the waves or watch the terns, to meditate. In two days, I will marry, take a new name, and move to land-locked Moscow, Idaho, over two thousand miles away.

Just the night before, I try to convince my husband-to-be that we should both change our names as we enter this marriage. "Rockefeller?" he proposes. "Kennedy? Or how about Koufax?" he says, in honor of his favorite Brooklyn Dodger. Exhausting the list of all his sports heroes from Johnny Unitas to Don Drysdale, he then suggests his favorite historical figures, with Jefferson topping the list. "Susan Koufax Jefferson," he offers, "how does that sound?" After I reject all these possibilities, he asks, "Well, what do you suggest?"

Despite the fact that I have initiated this conversation, I am unprepared to respond, and so when I blurt out "Montauk," it surprises both him and me, and yet I can imagine it. I see myself as this new person, Susan Montauk, who forgoes graduate school, takes up residence at the beach, and makes a living by the shore. While not panicked about getting married, I am terrified of leaving the coast forever. If I incorporate "Montauk" into my name, into my future identity, I might not lose my shoreline, my sense of place. Renaming myself at this moment feels necessary.

"No," my future husband declines. After all, we sorted out this issue with the rabbi and our mothers, and everyone agreed that I would take his name as my new name.

Storm Surge

My daughter, Sara, is eight years old. Ordinarily a late sleeper, she is tugging me out of bed to go for an early morning walk on the beach. She's eager to see Hurricane Bob's aftermath. We are in Montauk visiting my mother, who fifteen years earlier built a small house here for her retirement. For a few weeks of every summer of my daughter's life, we set aside our ordinary suburban District of Columbia lives for shore time. Sara wastes no time this morning brushing her unruly hair or putting a teeshirt and shorts on over her bathing suit. Dressed only in her flip-flops and bathing suit, her hair flying, she hurries me out the door toward the beach.

Hurricane Bob is her first hurricane experience, and all day yesterday she begged to go outside. She listened intently to the wind, alternately melodic and frightening. She watched as tree limbs and other yard debris flew past our windows, and she opened the sliding doors on the deck allowing a small flood into the house. This morning she races ahead of me on the quarter-mile walk down to the beach, overflowing with questions about what we might find. I cannot slow her down as she runs down the hill, so I find myself jogging a bit to keep up with her.

When we reach the top of the dunes, we cannot find the narrow path we usually walk to get to the shore. It is gone. The dune grass and Sara's unbrushed hair share a certain similar wildness; there is no part to be found anywhere. We eventually decide to create a new path approximately in the place where the old path might have been. "Watch out for ticks," I remind her. "Be careful where you step," I call ahead. Is this really me calling out all these cautions to my daughter? How, I wonder, did I turn into that person who wants my child to slow down?

Sara, through instinct and excitement, finds the remnants of the old path and reaches the beach first, but when I catch up to her, we are both silent. This is not our beach or at least not the one we felt we understood. Rachel Carson opens *The Edge of the Sea* with this comment: "The edge of the sea is a strange and beautiful place. All through the long history of Earth it has been an area of unrest where waves have broken heavily against the land, where tides have pressed forward over the continents, receded, and then returned. For no two successive days is the shore line precisely the same." The day after a hurricane, the changes to our shore are astounding. Whole sections of the beach are gone, the cliffs are reconfigured into patterns like witches' fingers, and small pools of still water have formed to the east of where we stand. Shocked to discover that the waves are breaking directly against our feet, directly against the dune cliffs, we look for any familiar image or curve of the shoreline, but we cannot find our beach.

So we go walking. We walk the two miles into town and then turn and head back home. The sandy portion of our beach remains hidden, but

Sara the Scavenger discovers strings of seaweed, crabs, shells, piles of smooth white rocks, lost footwear, and all sorts of odd debris. We are relieved to see the bank swallows emerge from their small oceanside dwellings, and for a while we watch the flickering patterns they make against the sky. The aftermath of a storm, we learn, is a tangle of new and old images, and we are forced to reimagine a landscape we once took for granted.

For me, the most familiar aspect of this morning scene turns out to be a mother and daughter walking along the shore just after sunrise. The daughter, my daughter, is singing a little song to herself as she walks with one leg in the water and the other on the sand. The mother, me, watches as her daughter tips sideways with every step. She walks and sings and navigates the tides while I daydream about my childhood and walking with my father on this very beach and then sort through my worries about the return of my mother's breast cancer. My mother was diagnosed with breast cancer while I was pregnant with Sara and was in remission for seven years. Recently, the disease returned, and this summer she has come to the beach to rest after yet another surgery and more chemotherapy. Walking along the newly configured shoreline with both the familiar sounds and smells and the unfamiliar damage, I walk and think and let my thoughts drift.

After a while, I move closer to Sara and try to imitate the off-kilter rocking pattern of her footsteps. I want to know what imaginary world she has created. She is singing a pirate song complete with the requisite "yo-ho-hos." She then tells me that she is not Sara at all, but "Captain Long John Peg Leg Black and Blue Beard Hook," and she has been washed ashore after the hurricane. "It was a terrible storm," she tells me, "with fierce navy-blue winds."

"Long John Peg Leg Black and Blue Beard Hook?" I smile recalling my own childhood penchant for creating alternative names. "That's quite a mouthful. Do you have a nickname for short?"

"Of course not, Mom. That would be disrespectful. I am a ruthless pirate captain!"

I'm not sure what makes me happier this morning, having an eight-year-old child who uses words like "navy-blue winds," "ruthless," and "disrespectful" or having an imaginative child who responds to a hurricane with a wild new persona.

We linger on the shore for as long as possible before returning to my mother's house. There is much to do at the house in the aftermath of the hurricane: go to the firehouse to fill our water jugs, clean up the debris from the yard and deck, pull the tape off the windows, help my mother change her bandages. Both Sara and I have had to accept illness as part of our childhoods. When I was five, my father was diagnosed with Hodgkin's disease, and Sara at eight years old struggles with her adored grandmother's breast cancer. Like me, she will always connect this shore with freedom, imagination, sorrow, and loss.

Recurring Tides

The next night, still without water or electricity, Sara and I trek out to the lighthouse, in part to escape from the troubles at the house and in part to sit on the jetty to star-gaze. We perch on a large rock directly beneath the revolving Fresnel lamp of Montauk Light. The waves, still stirred up from the storm, wash over the rocks, but the night sky is clear and star-filled. We don't talk much at first. Sara slips into humming songs while I consider the string of years I have been finding my way across these slippery rocks behind the lighthouse. At twenty-three, when I married and moved to Idaho, I did not realize that I would find a way to return to Montauk every year, that I would become a migratory being who arrives in late spring with the terns and leaves just before autumn.

I want to understand how specific places shape individuals. How is it that we resist the imprint of one place and accept the imprint of another? What factors have to merge to create those of us who are place-oriented—some of us connecting to the mountains, others to urban environments, some to deserts, and some, like my daughter and me, to the coast?

Many have written about the connection between place and identity, and others have studied the role of imagination in forming one's personality, but it seems to me that a place that triggers one's imagination has a better chance of settling into one's identity. No matter where I live, somewhere inside I will always carry Mermaidia Oceanica, Queen of the Absolutely Amazing Atlantic Ocean—a little girl version of myself who imagined great and heroic adventures that all began at the shore. The runaway teen self resides here, that birdly teenager drawn to the shore for solace and life lessons. The older self is here, too—the young woman on the edge of adulthood and marriage, empathizing with the restlessness of the tides, and the mother-self surprised by her daughter's intense empathy with the ocean. I did not anticipate having a child who shares my affinities for the shore, whose call to the water is as strong as mine, who needs to sit by the ocean to sing songs and create sea stories.

When I was a little girl, I believed that Montauk was the end of the world, the place where maps stopped and stories began. Maybe that notion still holds true, but sitting with Sara on the erosion-control rocks just behind the lighthouse, I revise my childhood sense of place and consider the role of the tides. The destructive force of a hurricane may reconfigure and disrupt an entire ecotone, but such destruction is rare. On a daily basis, tidal currents ebb and flow with a reliable precision and tumble and heal the coast. Tidal cycles teach how to adapt, to change, and to cope with a frightening beautiful place. The shoreline, while in child-logic might seem like the end of the mapped world, turns out to be a fertile place for a child's imagination to expand and develop a connection to place. After sitting on the rocks for a long while, watching the lighthouse beam roll across the water, I say to Sara, "Can I tell you a story about a mermaid named Mermaidia who was saved by a ruthless pirate from a fierce hurricane, many many years ago, before lighthouses were ever imagined?"

"Yes," she says, "and his name was Captain Long John Peg Leg Black and Blue Beard Hook, right?"

5

The Toad Not Taken

Jeffrey S. Cramer

The three egg cases came sealed in a plastic bag. Kazia and I searched for just the right nesting place for them. One we tied to the underside of a maple branch, one under a peony stalk, and one in our grape arbor.

Hatching mantises takes a long time. First, you order the egg cases, wait for them to arrive, unpack them, tie up the cases, and then wait again. This is followed by more waiting, and when you think you are done, ready to witness the emergence, it is time to wait some more. You soon reach a time when you anxiously begin to check the egg cases daily. The one on the peony stalk had disappeared; the one in the maple had fallen to the ground and needed to be resecured; the one in the grape arbor remained secure and untouched.

In the early light it was difficult to tell if anything had changed, but one morning I could feel that there were praying mantises about. The egg case in the arbor looked as if it had exploded; yet I could not easily tell if anything had hatched. After a few minutes I saw what I had originally mistaken for a twig, brown and thin, begin to move. Looking closer I could make out the familiar shape of the praying mantis, like the adult, only done in miniature and shades of sepia.

As my eyes adjusted and I became familiar with the shape I was looking for, I began to find more. I could spot ten or twenty. There were supposed to be hundreds. One case was still untouched; one was missing. Like a hidden-pictures game, it was fun for my wife and me and our two daughters to try to find the mantises. For a day or two we became quite adept at it, and then there were none. Where did they go? Was this it? For days we didn't spot any more.

By our back door sits a large muck bucket in which we attempted to grow beans. Originally it was set up not only as a source for a fresh, organically grown vegetables but as a way of teaching our oldest daughter, Kazia, about the joy and exuberance that accompanies growing food from seed. We had hoped that by participating in this minigarden, by mixing the dirt in the bucket, planting the seed, and watering it, she would grow to love the plant and enjoy eating the bean that she had helped to produce. Instead, we succeeded only in teaching about drought when we failed to water the seeds, with an occasional lesson on flooding and poor drainage when it rained. The perfect beans and leaves shown on the seed packet were only distantly related to the stilted and insect-eaten growth by our back door, which we still insisted on calling a bean plant.

Nevertheless, beans or no beans, one lone mantis made this muck bucket its home. I brought Kazia out to see it. There it was, sitting on top of a leaf, its hands held in the position that gives this mantis its name, eating a small black insect. There was a brief moment of interest for Kazia that soon faded. I, however, could have watched the mantis all afternoon. After all, this was what we had been praying for, the chance to watch an insect grow, to observe its lifecycle, to know it not as something foreign to be ignored or feared but as something natural, familiar, close at hand.

I didn't want my children to grow up with the same kind of fear and ignorance of nature that I had—that all insects were disease-ridden and those that weren't were anxious to bite or sting; that nature stuff was either too cold or too hot and often wet; and that dirt was, well, dirty.

It was important that our children experience an original relation to nature, not one based on either fantasy or horror or, to encompass both extremes at once, Disney. I wanted to change our own attitudes, my wife's and my own, so that their response to the natural world around them would be a positive and exciting one, not a negative and exterminating one.

I longed to introduce both our daughters to a nonfrightening natural world—one where the spider in the garden would not sneak into the house and ascend two flights of stairs to attack them; one where a bee would not sting unprovoked; where a snake's slither was mysterious, unique, and natural. I had hoped that the praying mantises would do it and had just about given up on them as a catalyst when one day Kazia insisted on showing a friend the mantis on the bean plant. The excitement was contagious. It was only the beginning.

Somewhere in our backyard lives a garter snake, seen only occasionally.

"Here it is," I tell Kazia, after hunting by the stone wall.

She runs to see it as it tries to hide. Curling itself in and around the stones, it hopes to be hidden. We stand and stare at it, crouching closer and closer.

"Can I touch it?" she asks.

We bend closer. We can see its tongue, its cold eyes. I know it is feeling fear and that it is wrong for us to frighten it more in our desire to touch it, but we lean forward and Kazia puts out her hand. She barely touches it when it slithers off.

She is ready to touch anything now. Whatever we find in the house or the garden, she wants to touch—ants, spiders, beetles. It was a small achievement. No trumpets heralded, no sun broke through the clouds. The reporters were conspicuously absent. And yet it was what I had wanted. Now, when I find an insect in the house, before I try to catch it and set it outside, there is Kazia with her hand out, waiting.

Self-motivated interest, as I have come to observe, is the strongest impetus to a child's, or anyone's, learning. It is that which makes the idea of child-led learning appealing, and it is why we homeschool our children. Discovering something on one's own—without being led to it, without being taught it—can fill a person with curiosity and a natural desire to learn. Thoreau tells the story of how his free time in the fields, out of his Concord classroom, led him to further study:

I well remember with what a sense of freedom and spirit of adventure I used to take my way across the fields with my pail, some years later, toward some distant hill or swamp, when dismissed for all day, and I would not now exchange such an expression of all my being for all the learning in the world. . . . I suddenly knew more about my books than if I had never ceased studying them. I found myself in a schoolroom where I could not fail to see and hear things worth seeing and hearing—where I could not help getting my lesson—for my lesson came to me. Such experience often repeated, was the chief encouragement to go to the Academy and study a book at last.

This is just one example of how experience leads to learning, not the other way around. The real world versus the world of the classroom: there is no competition. All nature is my classroom. Perhaps, in part, this is why children in a classroom are often made to sit with their backs to the windows.

There were no cries. There was no noise but the occasionally frantic fluttering of wings. Voiceless, so as not to attract predators, it struggled in the net. How long it had been there, I did not know, but by the way its right leg was completely immobilized by the twisting of the net and some of the netting had entrapped part of its left leg, its wing, and tail, it had to have been there a while.

Our neighbors were away for the weekend, and while Julia and I were outside playing with Kazia, we noticed a bird caught in their downed volleyball net. I went over to take a closer look. By the time we found it, it would struggle only when it suspected danger. As I approached, it began a frantic attempt to escape, jumping, flapping one wing, with each useless push away from me only succeeding in further tightening the net's grip.

Slowly I wrapped my hand around it. In my hand it stopped struggling. With one finger I stroked its head, at the same time making a soothing "sshhhhh" sound as I would to a cat or a child. Try as I might, I could not disentangle the bird from the net. Julia and Kazia came over, and together we still could not free the bird.

While I still held the bird, somewhat calmed, in my hand, Kazia gently stroked its head. It was one of those brief moments, rarely offered, when she might be able to make contact with, to touch, a free and natural creature. It was not domesticated, it was not caged, and it allowed her, by not struggling or showing fear, to touch it. She touched it, unknowing of the gift offered her, and I knew that it would soon be forgotten in the days to come.

We knew we couldn't untangle the net enough to free it. Do we dare cut our neighbors' net? Would the bird live if we did? Its right leg seemed immobile, perhaps broken. If it had to die, wouldn't it be better to leave it there for our neighbors to find, to teach them what carelessly leaving this net on the ground can do? And if we did leave the bird there to die, plainly in view from our dining room window, what kind of lesson were we teaching our children?

I began to tell her that no matter how hard we might try, we would not be able to get the bird out of the net, that sometimes we can't help no matter how much we want to, that things die. We walked away.

I knew I was calculating the cost of a new net against the life of this bird, the destruction of our neighbors' property, however small and replaceable, with the saving of another kind of neighbor, small and irreplaceable. It seemed hypocritical to give money to save a whale, save a rainforest, save the planet, and not be willing to do something in a more tangible way. I knew I was doing something incalculably wrong by walking away.

At home we called a local department store to find out the price of a new volleyball net. They quoted us $15. Would we pay $15 to save the life of one bird? We didn't even know what kind of bird it was.

We got out the guidebook. A juvenile European starling. A descendant of one, actually of two, of one hundred starlings—sixty one year, followed by another forty the year after—introduced in New York City a century ago. Very adaptive, these immigrants made a strong foothold in North America, increasing more than a millionfold. Considered pests by some, these birds are here to stay.

I know of a woman who has done much for helping bluebirds, but she does this at the expense of other birds. She has no qualms about destroying a starling's nest because they are interlopers, nonnatives who have taken over the habitat of bluebirds and others. When I heard her calmly tell of destroying these nests to protect her chosen species, I was indignant. Who made her the savior of the bluebird, and what savior has the right to bless with one hand and smite with the other? It was easy for me to ask, "Who did she think she was who could say which species could live and which could die?" Now I had to ask, "Who did we think we were?"

It seems a fact, one that we as a species should be ashamed of, that helping is no longer an instinct, that it is something we must think out and plot the costs and the consequences of. We rarely reach out to help without considering the most far-reaching repercussions. We are unwilling to take responsibility for actions that may not, in the final analysis, bring about the beneficial solution we had desired. We have become unwilling to be wrong, and so, in many cases, we have simply become unwilling to respond, period—to other creatures, to other people, to ourselves, to our children.

We went back, scissors in hand. We put twenty dollars in an envelope with an apologetic note and slipped it into our neighbors' mailbox. The starling struggled again as we approached but quickly calmed in my hand. I held it as my wife cut and unwrapped pieces of netting until, with a push of its legs, the starling leapt from my hand and flew away. I longed for some Disney-esque ending in which, free at last, the starling would look back, tilting its head in comprehension, before flying away—some anthropomorphic sense of gratitude. Instead, it disappeared quickly, with a no-nonsense, self-preserving efficiency that in itself was a joy to watch.

As parents my wife and I want to regain responsibility, to share the mantle of responsibility with our children for their education and their lives. Learning at home is not just about learning to read or write. It is about learning to live, to interact, to be a part of a community that is comprised not just of children doing children things but of people doing people things. Homeschooling encourages children to question and then to search for solutions and answers. It encourages children to challenge first and then accept, or not, afterward. It enables children to follow their instinctual desire for learning and discovery and to work toward a fulfillment of their personal needs and interests. Homeschooling empowers them to explore with the sole purpose not of achieving teacher or even parental approval but of achieving knowledge, understanding, and a love of learning that will not stop when the bell rings. Because learning for us is not compartmentalized into subject and theme, because we are not regulated by lesson plans and schedules, because education is prepping not for an exam but for life, when the starling flies away, that is only the beginning.

We are collectors, touchers, takers. We are fascinated by things, and so we touch, taste, feel, look and smell, but most of all, we take—to look at later, to experience again and again, to share with a select few, to hoard, to make our own. We travel to distant lands and to some not-so-distant lands, and it is part of who we are that, as we do not like to be left behind, we do not like to leave things behind us. It defines who we are. Perhaps it is part of our heritage as hunters and gatherers that we collect as we walk.

Because our memories are scanty at best, often failing us, we rely on outside stimuli to help us remember. Taking photographs is one way to take something with us at the same time that we leave it behind. We sketch. We write in journals. We write insipid, flowery verse. These are ways to preserve without affecting the subject. When we leave, nothing externally has altered but our vision.

Thoreau knew when someone had called at his Walden cabin while he was out. When he returned home from whatever errand had called him away, he would find broken twigs or forgotten flowers, sometimes elaborately twined or wreathed, left on his desk. "They who come rarely to the woods," he wrote, "take some little piece of the forest into their hands to play with by the way, which they leave, either intentionally or accidentally. One has peeled a willow wand, woven it into a ring, and dropped it on my table."

The landscape should be entered responsibly, respectfully, so that when we leave, it is as if we had not been there. It should not be obvious that we have passed by. I do not want to make my way unconsciously through the world, leaving little crumbs along the trail or marking, like a dog, every tree. This is not an easy thing to achieve. It is more than just taking our trash with us, scattering our ashes, or covering our tracks. It is more than not having a negative impact. We are unable to predict the consequence of a positively inspired action. The opposite of negative impact may be neutrality—no impact. Too much damage has been caused in the name of improvement.

We must be awake to our surroundings. As we walk, we often do not know where we are. We are absent-minded, unaware. We break twigs and pick flowers. We crush something underfoot—an insect, a wildflower, a nest. We expose something that needs to remain unobserved to survive. We make our way clumsily through the world without purpose or definition.

Sometimes it is difficult to see the harm of our actions: they seem minor as we look at the abundance around us. It is even more difficult to explain those actions and nonactions to our children. We live in a country celebrated for its abundance, and this land overflowing with bounty has been exuberantly described and honored. Perhaps because of this, we also live in a country that has not taken its role of stewardship seriously. Ever since the rediscovery of North America by the white man, the resources of this land have been considered unlimited, and through this myth a consciousness of waste has been ingrained in us that is difficult to adjust, whether we are in a neighborhood park, crossing our own country, or visiting other lands.

Coronado, an early tourist to America, described "such large numbers of cattle that it now seems incredible. . . . Traveling over the plains, there was not a single day until my return, that I lost sight of them." Pattie, an American trapper, saw an endless plain of plenty: "As far as the plain was visible in all directions, innumerable herds of wild horses, buffaloes, antelopes, deer, elk, and wolves fed in their wild fierce freedom." Arthur Barlowe wrote, "I think in all the world the like abundance is not to be found. . . . This island had many good woods full of deer, conies, hares and fowl, even in the middest of summer in incredible abundance."

Facing such abundant resources, it is hard to imagine a need for a conservation ethic. Given resources of an unlimited nature, there can be no conception of anything but illimitable waste.

If waste, by its very meaning, as Webster defines it, is "to cause to shrink in physical bulk or strength: cause to become consumed or weakened. . . . to wear away or impair," then it becomes the simplest of logical conclusions that you cannot diminish what is unending, lessen what is greater than we can imagine. It is like removing a grain of sand from a shore, a drop of water from the ocean, a star from the heavens.

At one time in North America, flocks of passenger pigeons could literally blot out the sky, creating an ornithological eclipse. Alexander Wilson observed a flock in 1810 that he calculated to be a mile wide and over 200 miles long, containing more than two billion birds in flight. Audubon saw dung falling "in spots not unlike melting flakes of snow, and the continued buzz of wings had the tendency to lull my senses into repose." The seemingly unlimited supply and ease of capture made them a common and cheap market staple. In 1857 a law was proposed in Ohio that would protect the passenger pigeon, but the Ohio state senate decided the bird needed no protection. They called it "wonderfully prolific" and mistakenly concluded that "no ordinary destruction can lessen them or [cause them to] be missed from the myriads that are yearly produced." Just over forty years later the last known wild passenger pigeon was shot.

Julia and I took Kazia and Zoe to a nature sanctuary north of Boston to see the tide pools. We gathered shells and rocks and bits of seaweed. Our pockets began to bulge. Then we saw the sign: "Please do not remove any objects." Unable to explain satisfactorily to our children the harm in taking a few small shells from this infinite shore, I asked one of the guides there. She explained that they welcomed a large number of visitors every day, that a considerable number of schoolchildren were bussed in, and that if each person took only one or two mementos, the beach would soon be stripped clean.

It was a simple concept. I was one, we were four, but we must look at the possibility that every person has the potential and the right to do the same thing we do, that we are not exempt because we are only one (every person is only one, every action is only once), and that consenting to one is consenting to all. What is here for one is here for all to share. Infinitude is merely a mathematical concept. In reality everything is ultimately finite.

It is a wonderful life, and the wonder is how far-reaching every action and thought may be. This isn't to say we should never pick a wildflower or pocket a shell, but we must do so responsibly and consciously. As stewards we must make sure there are always enough buds to flower and go to seed and not pick a field clean. When collecting shells or rocks, we must not leave a barren shore. We must not take just for the taking, pick for the picking. When it comes to wildlife—whether an insect, a snake, a toad, or a bear—look at it, observe it, hold it gently in your hand if you must (okay, maybe not the bear), and then put it back. One snake seen slithering through the underbrush is worth a hundred held in a terrarium.

One man brought a hundred starlings to New York and changed the face of North America forever. A small group of men stocked the Colorado River with trout, and the fate of the humpback chub was irrevocably altered. Many men but one conscience almost completely wiped out the plains bison from our continent and did succeed in removing the eastern bison, the passenger pigeon, the Carolina parakeet, the auk, and other unique forms of wildlife from our lives forever. Forever. When it is love we are talking about, forever may be a heavenly eternity, but when it is referring to an unredeemable loss, it simply becomes hell.

One summer day, paddling down the Concord River, doing my best Thoreauvian impression, I could see a school of sunnies swimming under my canoe. I took a cracker from my backpack and held it under the water. The fish began nibbling at the cracker, with an occasional gentle tug on a finger. I was in awe as these fish fed from my hand. It was a gentle reminder of the power of nature to hold us enthralled as I interacted in this simple way with the wild, however mild and innocuous that wild happened to be.

I have been lucky enough to hold a starling in my hand; to steady a raccoon with my gaze as we sat and watched each other at five in the morning in my backyard; to see a fox run unharmed across a busy suburban road during a rush-hour sunset; to give a soon-to-be-run-over turtle a life-saving ride to a river in my car; to observe two spiders share one large juicy fly for a noontime repast; to have a gentle garter snake sun on a board behind my house; to have a luna moth balance on my finger. I want my children to be able to say the same thing and their children after them.

Whether we are exploring a neighborhood wood or a neighboring country, whether we are crossing the street or crossing the continent or the globe, we are guests. Whether we are on our land or on the land of others, whether we have a deed giving us an implied legal right to the land or have paid the toll and can show our ticket, we are not truly tenured but are tenants temporarily on common ground.

The thing we take with us today is gone for everyone else tomorrow. If it lives, the toad not taken is there for others to observe, for it to mate and give rise to more of its kind or to be eaten by a bird or animal or to return to the earth in an endless cycle. It is a cycle with which we should not interfere.

When we can observe and then walk away, resisting the all-too-human impulse to take and make our own, responsibility begins. When we pass that responsibility on to our children and with it a sense of our innate moral accountability, then stewardship and all that it stands for truly begins.

6

Of the Fittest

Janine DeBaise

It began with my seventeen-year-old niece Erin and her love of reality television. She'd been watching *Survivor*, the television show that plunks carefully selected strangers into the wilderness and then follows them with camera crews as they scrounge for food and make snarky comments while practically starving to death. This show captured the imaginations of the American public that summer, which I suspect says more about the average person's love of snark than our culture's grasp of what it means to live within the limits of place.

We would play our own Survivor game, Erin decided. By *we*, she meant my extended family, who gather at my parents' camp in upstate New York for a week every Fourth of July. How did she know we'd all be willing to play? Well, there was some precedent. In the early 1970s, long before Erin or any of the grandchildren were born, my parents went on a Euell Gibbons kick. Armed only with the book *Stalking the Wild Asparagus*, they talked about how we were going to "live off the land" for the whole week. We didn't end up going whole hog (or whole asparagus, you might say), and some meals included hamburgers cooked over the fire. But mostly, we spent a lot of time scrounging for food that summer. Most of it tasted pretty good too—milkweed pods cooked in hot water, the white parts of cattails marinated in salad dressing, and watercress plucked out of the lawn.

My parents' camp on the Saint Lawrence River isn't exactly wilderness. To get there, you drive a few miles from town and take a turn off the highway. Their land is a peninsula set amid acres and acres of cattails, all protected by the 1972 wetlands legislation. I still remember the first time my father saw the property. Most people who buy land on the river want big rocks and deep clear water. But my father loved the shallow muddy water, where little kids could chase after frogs and snakes, the acres of waving cattails that made the land completely private, and the oak trees that have stood there since native people camped underneath. He said to my mother, "It's a paradise."

My parents are the kind of people who have read Henry David Thoreau's *Walden* one too many times, and their camp bears a remarkable resemblance to the cabin where Thoreau lived. It's sixteen-by-sixteen feet, with a wooden table, a propane stove, and a single light bulb for playing cards at night. The only luxury is the big refrigerator, which comes in handy when you're feeding five kids, four in-laws, and ten grandchildren. Each year, during the week of July Fourth, we bring tents and set them up under the pine trees.

It was here Erin set our version of Survivor 2001: The Thousand Islands. She was sure it would be just like the television show. Well, minus the camera crews and the auditions and the insane publicity.

Erin designated July 6 as Survivor Day. The evening before, she put up signs on my parents' cabin, the outhouse, and several big trees near the fire pit. There were rules.

From 8 a.m. until 8 p.m., the tents, cars, and my parents' cabin would be off-limits. No store-bought food. Erin posted a sign on the refrigerator that said, "Don't even think it." She banned electronic devices of any kind. She announced that she would split us into two tribes, and each tribe would be given one metal cooking pot, six matches, one small bag of rice, and one canoe.

Each person was allowed one personal item, which had to be chosen the night before and approved by Erin. She announced that there would be four challenges—or contests—during the twelve hours of the game. She hinted that there would be prizes.

My brother-in-law Larry, who grew up in a wealthy family on Long Island, read the posted rules and gave the rest of the family an incredulous look. He summed up his stance in one simple sentence: "Starving myself is not my idea of a vacation." He and my sister Laurie volunteered to take the three youngest grandchildren to town for the day. I felt a bit relieved that I wouldn't have to watch my six-year-old go hungry.

Everyone else would remain. Twelve people in all, pitting themselves against the fierce nature of the North Country in July.

Thursday, 7 p.m.: The Game Begins

Erin's tribal division is ruthless. She separates all the usual camp pairs: Devin and Emily, the inseparable ten-year-old cousins, co-owners of an imaginary bakery on the big rock ledge; Shannon and Jaime, the teenage cousins who spend hours talking and brushing each other's blonde hair; and the old folks, my parents, who still like to hike together after forty-three years of marriage. Members of both teams express relief that my father and I are on separate teams. Everyone thinks we argue too much.

Here Is My Tribe:
My mother (age sixty-nine). Perhaps the most valuable member. She knows which plants to eat, she knows the kind of naturalist trivia you get from books, and she has decades of experience cooking over a fire. She will emerge as the leader. Her only weakness is a tendency to faint if she goes more than two hours without food. She chooses a raft as her personal item, in case we want to go swimming.

My husband, Bill (age forty). Not the camping type. He grew up in the suburbs and gets restless at camp. His most important talent is that he can do spot-on voice impressions—from Henry Kissinger to Elvis Presley to Robin Leach. We're not exactly sure how that talent is going to help us survive in the wilderness, but he's entertaining. He plans to drive into town early the next morning to buy the newspaper for his personal item, a choice he defends by saying we can use it later to start a fire.

Me (age forty). Like most well-read people, I know lots of interesting but useless facts. My role is expected to be minor, unless we use the canoe and raft. Like my mother, I need to eat every couple of hours, so the whole tribe is nervous about my getting a migraine. I choose my journal as my personal item. The rest of the tribe accuses me (kiddingly, I think) of not being a team player. My sister Colleen defends my choice by saying she wants the pen to do the crossword puzzle in the newspaper.

My sister Colleen (age thirty). Urban, sophisticated, high-strung, she dresses like a fashion model. Some of us suspect that years of living in Manhattan have not sharpened her wilderness survival skills, but she's so much fun that we are happy to have her on our team. Besides, she is training for the Chicago marathon in October, which means she is in great shape for the physical challenges. After being nudged by my mother, Colleen chooses a sharp knife.

My daughter Shannon (age fifteen). Her most valuable skill is her ability to manipulate her younger brothers. And unlike her brothers, she will eat vegetables. She rolls her eyes when she finds out that she's in the same tribe as her parents. She chooses a red sleeping bag.

My niece Emily (age ten). When she pulls her blonde hair back into a ponytail, she's ready to tackle anything. She's so cute that she'll come in handy if we have to beg food from strangers. She chooses a red water bottle. Our team color, we decide, is red. I even have the foresight to demand the red canoe rather than the green one, a strategically important triumph for team morale.

Our first task as a tribe is to choose a name. My mother tosses out a suggestion right away. "How about the Gananoques?"

"I think it means something in the native language," I volunteer.

"Something about a river," my mother says, "Or hunters, maybe."

Shannon shrugs. "That's cool."

My mother invents a cheer to go with the name. The cheer sounds suspiciously like the chant she and Shannon use when they play on a team during our evening card games. Meanwhile, Colleen announces that she doesn't know how to drink out of a water bottle and demonstrates her inability to do so. She leans back at a peculiar angle and squirts water into her eye. We use up all of our strategy-planning time trying to teach Colleen how to drink out of the bottle.

The Other Tribe:
My father (age seventy). He has lived in upstate New York his whole life. He's camped, hunted, fished, and sailed in this area since boyhood. Tough competition. He wants to choose his sailboat for his personal item, but Erin says no. Instead, he chooses a cleverly designed device that folds flat and has four cups nestled inside.

My sister Carroll (age forty-two). The oldest of my siblings, she is likely to emerge as the leader. Anyone who has played Monopoly with her knows that below her easygoing surface lies a fierce competitor who goes berserk if she doesn't get all the light-blue properties. She pulls out the book *Stalking the Wild Asparagus*—which she just happens to have—as her personal item. She is accused of having insider information.

My brother-in-law Jimmy (age forty-one). A laid-back guy with a soft Maryland accent who runs marathons and likes to cook. He's an uninhibited guy who will egg on his nephews when they make inappropriate jokes. He chooses his fishing pole.

Colleen and I decide we are not intimidated by the other team's potential to catch fish. I'm a vegetarian, and she thinks eating fish is gross.

My niece Jaime (age nineteen). Blonde and beautiful. The television cameras, if they actually existed, would love her. One year of college has not turned her into a cynic. She proudly produces a cigarette lighter as her personal item. Since no one in the family smokes, we are suspicious. Clearly, Erin leaked information about Survivor Day to the rest of her family.

My son Sean (age thirteen). Good-natured, strong, not likely to get tired. He would wear the same black tee-shirt and shorts all summer long if his mother allowed it, and the lack of plumbing at camp has never bothered him in the slightest. He's a kid who is growing fast, though, so feeding him from the wild could pose a problem. He chooses a pocketknife.

My son Devin (age ten). A face full of freckles, lots of enthusiasm, and a high-pitched voice more shrill than a smoke alarm when he loses his temper. He'll take the game very seriously, and he'll do anything his Aunt Carroll tells him to do. He chooses a deck of cards.

Their tribe calls themselves the Ospreys and devises a clever bird call that is supposed to sound like an osprey. While swimming at an island the day before, we'd watched an osprey circling around, gliding, and then dropping rapidly to pull a fish from the water, a fish so heavy he could barely lift to the sky again. This name choice strikes us as terribly clever, and we feel that the other tribe already has the upper hand.

Friday, 7 a.m.

Both teams nervously prepare for the 8 a.m. start to Survivor Day. At the picnic tables, the kids madly gulp bananas and cereal. I drink about a quart of orange juice that came all the way from Florida. Potassium, I say to myself. My sister Colleen keeps chanting, "Carbo-load! Carbo-load!"

The other tribe begins to make us nervous. They gather in little groups, chuckling, whispering, and looking very smug. Colleen and I call a hasty tribe meeting. "What about food? Shouldn't we have a plan?"

Ten-year-old Emily looks around furtively and whispers, "I know where there are some berries."

"Perfect," my mother says. "And the field by the dirt road is filled with milkweeds."

We need to move quickly after the 8 a.m. start to beat the other tribe to the obvious food sources. Cattails can wait; we are standing at the edge of a marsh that stretches half a mile to meet the river, so we have an endless supply. Once we come up with a food-gathering plan, we turn our thoughts to more important concerns.

Clothing. It's an unusually cold and windy day, but we hope it will warm up. The men keep snickering about how uncomfortable it is to wear a bathing suit under their clothes. My brother-in-law Jimmy announces, "I'll just swim naked. I've got no problem with that."

The true survivor look, according to fashion expert Colleen, consists of a colorful sports bra and short shorts. But it is too cold. The teenage girls brought sarongs to wear over their bathing suits, but in this cold wind, they wrap them around their heads like turbans. Colleen, having abandoned her sleek urban black in favor of jeans, sets the fashion tone for the nonexistent cameras. She braids her hair, streaks charcoal on her face, ties on a purple bandana, and tops this off with sunglasses.

7:50 a.m.

Colleen opens the door of her rental car, parked near the picnic table. She yells: "Time to get pumped!" She cranks the music as loud as it can go: "Cowboy" by Kid Rock. Family members, young and old, start dancing wildly and brandishing their personal items in a scene that looks like something out of a Maurice Sendak book.

8 a.m.

Colleen shuts the car door. Erin gives the signal. The game begins.

My tribe disperses quickly, according to plan. Colleen and Emily disappear into the woods, searching for berries. My mother, my daughter, and I sneak to the field to pick milkweeds. My husband, who was somehow left out of the planning session, sits on the red sleeping bag reading the newspaper. The other tribe suspects he's a spy and move cautiously away from him.

Once in the sheltered field, we move into a rhythm of picking milkweed buds and talking. I take off my red sweatshirt to use as a bag. Shannon looks nervously at the buds. "These things," she asks. "We're going to eat them?" My mother shows her how to avoid the ones that have already begun to flower.

The Osprey tribe—all six of them—come strolling by on the dirt road, looking smug. My father is in the lead, walking briskly, wearing his winter ski cap, a ragged flannel shirt, and a down vest patched with duct tape. My sister Carroll carries their cooking pot. My son Sean swings his pocketknife. My brother-in-law Jimmy makes osprey noises. My niece Jaime has added gull feathers to her turban. Ten-year-old Devin is so excited that his freckles are moving.

They march past without saying a word, looking at our milkweed buds with disdain. I can tell from my father's pace and expression that he has forgotten about the Survivor game and is just excited to take them on a long hike. Back at our tribal meeting spot—the red sleeping bag spread on the ground under the white pines—we find the rest of our tribe. Colleen and Emily return with six berries and a handful of bright orange daylilies. "A nice little spread," Colleen says brightly and strips off her fleece to sun herself. She has her priorities, and getting a tan is the top one.

My husband looks curiously at the milkweed buds: "What are those?"

"Lunch," I explain.

Bill looks again. "You've got to be kidding."

My mother and I cover the milkweed buds with cold water. An hour into the game, we are already getting hungry.

10 a.m.

We decide to conserve our energy. That wind is still cold. The women cram onto the red sleeping bag. "You know, lying down on the ground on a cold day means putting your body into the boundary layer of the Earth's surface," I say, "It's warmer here than the climate just six feet higher." Shannon kicks me and says, "*Mom!* I'm trying to sleep."

I write in my journal and watch the clouds overhead while family members use my body as a pillow. As the scent of the pine trees wafts across the sleeping bag, I offer to make the group pine needle tea.

"We made it once when I was a kid."

"Did it taste good?"

"No, it was awful. But it's full of vitamin C."

No one thinks that scurvy is imminent. Emily and I munch the bright orange petals of the daylilies. "I eat these all the time at home," Emily says cheerfully.

It's true. Often, I have watched her and Devin, sitting on the grass outside her city home, pulling the petals off the daylilies in the front garden.

We goad Bill into reading the newspaper aloud. He picks obscure little articles and reads them in different accents. An item about the royal family, read in a snobby British accent, gets Colleen and my mother rolling about the sleeping bag in hysterical laughter. Bill warms up to this appreciative audience and starts ad-libbing like crazy, scanning the paper for the most ridiculous stories. "Woman shoots self in foot in trailer park."

He reads a letter to Dear Abby from a pathetic woman who cannot decide between loyal Monroe or hot-looking Lance. Mom shrugs: "She needs to look elsewhere." Shannon thinks Lance deserves a chance. "Maybe he's smarter than he looks." My sister Colleen and I scream: "Forget them both! Go to grad school!"

Eventually, the Ospreys return. Raspberries and blackberries fill their cooking pot. We stare enviously. My father, who is muddy up to his knees, swings a rusty leghold trap and brags that he could hunt wild game. Jaime, who has stripped down to a tank top and added sprigs of pine to her turban, carries an old wooden box. Jimmy holds up a neat pile of green cattail punks. "I can get some fish to go with that," he says.

I can tell that my sons are bursting to tell me about the walk—but they won't cross tribal lines. Devin bounces up and down, hanging onto his Aunt Carroll and whispering into her ear, a new shade of pink across his freckles.

"They're having fun," Shannon says, giving me an accusing look. "And they have berries."

"Don't worry," Colleen says. "We'll win the challenge."

"Yeah," I say, "I think there's some kind of food prize."

Our team is getting pretty hungry. Daylily petals are not that filling.

11 a.m.: The Mental Challenge

Erin instructs us to gather under the pine trees for the first challenge—trivia questions about camp. Mom, Colleen, and I look at each other confidently. We read the camp journal the most often. We remember details. We can carry the whole team.

But Erin decrees that we can't help team members, which means we lose our advantage. The questions come fast, like bullets. How many times have we rebuilt the outhouse? Who is the only person to swim around Third Brother Island? How many times has cousin George fallen off the dock? Suddenly the Ospreys take the lead.

They win it. All six jump to their feet, cheering and dancing, celebrating in the most obnoxious way. My sister Carroll and my son Sean high-five each other. I hear my brother-in-law Jimmy say to Devin, "Want me to moon the other tribe?"

Erin hands them the prize, which turns out to be random items she scavenged from the camp—one cold beer, one sleeve of graham crackers, six marshmallows, and six squares of chocolate.

Six squares of chocolate. Colleen and I look at each other, sharing the pain of the moment. Six squares of chocolate.

The agony of defeat. "That was the mental challenge," my daughter says. "Our only chance." She gives me an accusing look, as if I am responsible for the loss. Colleen and I throw ourselves on the ground and talk about our favorite ways to eat chocolate.

"I would have heated up water," I say, "then put the square of chocolate on my tongue, and then sipped the hot water slowly and let the chocolate melt gradually."

"I would have dug up chicory roots, roasted them, and made chicory coffee and then melted a square of chocolate into the coffee."

While Colleen and I grieve the loss of chocolate, my mother calls my sulky daughter over. "Help me make a fire. It's important we use only one match."

Shannon rises to the challenge, and soon the pot of milkweed buds is boiling nicely. My mother shows Shannon how to change the water to get rid of any bitterness. We start hunting for sticks to use as chopsticks, even though my mother—who grew up in the New York City area—is the only one who can use chopsticks in any kind of meaningful way.

My father, still in his tall rubber boots and ragged flannel shirt, comes dancing past the red sleeping bag, dangerously close to crossing the tribal line. He's humming a Glen Miller tune. Smiling smugly, he waves his square of chocolate near me. I am sorely tempted to punch him.

The milkweed buds are quite tasty. Or maybe it's that we're starving. I give up on the chopsticks and start grabbing buds with my fingers. We eat out of the one pot—no one has the energy to fashion bowls from leaves or bark. Colleen attempts to drink out of the water bottle and drenches us all.

"You're a runner," I say for the tenth time. "How is it that you don't know how to drink from a water bottle?"

She shrugs.

After the milkweed buds, we cook our rice—about a cup of it split among the six of us. When my mother spills some onto the picnic table, we rush to pick up every grain with our fingers.

We brainstorm for other food sources. Too late for strawberries. Too early for apples. The dandelions and watercress would be bitter this time of year: we weren't *that* hungry. We roast some green cattail punks. Cooked over the fire, they taste—well, they taste like cattail punks, with fluff that sticks in my teeth.

Clouds move across the sun. We huddle on the sleeping bag. Colleen and Bill work on the *New York Times* crossword puzzle. My mother is the only one who knows any of the answers. Emily and I find more day-lilies and drink water to fill our stomachs.

The other tribe gathers over near the fire pit under the oak trees. Sneaking a peek, I am startled to see both my sons happily devouring milkweed buds cooked by their Aunt Carroll. "Hey, these are good," Sean says. I imagine his reaction if I had served milkweed buds for dinner at home.

Jimmy walks past us deliberately, fishing pole in hand. "I'm not that hungry," he says smugly. "We'll probably just throw the fish back in."

1:30 p.m.

Erin announces the culinary challenge. Each team has ninety minutes to prepare a meal from the wild.

"They've got berries," Shannon whispers in a tragic tone.

"Erin is the judge," Emily says mournfully, "and she likes anything sweet."

The morale of our tribe is at an all-time low. My mother suggests we take a walk to see what we can find to jazz up our meager food offerings. "Presentation is everything," Colleen points out.

We tramp along an old dirt road that leads to some small camps built on Goose Bay. To our right, trees hang over rock outcroppings. On our left, small clearings for docks occasionally break the long stretches of cattails. The sun comes out as we walk along, and I look across the bay to islands with gray cliffs and pine trees. Then I turn to my niece Emily: "We can win this challenge."

As we meander down a grassy road, Mom and I point out family history to Emily and Shannon. Old Mr. Clark, dead before Shannon was born, told us this spot here was an Indian burial ground. The summer I turned thirteen, my sister Laurie and I met two boys in that camp over there—two boys from Rochester who fell madly in love with us.

Passing a camp with a small vegetable garden causes an ethical dilemma. Should we steal a zucchini? The neighbors wouldn't care. Squash grows so fast in upstate New York that people give away the stuff. (How do you know if someone in upstate New York has no friends? You see him buying zucchini in the supermarket in August.) But our high moral standards prevent us from becoming vegetable thieves.

Colleen gathers wildflowers—armfuls of purple vetch, yellow buttercups, white daisies, orange daylilies—and gives them to Bill to carry. He keeps saying, "Shouldn't we have some kind of food as part of the meal?" We ignore him.

At the waterfront stand small trees with gracefully curving branches and long leaves.

"Mmmm," I say, "What about sumac lemonade?"

My mother points out the obvious: "The sumac isn't even close to being ripe enough."

"Let's do it anyhow," says Colleen. "We'll get points for creativity."

I take off the red sweatshirt, and we fill it with sumac berries. Meanwhile, Emily discovers an old stump with curved bark. The bark will make a lovely bowl. Oh, things are coming together nicely.

There is just no end to our brilliance. When we get back to camp, I rip a page from my journal to write a formal menu: *Fresh milkweed buds fire-roasted, drenched in butter, garnished with bright daylily petals. Native marsh cattail hearts. Moulin Rouge Lemonade made with organic sumac. Raspberry jubilee.* Colleen, Shannon, and I luxuriate in the fun of choosing words. We are good with words.

My husband Bill says, "But you know, she has to actually eat this. Shouldn't we have some actual food?" We ignore him.

Near the fire pit, the other tribe works furiously. My sister Carroll boils small green apples into sour applesauce. "I need some sugar to work with," she moans, but the concoction still looks impressive and practically edible.

Colleen and Shannon hide behind the pine trees, arranging wildflowers into a lavish display that hopefully makes up for the fact that we have little real food to offer Erin. My mother takes Bill and Emily down to the dock to pick cattails, trying to find the tender white parts inside the green stalks. As Bill has never eaten these before—and never plans to—he has no idea what to look for but helpfully yanks cattails out anyhow.

"Presentation is everything," Colleen repeats. She stops to admire her work. "I could be a caterer. I'd be good at it."

"I want a job at a flower store," says Shannon. "I'd be good at it."

My mother goes back to the fire pit to cook the choicest milkweed buds. At this point, I am so hungry that I start to resent the amount of time we've spent cooking this meal for Erin—who has had access to food all day. I tell myself the victory will be worth it.

3 p.m.

We gather at the picnic tables to unveil our entries. I suddenly remember, with gut-wrenching clarity, that Carroll and Dad are both artists. Carroll has worked in restaurants for years, and Jimmy is the son of a chef.

We don't stand a chance.

Their tribe used big lily pads for plates on a birch-bark placemat. Wildflowers rest in a decorative glass bottle, which they claim they found on their hike. The food—which actually looks tasty—is arranged nicely. Young green cattail punks, cooked until tender. Milkweed buds. A mound of green apple jam, surrounded by lots of big ripe berries, both purple and red. I salivate, staring at those berries.

Our entry, on the other hand, looks like a floral arrangement— something you admire while standing in line at a funeral home, not something you want to put in your mouth. It takes some work to find the edible parts. And the sumac lemonade, which turned a strange greenish color instead of a lovely shade of pink, tastes so horrible that Erin spits it out.

We lose. Again. Oh, the humiliation of defeat.

We take solace in the fact that the prize is pathetic. They get forks, spoons, and one granola bar to split among six people. I realize that Erin is coming up with prizes by scavenging through the cabin and cars. If we do this again, I'll make sure to supply chocolate chip cookies.

"The next challenge is in an hour," Erin announces. "At four o'clock."

Another challenge? But we are starving. My mother and I fan the coals. "We can get the fire going again without matches," I brag to Shannon. She is not impressed. But she helps her grandmother cook a pot of milkweed buds.

Bill doesn't even pretend to eat any. "I'll let you have my share—so you don't get a migraine," he says generously. The rest of us crowd onto the red sleeping bag, eating the buds with our fingers. As I raise a clump to my mouth, I notice a dead green and black caterpillar tucked under the bud.

A monarch caterpillar, I realize. They eat milkweed. We're competing with local caterpillars for food.

The wind rises again. I sit between Emily and Shannon for warmth. Bill and Colleen sift through the newspaper. The other tribe, also huddled together for warmth, plays pitch, a card game my father began playing as a kid. Rumors spread that some members of their tribe are suffering the effects of the green crabapple sauce. We hope it's true.

4 p.m.

Erin announces the physical challenge—a relay race. We have one minute to pick our four strongest runners.

My mother hurt her knee three weeks ago, so she's out. Colleen and Shannon are definites. And Bill has the longest legs at camp. I look at my ten-year-old niece Emily, who is listening to the discussion and not saying a word. "My left leg's been hurting," I say. "I'm out."

Emily jumps up, eagerly: "I can run fast."

Over at the Osprey camp, my sister Carroll and my father back out quickly to give my ten-year-old Devin a chance to run. I think we are all losing our competitive edge. Perhaps the hunger is wearing us down.

Erin wants to start the race, but Colleen demands time to train her fellow tribe members on her technique for passing off the pine cone. She turns to us and whispers dramatically: "This could win us the race." Hidden safely behind a pine tree, she demonstrates the proper way to pass the pinecone, using such exaggerated gestures that Emily and Shannon spit out their water.

Erin leads the eight runners away to assign them spots along the dirt road. The rest of us gather near the green bench, the place where we sit on nice evenings to watch the sun set over the Saint Lawrence River. My mother and I look through the oak trees to try to spot the runners. My father wanders down to the dock, casting longing looks at his sailboat. I talk to my sister Carroll for the first time that day, checking in with her about my sons. "They're loving it," she says. "You wouldn't believe how seriously Devin is taking this."

Erin appears, and we separate guiltily.

When the camp dogs start barking, we know runners are approaching. Then suddenly, out of nowhere, they appear—Jaime and Shannon, hurtling down the narrow path. And my tribe member is in the lead!

We win! Finally we win! The Gananoques leap around ecstatically. The runners gather to tell their stories, to relive the whole race again and again. Emily and Devin, the ten-year-olds, emerge as the true heroes, running bravely against experienced runners many inches taller.

Erin hands us the prize—two stale donuts (to be split in six pieces), six empty cups, and four packets of cocoa. "We need better prizes next year," Colleen says. My niece Jaime looks over at our winnings and laughs: "Yeah, that sucks."

My mother cuts up the donuts. Bill lets Emily have his piece, but I am incapable of that sort of sacrifice. I savor my bit of donut, chewing it slowly to make it last.

But the best part comes a few minutes later. My mother heats the pot of water on the fire. Then sitting by the fire, with the wind still keeping things cool, we huddle and sip the chocolate liquid. My mother and I go on and on about how great the cocoa tastes until our own tribe members tell us to shut up.

6 p.m.

We drift closer to the fire, tribal lines blurring. Devin leans against his sister, Shannon, and my father tells Emily a story about the first car he ever owned, a 1936 Ford. The sun moves toward the edge of the cattails.

Before we can get too complacent, Erin steps briskly up to the fire pit. "One more challenge," she says. Jimmy rolls his eyes. "I'm not even hungry," he says.

"And the prizes suck," says Jaime. She sticks her tongue out at her sister.

"A scavenger hunt," Erin says firmly. "In one minute, I'll give each tribe the list of items. Whoever gets them first wins."

Quickly, my tribe moves away from the fire and into a huddle. "We'll divide up the items," whispers Shannon. Despite the wind, Colleen dramatically pulls off her warm clothes to display her running outfit—navy blue halter and shorts. "I'm ready," she says, poised like a superhero about to do battle.

Erin hands Shannon the list. Looking over her shoulder, I scan it quickly. A maple leaf. A blue stone. A branch with two berries. A branch with a pine cone attached. A cattail punk. A pink flower: wait, there are no pink flowers around here.

Colleen looks around furtively and whispers: "Remember that geranium we saw on our walk? In a planter near the island camp. It's probably a mile away, but I'm fast." She slips quietly through the pine trees and runs down the grassy road.

"Mom, you get the maple leaf," Shannon orders. "Emily, you get the blue rock."

There's a single maple tree hidden among the oaks on the path that leads to the dock area. I find my Dad already there, reaching up to take a maple leaf for his team. He looks at me. "Here, you need one too?" We cross tribal lines to walk up the path together, moving close to avoid the lush poison ivy that lines the narrow strip of hard-packed dirt.

"Devin is so serious about this," my father says, "You should have seen him at the race. He put his whole heart into that run." He stops near the cabin to upright a fallen water jug and ambles over to his tribe.

Everyone waits at the fire pit—except for Colleen, who is nowhere in sight. "We've got everything already," says my niece Jaime. "We've won."

I look at the items the Osprey tribe spread out on the bench. Their pink flower is not pink. It is a white and purple morning glory! Not even close.

Erin, in a blatant act of favoritism, declares the Osprey tribe the winners. "It's not pink!" we scream. She shrugs. My father holds the flower up and says in a philosophical tone of voice, "Well, you know, there is a whole range of pink. Some are closer to red, some near to purple."

Moments later, Colleen bursts through the pines, panting, clutching a pink geranium. "Here it is!" she exclaims. "I risked public embarrassment, I risked arrest, I risked messing up my training with a two-mile sprint, but I have the pink flower. We will win this."

No one wants to tell her. We stare at her in silence, and then, as if triggered by an invisible switch, everyone starts arguing. Erin shrugs. "My decision is final."

Colleen stares at the white and purple morning glory in disbelief and horror. "This is not pink," she says. "How could anyone think this was pink? This geranium—this geranium is pink, a true pink, the only pink for miles around."

We move closer to the fire to listen to Colleen's story—her keen observation of wildflowers earlier in the day, her quick decision to make the run (sacrificing all for her team) for the only pink flower around, and then an unfortunate incident with the old man watering said flower when she arrived wildly out of the blue to pick it.

There is more—a formal tribal council, secret meetings, dramatic monologues by both my father and my husband in attempts to sway the vote, an argument about whether a certain tribe rigged their vote—but mainly we sit around the fire, rehashing the day, telling our favorite parts, giving each other compliments on our survival skills. The Osprey tribe continues to brag about their incredible hike. "We turned the corner," Carroll says, "and it was like walking into a painting. The light was just perfect."

"I'm not even hungry," Devin says.

"We could live off the land if we had to," Jaime says.

"We'd need to hunt and trap for the winter," says my father.

I think the kids and teenagers are amazed that we could do it. They got a glimpse of what it's like to forage for food, to live within the boundaries of place.

Emily and Devin, the youngest members of each tribe and underdogs from the start, find themselves tied as winners, awarded bonus points for energy and effort. Erin produces the grand prize, something she bought with her own money—a green folding chair, perfect for sitting by the fire. It seems quite grand after the previous lame prizes. Emily and Devin set the chair up by the fire and squeeze onto it together.

8 p.m.

We survived the day. We hug each other and cheer. Colleen opens her car door and cranks up the music. Everyone dances wildly. We dance to Kid Rock, to the Beatles, to the Beach Boys.

Bill and Jimmy drive to town and return with steaming cardboard boxes of pizza, French fries, and wings.

"We don't really need that food," everyone keeps saying. "We could survive without it." And then we sit under the oak trees and eat.

7

A New England Childhood

Alison Hawthorne Deming

I grew up in the 1950s in rural Connecticut in a town of farms and woods. The suburbs were beginning to expand. The malls had not yet arrived. Everyone was happy when a supermarket was built. The drug store had a Formica ice cream counter with tall round stools, where I liked to order a vanilla ice cream soda. I also bought my comic books there. My favorites were *Casper the Friendly Ghost* and *Little Lulu*. People drove to Hartford to work for the insurance companies. My father worked for a radio station and was a popular talk show pioneer, starting with *The Morning Watch* radio show in 1934. He wrote skits about various characters he played, like The Old Man of the Mountain, a wise and ornery Yankee codger, and The Motorcycle Mouse, his spinoff of *Stuart Little*. He conducted conversations on air with his pet cow, Bessie Bossie, and showed up as a personality at local fairs and beauty pageants with a real cow by his side, although everyone must have known that his radio companion was a child's toy he tipped over to let Bessie's lowing loose on the airwaves. How I loved to hear his corny jokes morning after morning. "Well, what do you think, Bessie, about today's disturbing news?" "Moo-oooo." Bessie had a way of putting things in perspective.

He ended his career in the mid-1960s with *It's a Pleasure* on television, where he interviewed politicians and public figures, and *What in the World*, a quiz show about travel and culture in which art-smart panelists raised money for local charities by riffing on statues, monuments, cathedrals, and paintings from that week's chosen locale. He had wanted a career as a stage actor and had worked in New York—mostly bit parts and walk-ons. His big role was Herod in Oscar Wilde's *Salome*. He toured in a road company with Clifford Odets, sleeping in barns in Pennsylvania and living on soup and pie in diners. He never really found great success as an actor, but he was beloved in his radio and TV days for his magnetic charm and general fondness for all people.

My father did not like crows. He spent many hours working in his vegetable garden. It was his solace. He started corn from seed, germinating Golden Bantam stock in Dixie cups, then transplanting it into hills he had hoed up in the rocky soil. As soon as he tamped the seedlings into the ground, the crows flew in to pluck the tender greens. I saw him storm out of the house with his shotgun many times to teach them a lesson. I'm sure he failed. I was never shocked to see his rage. I empathized with his feeling of helplessness against the forces of nature that riled him, although I did not share his hatred of crows. Every summer there seemed to be plenty of corn on our table. My father's passion to make sure that we had that corn impressed on me the importance of his gardening. We had a dog named Bear and a cat named Tiger. The biggest threats in our backyard were copperheads that lurked in rusty leaf beds, skunks, and porcupines, all of which made our dog suffer pain and humiliation but left the bipeds pretty much alone. It was a childhood filled with the sense of wonder at the presence of natural beauty, abundance, and the pleasures of horticulture.

What I didn't know in the pastoral dream of my childhood—it is not information that shows up on primary school maps showing dairy farms in Wisconsin, maple syrup in Vermont, and oranges in Florida—was that our state was becoming rich by successfully following President Franklin D. Roosevelt's December 1940 urging that America become "an Arsenal of Democracy." Hartford had a head start as the home of Colt's Patent Firearms as early as 1836. As a young man, Samuel Colt sailed to Calcutta and carved a wooden model of a pistol inspired by the ship's capstan. The pistol's revolving cylinder held five or six bullets, and it revolutionized shooting. Until then a shooter used a one- or two-barrel flintlock musket. Colt made it possible to shoot and shoot again six times without reloading. He also implemented mass-production techniques for guns. According to the company's Web site, Colt's "post–Civil War slogan" was "Abe Lincoln may have freed all men, but Sam Colt made them equal." As of 2010, the company had produced over 30 million revolvers, pistols, rifles, and automatic weapons.

In my little farm town of Avon, Connecticut, the red brick plant of Ensign-Bickford sat beside a bucolic stream that fed into the Farmington River. As kids, my friends and I used to gather in the factory's shadow to swim in a dammed up pool, which I now realize must have been, in the environmentally blithe 1950s, tainted with industrial effluent. But for us, it was just a swimming hole—a site for cannonballs and swan dives, for flirting and bullying, for kids to be kids on their own, benign and unsupervised. Were we told anything in school or at home about what the company manufactured? "Safety fuses," I recall from somewhere, but I do not remember if I knew that as a child. The building was just another pretty New England mill along a riverside, and it might have made anything from cotton batting to screwdrivers. According to the company's Web site, William Bickford invented the miner's safety fuse in Cornwall, England, in 1831, and it lauds the "humanitarian basis of the invention." From that acorn of good intentions, a multinational corporation has grown. Today the old brick factory building is an upscale shopping mall. Corporate headquarters has moved one town away. It's difficult to tell what the company and its subsidiaries make today: they have interests in "adaptive ordnance systems," aerospace and defense manufacturing, chemical manufacturing, renewable energy, real estate, and pet food. A shell game of commitments, primarily related to killing and destruction, with a profit hiding under a sufficient number of shells to keep the company profitable—and a few feel-good industries to detox the public image.

Connecticut's defense industries flourished during World War II and the cold war. Pratt and Whitney made jet engines, Sikorsky made helicopters, and the first nuclear submarine was built in our state. Military-related employment in the state in the late 1980s accounted for nearly 100,000 jobs; by 2003, that had fallen to 48,000. Even so, the U.S. Defense Department spent $6.2 billion here in 2002, which is more than twice the national average for a state, and $4.8 billion in 2009. Black Hawk helicopters, F-22 Raptor fighter jets, F-35 Joint Strike Fighters, two submarines per year, spare parts, and engines. Connecticut remains one of the top ten defense-industry states in the nation. Our comforts were built on the business of war. What did I know? It's a wonder I remained innocent of this sense of the place for as long as I did, given that I grew up during the heyday of nuclear proliferation. Yes, my childhood was filled with wonder in nature and that bedazzlement made the militaristic facts of American life almost unbelievable to me. If the world was so beautiful, how could so much human intelligence be devoted to violence and destruction?

Crows are ubiquitous in the Connecticut hills and fields. Their feathers shine in sunlight like obsidian. Flying over a cornfield, a flock of crows is an elegance. Gleaning grubs from a fallow field it is a society of peasants. Crows fly with patience, their flapping never belabored. Sometimes they glide. They make their own clothing, feathers grown from their skin, every keratinous cell of the calamus, every black silk fiber of the vane, made by the crow, thoughtlessly and without effort. There is a hollow place in the quill, a space used by veins to supply nutrients while the feather is alive and growing. But the feathers are dead when the crow wears them, a head dress, wing dress, body dress, basic black, and bearing the lovely sheen of life. For forty million years, the iridescence of bird feathers has graced the earth.

But it was the sound of crows that I loved as a child. Caa-aaw. Caa-aaw. The throaty, emphatic call announced their presence. It rose from cedar trees on the edge of the yard. From a place in the sky just out of sight above the hickory tree or behind the house, it entered the open window of the school bus or the chaotic playground during recess at school. The caws announced some work to be done, some passage to be flown, some sight to be seen, some news to be shared. What made them call from the air as they passed on their way? Caa-aaw. It was a sound I knew well and a voice that made me feel that the world was right—that some lives beyond my life were going about their business, being with their being—and I felt suddenly larger than my small self. Even now remembering it, I feel as if I am opening the door and stepping outside into the wonder of things.

Thunderstorms were a pleasure I shared as a child with my father. When I was afraid, he'd invite me to go outside and watch the storm. Little was said. We sat under the sloping porch roof, a safe redoubt from which to watch torrents of rain whip across the lawn and flagstones, pelting the thicket of laurels he'd planted. Light exploded inside the clouds, thunder bouldered around us and clattered through the woods, cold mist splattered our faces, and the ozone scent, fresh and electric, replaced the humid dullness of a Connecticut summer afternoon. Our house was perched on top of a wooded hill—a lightning magnet. Although my instinct was to retreat, for my father the storms were a chance to feel the familiar landscape anew. In the safety of his companionship, I began to look beyond my fear. We sat in silence to watch and listen to the storm. My father taught me to count the interval between flash and rumble to learn how many miles away the storm was. With this method, I calmed myself when I was alone and the sky's violence was near.

The yard was a handmade landscape. My father had dug and stacked fieldstones, dug and hauled dirt, dug and carried laurels down from the rocky woods, their roots balled in burlap. Transplanting was a skill in which he took pride, and I recall many excursions into our woods, single-file parades of laurel scouts seeking wild specimens among the twisted shrubs that looked like good candidates for domestication. My father had many friends and admirers in his public life. Yet the skill I most admired was taking friends and family into the woods to hunt for shrubs. To this day, I follow his example in my own efforts to make a patch of ground fruitful. Dig hole. Add compost. Add water so disinterested roots take immediate hope in their future. Add soil and tamp with feet to firm the bedding and press air out from the watery soup. Water again and tamp again to secure the transplant against wind and flooding.

This nurture I suppose my father learned from his father, an amateur horticulturalist who hybridized fruit trees and tried to save the American chestnut from blight. The nurture of plants was a domestic pleasure for these men, who found the outdoors a refuge from the tensions of domesticity. For my grandfather, it was a civic duty. I have copies of his speeches as president of the Northern Nut Grower's Association. In her nineties, my father's sister remembered their father walking among the trees in his orchard, a small pot of melted paraffin tied to his belt, loops of raffia to bind the slips to their host plants. This story came to me late in life, but my father must have carried it in his memory, both men long gone, and now it lives in me as a story that feels like my personal past. And so family stories become grafted onto our own individual ones, giving us a sense of continuity and consolation in times of loss.

I wonder when my grandfather fell in love with trees? I see him now, a dour man, a pinched New Englander who was made hard by the hard hills, who said little and rarely smiled, a country doctor with an office beside a mill, a place where a doctor would come in handy in 1900. Now both the mill and office building are derelict, but I can picture the old man as he walks in the orchard scoring the rocky hillside of the family homestead, the little pot of wax kept warm with Sterno, strands of raffia tasseling off his canvas belt, the man cultivating his plot of land with homespun, hands-on science—one of the small wonders of the world.

When I was a girl, my mother took me to a gladiolus farm in Plainville. How extravagant those flowers were. Glamour girls. Drag queens. Scarlet bugles. Magenta cornets. Rosy sirens. Like my mother, a writer and theater director, the glads outdid themselves in grandiose gesture. How I loved to visit that farm. We walked drab rows of stalks that had not begun to release their packages of sexual heat. As a girl, I did not see the sex, but surely I felt in the glads' packaged intensity the wish for some explosive joy in myself. The glad field was set back from the road, a nondescript place with a shed for wrapping bundles of the cut stalks in newspaper for swaddling them, my mother carrying the bundle in her arms like a baby.

My mother loved all kinds of flowers and grew extravagant beds of roses, peonies, sweet William, iris, and tulips. She was a New Yorker who had taken to country ways, although she never lost a cosmopolitan flare that found expression in the theater. She loved best the tiny blooms of trailing arbutus that showed up of their own accord beside the forest path in spring. Pink clusters, tissue paper thin, fragrant in a gentle way that drew you to them, not cloying like the narcissistic lily. Did I hear that they were "endangered"? I'm not sure, though I knew as a child they were a rare thing and we were privileged to see them and responsible for protecting them. The arbutus employed a dampened down means of seduction—a flower that didn't have to brag about itself to get attention, once you knew its name. I loved hearing the word *arbutus* emerge in that one season each year as much as I loved seeing and smelling the flower. Why did that word fill me with wonder? In our family, a flower—or an unusual mushroom or bird—roused more than happy admiration. Out came the *Guide to Woodland Flowers*, the magnifying glass, *The Book of Knowledge*, the clipping from a magazine that told us the stinking mushroom we'd found beside the root cellar was a "fetid wood witch." There was joy in the sighting, in the hunting for knowledge, and in the satisfaction of that hunger. This is the way of the old New Englanders, transplants from across the Atlantic who believed they'd need to know the new land in order to survive on it. My mother bent with a glass to inspect the flower's parts. "I can't imagine how such a thing can grow from a single seed," she swooned each time she bent to the sepals and stamens. The seed was God to her because it contained so much. And so much of what it contained was a mystery.

Wonder stirs admiration, amazement, a rush of recognition, a sudden imperative to pay close attention to some thing. Wonder ignites curiosity. Descartes saw wonder as the first of all passions, the impassioned state that makes learning possible. It must be one of nature's greatest gifts to the human condition, the engine of our capacity to learn from experience and to adapt. Rachel Carson saw wonder as "that true instinct for what is beautiful and awe-inspiring" and worried that the loss of wonder that many people experience in adulthood leads to "the alienation from the sources of our strength." What she hoped to nurture in children was a feeling for one's natural surroundings, an indestructible respect that went deeper than the acquisition of fact, a renewable resource of human spirit that would last a lifetime.

The shine, silver mottle, rose and blue moons shedding haloes on one another. The lean, muscular, spangled bodies. My father laying the string of brook trout on the grass in front of our cottage on Grand Manan. Fourteen silver and olive green beauties, mooned with pastels—and the scent of them, forest and sun-dapple and freshet. At such moments my father became a messenger from a world so close to ours yet distant and inaccessible to me. A parallel world, like the one in children's books where animals could talk and a story could quell all dangers. That he knew the forest ways made him a hero. My mother coated the trout with corn meal and fried them in butter for breakfast. The meat, like vanes of a feather, those narrow wedges of flesh, fell from the spine, the geometry of life falling away from the touch of my knife.

My father must have learned his fishing skills from his father by winging dry flies onto the Housatonic River as it wrestled its way through the Connecticut hills. The practical knowledge passed from father to son, on back for ten generations in this landscape and back to their ancestral English rills. But where did it begin? A man comes home from work tired and wanting a drink. A man comes home from fishing having been awake before dawn, walked through the dawn chorus, and conspired with his intuition to read how water moves and how fish move in that water. With his modest kit of tools and skill, he brings joy back home to his family for breakfast and carries the peace of solitude in a wild place into his day.

My father has been dead for two decades, and more years have passed for me than I can claim for the future. It comforts me to see a photograph of my child self wearing a homemade polka dot dress and kneeling before the string of brook trout to admire them, and to know how ordinary and necessary a thing it is, this joy in animal being.

What was missing, I wonder, in those years of innocence? Surely there were rages that engulfed me and sent me screaming in tears to my room. But there was always some solace near at hand, some consolation in the beauty that surrounded me, something larger than myself to hold me in its embrace. I did not understand suffering, neither my own nor that of others. I felt overwhelmed and immobilized by it. When the hurricane floods of 1955 ravaged neighboring towns, rivers violating their banks and turning streets, light posts, porches, roofs, and rocking chairs into nondescript rubble, I toured the wreckage with my father. We looked upon the mess in wonder. How could three solid days of rain cause this much destruction? It was a material calamity, but I have no recollection of anyone speaking of the dead, the displaced, or the anguished who had lost homes, jobs, or loved ones. Perhaps at age nine I was not able to hold such anguish in mind. Perhaps I had to bury the suffering of others, as I had learned to bury my own miseries, because that is what a person does to get from day to day. Perhaps the adults did not speak of such calamity around the children, wanting to protect us. But I felt some quiet and terrible knowledge about the world as I looked at house after house that had fallen into the river, a main street with its shops and flower baskets that was simply gone.

Yes, this too was wonder, its darker manifestation, making one fall silent before the vulnerability of being human. How could the beauty and orderliness of life become so ugly and cast into ruin? I am grateful to have seen the destruction by my father's side, who turned the astonishment to good use in reporting the news on radio. The facts and numbers have dissolved for me, but what remains is a child's awareness that such calamities can happen, that they are terrible and stir a dreadful sense of wonder at nature's power, and that we'd better all stick together.

One incident in my childhood strikes me as a time when my empathy for animals was awakened. Our dog, Bear, was a lumbering golden retriever who ruled the woods surrounding our house with proprietary zeal. Thunderstorms sent him off into barrel-chested barking and hopeless pursuit through the woods as he tried to warn away the invading presence. But he also possessed that sweetness of character for which the breed is known. One summer day, he brought home three baby rabbits, one at a time the tiny creature held gently in the dog's mouth. What a strange thing for a dog to do, we thought. Chances are he had killed and eaten the mother. What had induced him to bring the babies to our doorstep? He placed one on the porch steps, returned to the woods, placed the next and the next.

My father was impressed at the dog's apparent wish that we care for the orphans, so he built a cage with chicken wire left over from his pea fence, and we raised the babies outdoors under a sheltering lilac bush. I fed them lettuce through the lattice of the cage, transfixed to see the little noses wobble as they chewed, the whiskers vibrate like an acrobat's highwire. When it came time to turn them free, we worried that the dog might now find them worthy of chase, so we released them in woods five miles across town, a spot with fewer homes and dogs where the teenage rabbits would stand a chance.

The tenderness of this time has stayed with me, and I think now that the experience stirred up feelings of empathy that have expanded over several decades into an ethical sense of obligation to our fellow creatures. Children need an education in empathy because without this human capacity, the sense of wonder can devolve into an addiction to novelty or the captivity of self-involvement. Turning the captives free into the forest of foxes and owls was a terrible moment. I knew they were unlikely to survive and that nature was a game of chance and nurture, rare and short-lived. The letting go was hell. Then it was done, and we forgot them. Bear remained a hero to us for having shown gentleness. All we'd ever asked of him was that he become our family companion, but I'm grateful that his inbred bird-dogging skills emerged in facing the challenge of baby rabbits, his breed having originated in Scotland in the mid-nineteenth century, where retrievers were selected and trained to carry a shot bird back to the hunter with a gentle mouth.

What can the care of a small animal or two or three, the beauty of a landscape, the tenderness of a man or woman or dog tending transplants, add up to in the mind of a child in the early twenty-first century, when we must also ask that child to learn about carbon emission thresholds, climate chaos, the Holocaust, the terrorist attacks of 9/11, the genocidal foundations of our homeland and its now perpetual militaristic enterprise, and regions of our glorious continent designated by will or accident to become national sacrifice areas? We have a problem of scale when it comes to nurturing the sense of wonder. Asking children to be aware of human violence and natural destruction (and the growing relationship between the two in the era of climate disruption) from a young age violates that wellspring of spiritual strength that Rachel Carson envisioned. Adults who become mindful of this need and attentive to meeting it are likely to discover the unreasonable hope for the future that parents can muster. And one need not be a parent to take on this role of calling attention to the taming power of the small. The appearance of nesting swallows in a prison yard can keep an attentive convict alive during the debasement of his captivity, as Ken Lamberton has eloquently written. Literature does this by bringing our attention to what novelist Aurelie Sheehan calls "the remedy of the immediate."

I find myself unwilling to make a bold claim about how the sense of wonder might quell our human capacity for destructiveness, meanness, and avarice. The evidence of history and the present moment fills me with dismay. Yet we and our children and grandchildren need the rejuvenation of the sense of wonder more than ever. The cost of letting one's appetite for the world's beauty die, of failing to say what one has loved and why, of flagging in sharing one's admiration for amazing life would be the ultimate economic failure leaving the human spirit impoverished. The sense of wonder is shifting in this perilous time for Earth from being a noun (a given) to being a verb (an act). Bedazzlement is not enough. We are called to wonder what the future will bring for those who come after us and to treat the future generations, human and otherwise, as companions for whom we would offer hospitality in our household.

8

Child's Play: Finding the Green in the In-Between

Carolyn Finney

For Henry and Rose

In 2009, one of the U.S. national parks became home to the first black First Family. As the world in general and African Americans, in particular, reflected on these changes, I was struck by something my mother said to me the day after Barack Obama's November 2008 presidential election. At seventy-six years old, she had lived through the Jim Crow and civil rights eras in the South. With my father, she had moved North and raised three children while navigating a new life away from her family in the South and all that was familiar. As a family, we had talked ad nauseam over the years about the "state of things" as it related to black people, our ability to move and choose freely in our lives, and what it would mean if we *really* had that kind of freedom. Both she and my father never imagined that they would see an African American president in their lifetime. The image of a black man as the most powerful leader in the free world was surely one that my parents were reveling in. But when I asked my mother how she felt about the election, she told me that the image of two black girls living in the White House was what moved her most.

I've been thinking about that—picturing the First Daughters moving through the White House, living their lives as kids do. What does it mean when your backyard is the White House lawn? Do they play outside? Do they dig in the dirt, roll in the grass, and run around endlessly? How is their relationship with the outdoors moderated, constrained, and supported by the fact that they live in a national park? How do they navigate the many in-betweens—living in a place they call home that is technically owned by all tax-paying Americans and being the first black family to live in a house built by enslaved Africans but inhabited until now by white families? And how do the concepts of work and play manifest in their evolving relationship with nature?

When I was asked to write this essay about my childhood experiences of the outdoors, I jumped at the chance because I love talking about my *Sabrina*-esque childhood on a large estate owned by my parents' employers.[1] But as I've tried to write this piece, I have been stumped when considering how to talk about the ways in which my parents influenced my relationship with the natural environment. They did affect the way I think about and interact with nature. I'm doing the work I do today as a geographer primarily because of their influence on my thinking about land and place. A friend and colleague understood immediately what the problem was and told me that I was using one of two models that are typically invoked when trying to understand human and environment relationships in the United States—interaction with the natural environment through leisure and recreation (the other model emphasizes the natural environment as a supermarket of resources).[2] My parents' presence on the land we inhabited was predicated on work, so my experiences did not fit neatly into either of those models of understanding nature. What I remember is that for the first eighteen years of my life, my parents worked from dawn to dusk and that the life that my brothers and I lived as children was shaped by the how, when, why, and where of our parents' work.

I grew up in a gardener's cottage in Westchester County, New York, on twelve acres of scenic property that included a large pond and many kinds of trees, including fruit trees. The estate was owned by a wealthy family of contractors who were well known in New York (their name still can be found on a large building in New York City). In the late 1950s, my father returned from the Korean War and needed to find a job. Opportunities were sparse for a black man who had grown up poor in rural Virginia and had only a high school education. But his sister had become a nurse and was living in New York, and her husband, a contractor, had heard about a potential job opportunity. A wealthy Jewish family was looking for a young couple to live in a small home on their estate, care for the property, and perform additional duties, including chauffeuring and doing some housekeeping. My father's only other job opportunity was to be a janitor in Syracuse, New York. So my parents packed their few belongings and drove from Floyd, Virginia, to Mamaroneck, New York, where they began a fifty-year position as caretakers for the estate.

The land was beautiful, but it was far from everything that was familiar to them. The neighborhood was affluent and white, and we were the only nonwhite family living and working in the area. My parents—who grew up in a predominately segregated southern town where nearly everyone they knew and interacted with was black and poor—were constantly reminded that the only reason they lived on this privileged piece of geography was that they worked there. I remember the first time I became aware of how my presence on this property was seen by others. Police regularly patrolled the neighborhood—which included homes owned by people like the jeweler Harry Winston and the chief executive officer of Schaefer Beer—and one day, they stopped me as I walked home from school. I was in the fourth grade, a skinny girl with short hair lugging her book bag up the tree-lined hill. When the police officer wanted to know where I was going, I pointed down the street and gave him the address. He asked me, "Do you work there?" I remember feeling confused and replied, "No, I live there." I was only nine years old. What kind of work would I be doing? From that moment on, I was developing an active appreciation for the natural environment and was also learning that my presence in certain places and spaces was not expected, welcome, or "natural," and that my family's presence in this abundantly green neck of the woods was justified and legitimized primarily through work.

Spending lots of time outside was typical for my brothers and me. My mother couldn't always keep an eye on us because she had housework to do, either in our home or in the big house that the owners occupied on weekends and holidays. So my parents shared that duty. My father was almost always at home (much to my chagrin) because he worked on the property. He mowed several acres of grass, tended to the fruit trees (the apple, peach, plum, and pear trees had insect issues and leaves to rake), planted five or six flower beds, and cared for the garden (including the vegetables that we ate on a regular basis), the fish pond, and the swimming pool.

Some parents might think that my parents were fortunate to be able to keep their eyes on their kids at all times. But we three kids had twelve acres of trees, rocks, and small bodies of water to explore (and in which to escape from the prying eyes of parents). My parents made sure that my brothers and I knew how to swim at an early age. We had free lessons at Harbor Island, the local public beach that was a five-minute drive from the property, so by the time we were six or seven years old, we could paddle anywhere. It wasn't until years later that I realized that our learning to swim wasn't about providing us with greater recreational options, but making sure that as we ran around that property that my parents worked, we wouldn't drown if we fell in the pool or pond. It was purely practical and made perfect sense for parents who understood how their work shaped the possibilities (both good and bad) for their children.

Sometimes, my father would get additional job opportunities. He would be asked to look after other properties in the area by doing minor caretaking tasks, such as clearing land and mowing grass. If the extra job was on the weekend or during the summer, my brothers and I often went with him. It was always exciting. We got to see another big playground (Mr. See's house was a favorite), and the need for something new and different would be satiated for a while. There was always a certain comfort in our playing outdoors in a new place because my father would never be far away. We would hear the sound of the lawn mower, the pruning shears, and occasionally his voice admonishing us to stop doing whatever we shouldn't be doing. Our ability to play had everything to do with his need to work: we got to play outside because he had to work outside. And my brothers and I learned to roll with it.

One of my favorite things to do as a kid was roll in the leaves that my father gathered in autumn. These were very large piles of leaves because there were more trees than I could count. He used a blower to pile up the leaves and put them into burlap sacks, and then he hopped up into the seat of his yellow tractor with its green trailer to lug away the bags. That was fun, until he felt that my brothers and I were old enough to pitch in and work instead of playing all the time. My father had particular ideas about the roles of men and women. In his mind, outdoor work was for boys and men, and indoor work (such as housework) was for women and girls. Although I didn't have to rake leaves, I was not happy to be relegated to cleaning the bathroom or doing other housework with Mom. Without knowing it at the time, work became the lens through which I began to understand how the outdoors was gendered.

Although most of her work was done indoors, my mother's daily activities included some outdoor responsibilities. My parents had two gardens—one large vegetable garden that was a five-minute walk from the house and a small garden behind our home where my mother grew flowers and herbs for cooking. I often saw her, right before dinner, snipping something off that I knew would end up on our plate—rosemary for chicken, basil for pesto, and fresh mint for tea in the summer. My mother is a good cook, but like a lot of Southern women, she started out cooking tasty but not particularly health-conscious meals. Over the years, her cooking evolved to reflect new knowledge and new items grown in our gardens.

I also watched how my parents engaged with the local wildlife. My mother considered it part of their job to feed the birds on a regular basis.

But not all birds are created equal. My father saw it as part of his job to get rid of the geese that adored the pond but left piles of droppings that created more work for him. At one point, my father became so obsessed with the geese that he sat outside at night with his rifle, waiting for them to have the gumption to use the property as their personal bathroom. My mother bristled whenever he told her about some poor goose that he shot, but she understood that the geese interfered with his work and that his ability to do his work well was what mattered most. My father could work up a righteous anger so that he could shoot them where they stood, but he suffered from bad dreams of being attacked by large flocks of geese. He would tell us how he wanted to explain to the geese that he wasn't shooting them randomly or for his pleasure. I guess he believed that even the geese would understand the importance of prioritizing work above everything else.

In 1996, my parents' boss decided to sell the property to a new owner. The original owner was aging, her husband had died many years earlier, and her grown children didn't want the property, so the land exchanged hands. My brothers and I had long since left the estate, even though we visited regularly. This was home for all of us, but even more so for my parents. They had grown roots on this land while growing us kids. Through their work, they showed my brothers and me what a commitment to a piece of nature could yield over time, both literally and figuratively.

My parents stayed on with the new owner for another seven years, but they were aging as well, and it was increasingly challenging for them to manage the physical responsibilities that a large piece of property demanded. The original owner tried to work out an arrangement where my parents could stay on the piece of the land where the gardener cottage stood. She considered establishing a mechanism that would allow the hefty property taxes to be paid for as long as my parents lived. But instead, the owner helped pay for a new home to be built in Virginia, the state of my parents' birth.

My parents are now in their late seventies, and work—the practical and necessary-ness of work—continues to define their existence. They have a lovely home but only a half acre of land. My father, who works part-time at Costco, still spends hours outside tending to that half acre and its few trees and bushes. Their robust garden provides flowers, herbs, tomatoes, and peppers. But there is also a sadness present, particularly for my father, who misses New York and the piece of land on which they made a life. How do you leave a piece of land that you worked and loved? What did it mean to work outdoors all those years, only to lose what you worked so hard to maintain?

The Obama daughters are living in a place, a real park, that they call home but do not own. Their father, through his work, has made it possible for them to live there, and they are reminded of that on a daily basis because of the nature of his job. Through the work of their mother, they see the vegetables in the garden and the honey in the hives become dinner on their table. Despite the economic privilege that mediates their opportunities, the ethic of work influences their experience of the natural world.

I think we have a lot in common. We're from completely different generations and different geographical locations, the life experiences of my parents and theirs seem worlds apart, and our starting points as young girls were different. But their parents' commitment to their work will play a significant role in how those girls think about their relationship with the environment. One day, when they have to leave the land where they have lived and learned, they will remember the vegetables that their mother planted with her own hands, they will remember the privilege of living on a piece of land filled with history, and they will realize that the work and love of their parents made it possible.

Notes

1. *Sabrina* was a 1954 film starring Audrey Hepburn, Humphrey Bogart, and William Holden.
2. Conversation with Kaylynn Twotrees, artist and environmental conceptualist.

9

The Naturalistic Necessity

Stephen R. Kellert

Owl
Hope flies on silent wings.
Standing on that moonlight beam.
Big, but hopeful if it's seen.
Crouching down eyeing its prey.
Weaving its way through the trees
Under the moon
And that's how hope flies on silent wings.
—Ellanora R. Lerner, age seven

The irreplaceable role of children's direct experience of nature is integral to their healthy maturation and development, what I call the *naturalistic necessity*. All forms of experience of nature are critical in children's development. This includes direct experience (involving relatively spontaneous and free-choice contact with largely self-sustaining nature), indirect experience (such as organized and structured contact with nature that requires ongoing human input for its survival, like a garden, a potted plant, or a pet), and vicarious or symbolic experience (including representations of nature in story, picture, video, computer, and more). Despite the importance of all three forms of experience, direct naturalistic experience of nature is particularly vital and indispensible in childhood development. Yet mounting evidence suggests a potentially catastrophic decline in children's direct exposure and engagement with the outdoors.

Why should children's direct free-play experience of nature exert such an indispensable and irreplaceable effect on their development? Let's start with an illustration, a hypothetical encounter with a frog. We imagine an eight-year-old child who initially encounters just the picture of a frog—instructive about the creature's physical features, perhaps even captivating and interesting, but like all two-dimensional portrayals lacking detail, dynamism, and a sense of relational context. The child further learns about frogs through fictional stories, allegories, and legends—perhaps about a prince in disguise or a character on *Sesame Street*. Despite repeated and varied exposure, her understanding of and empathy for the frog remains fundamentally limited, not unusually distorted, at times largely viewed through an anthropomorphic lens. Despite the beguiling and instructional value of pictures, books, and stories, the real frog on its own terms in its own world remains elusive, unengaged, obscure.

The child has an additional chance to encounter a real frog in a classroom, at a nature center, or a zoo. The animal becomes real and alive and more dynamically revealed as the child takes better stock of the creature's remarkable nuance and variability of size, shape, color, behavior—a special and altogether unique quality of *frogness*. Yet the experience of the frog remains largely contrived, exotic, and controlled. It lacks detail and complexity, a subtlety of physical and mental quality, a behavioral and ecological integrity, or a connection to place, landscape, other creatures, human culture, and the child in particular.

But one day, the child encounters the frog in its own world through the guiding and mentoring hand of a significant adult—a parent, a friend of the family, or in this case, her grandfather. The child is guided to a wetland first in her backyard and then in a nearby park and introduced to previously hidden wonders by the wisdom and experience of a nurturing adult. They are initially drawn by an evening chorus of spring sounds that are so riotous that she can hardly sleep. They hear it again the next day, determined to track the sound to its source.

She and her grandfather work diligently, slowly approaching the source of the racket and learning that when they do so quickly, everything turns suddenly quiet, sound disappearing as if it had never been there before. Slowly, stealthily, with mounting skill, they crawl through uncomfortable grass, at times sinking into muck. Finally, poking their heads above old reeds and new grass, they spy the surprisingly small creatures who are responsible for all this noise: little frog heads poke out from a thin film of water. Edging closer, they wonder at strange circular movements and odd behaviors, the frogs congregating at certain parts of the pond, green egg masses nearby, an odd smell, their seeming cuteness. When the adult and child finally have to stand up, the frogs quickly disappear. The grandfather and child discuss what frogs fear, what they eat, who eats them, how they deal with snakes and raccoons and turtles, even what they feel about one another and other creatures, how they fit into this world and manage to survive through long cold winters, and more.

Another day, the girl and her grandparent catch a frog or two, examine it gently and carefully, find its sliminess discomforting, and soon let it go. When the child is afraid she might catch some disease, her grandfather provides comforting reassurance. Spurred by curiosity and the desire to know more, they read together about frogs, both real and imagined. They return again and again to spy on the creatures, learning more each time and getting to know something about the animal's damp world. She feels like their time together will never end and they will find more and more, as if they have entered a magic world where the more you explore, the more endless mystery you encounter.

The relative fullness and richness of this imaginary experience of nature hints at a distinctive and irreplaceable quality of direct outdoor contact, especially when compared with simply indirect or vicarious experience. Whatever advances might be made in electronic technology and however creative the modern zoo and nature center have become, the naturalistic experience continues to be an unrivaled context for maturation and development.

What constitute the critical elements of this context that often is instrumental in engendering a developmental response? The complexity of naturalistic experience defies a simple listing or comprehensive articulation. But the many dimensions of direct engagement in nature often provide children with an irresistible and irrepressible context for learning and experience. These unique characteristics include unrivaled diversity and information richness, mobility and malleability, dynamism and aliveness, attraction and aesthetic appeal, curiosity and imagination, unity and connection, surprise and unpredictability, mystery and challenge, as well as uncertainty, anxiety, aversion, unattractiveness, dread, fear, and more. All this and still more constitute innumerable opportunities for a myriad of developmental effects, including coping, problem solving, critical thinking, identity formation, self-concept, and self-esteem.

These maturational qualities are distinctively encountered through direct free play outdoors but are meagerly afforded through indirect and representational experience. Even ordinary settings like a small park or backyard habitat provide a cornucopia of sensory stimulation, variability, shifting circumstances—an unending source of intriguing and intoxicating qualities of life on its own terms. Children cannot resist this attraction, and creative and coping responses are developed as they adapt to this richness and dynamism.

Direct experience of nature also confronts uncertainty, discomfort, fear, and other aversive qualities that are rarely encountered through structured, organized, and vicarious experiences of nature. These negative reactions and the responses they engender are also the stuff of learning and development, offering critical opportunities for challenge, confronting the problematic and uncertain, learning from failure, exercising perseverance in the face of adversity, and even demonstrating fortitude and courage. Children's direct experience of nature attracts as well as repels. It is rarely boring or easily let go.

Autonomous, free-roaming, self-sustaining life is also a critical irreplaceable element of the outdoor experience that is rarely if ever duplicated by indoor, vicarious, or structured experience of the nonhuman world. The crux of the child's naturalistic encounter is essentially the experience of the sentient, familiar yet fundamentally different, and often surprising and ultimately mysterious. It is a source of wonder and the formative basis for emergent feelings of caring and compassion.

Through trial and error, reaction and response, at play and at *make-believe*, the child becomes acutely aware in the out-of-doors and the constraints of its reality. The outdoors is the *real* world, in contrast to the essential artificiality of the indoors. The child in nature encounters inadequacies and setbacks but also triumphs. These failings of self and other organisms can reveal pain, suffering, injury, and sometimes death. Children cope with these aversions and fears through free play outdoors in a modicum of privacy at times involving peers and adults serving as guides and sometimes role models. All this organizes and facilitates growth, an evolving capacity for coping, where sadness and suffering are as much a part of reality as pleasure and happiness.

A Diminishing Reality

Children's direct experience of nature assumes countless expressions, and samples are reflected in the stories that follow. But there is a worrisome trend of rapidly declining direct contact with nature today among many if not most children. The scale of this decline is so ominous that Richard Louv has labeled it *nature-deficit disorder*, and biologist Robert Michael Pyle has called it an *extinction of experience*.

Is diminishing direct experience of nature a reality or an impression? Although sparse, the data reported in the introduction all point toward a reality in which children experience substantially fewer opportunities for contact with and access to the outdoors today. An equally discouraging and related trend is that few adults assist and facilitate children's contact with nature. In addition, other obstacles to children's contact with nature include the decline of the extended family, two working parents, the overstructuring of children's play time (especially organized sports), and adults who lack the skills and motivation to take themselves or their children outdoors. The naturalistic experience may be an irreplaceable necessity in healthy childhood development, but its occurrence in our modern world is precipitously, perhaps calamitously, declining.

Reversing these trends constitutes a tremendous challenge. I remain optimistic, however, that the creative capacity, intuitive good sense, and resilience of the human species will help us restore nature as an integral element of children's everyday life. The work of organizations like the Children & Nature Network, which reconnects children with the outdoors, supports this optimism, despite the ominous trends marching apace. I am further encouraged by my personal encounters with children that reveal their continuingly creative ways of engaging nature, despite many obstacles.

Narrative Illustrations

This chapter presents three fictional stories that illustrate the many ways children can experience nature as a critical component of their maturation. They illuminate how children, sometimes aided and sometimes hindered by parents and other caregivers, use the natural world as the raw material for personality and character development.

Of Forests and the Sea: 1955—Middle Childhood

I remember it as a mostly tumbledown world, geographic precision being of little concern to a six-year-old, when physics is more feeling than substance. All I knew was that my world had this peculiar pitch that gradually led down through outdoor furniture, wound through paths and thickets, and eventually reached the road. The path across the road passed through beach roses and poison ivy before entering spiky grass, where thousands of ticks lurked, waiting to pounce. You were almost at the beach here, although you still had many stones to cross. A few prickly plants grew in this sandy world beyond the tides and waves. In the spring, they formed a carpet of yellow, pink, and blue flowers. Beyond the rocks and plants lay the beach—exquisite, soft, stretching endlessly, a place where time passed so slowly that it almost seemed to stop and bend backward.

A trip to the beach often included Mom and older siblings and sometimes cousins, friends and their parents, and neighbors. It wasn't unusual to meet someone on the beach you didn't know but who became a friend. Even when by yourself, you never felt alone because there were many things to do and many creatures on the sand, below the sand, in the water, in the air—just about everywhere. The place crawled with crabs, beetles, terns, minnows, fish, cormorants, and fishermen. Although I rarely brought much with me, I was never bored. The beach provided endless adventure and exploration with few specific objectives or destinations.

It was just a big pile of sand, unending brown stretching unchanged to the horizon and complementing a gray sea. Yet it always enthralled us. We passed hours like minutes, punctuated by forays into the cool waters to shed the irritating heat or excess energy. We built forts, castles, channels, and moats, chased after crabs, and engaged in small but never unimportant acts. Why did this pile of sand enchant us? Perhaps it was because at the beach we felt intensely alive. We molded wonders from raw creation, modifying the world around us but never fundamentally changing or diminishing it. We simply reorganized its "beachness," enlarging its properties and boundaries.

The beach was a special part of our mid-1950s neighborhood, a small village by the sea. I have learned since then that people in cities can be as numerous as flies living close to one another but still be mostly alone and apart. In our neighborhood, everybody knew just about everybody else. People always seemed aware of one another, as if the place were alive. Not everyone liked everyone else, and we were certainly not saints. We had plenty of rivalries, jealousies, petty quarrels, and worse. Yet most of us operated in a kind of shared mutuality, a respectful alliance and feeling of responsibility for the whole, especially for the young.

We kids were also aware of our physical world, taking pride and even a measure of identity in our blending of the human with the natural. Most houses were covered in unpainted cedar shingles, and the weathered gray textures merged with the land and the muted colors of the sea. Most homeowners left largely untouched the surrounding forest of pitch pine and scrub oak and understory of bayberry and blueberry bushes rather than convert them to grass and ornamental shrubs. But nearly everyone had a small lawn bordered by flowers and gardens that thrived in the humid air. The area was known as the Pine Barrens because few trees and plants survived in its mostly sandy soil. Yet people seemed to like that simple forest as if it defined what was normal and expected about our neighborhood. They were reluctant to get rid of the trees, perhaps captivated by the sounds of prairie warblers and bobwhites in spring and of screech owls and cicadas in summer or by the way that the trees cushioned the biting winds and northeasters of fall and winter. I suspect that the adults also responded to the wonder shown by the kids in response to the forest and sea—and perhaps by the kids they still carried around in themselves.

For us children, the forest and sea were our neighborhood, our place of unending exploration, adventure, and discovery, perhaps even the birthplace of our sense of beauty and respect for creation. In its bushes and brambles, we constructed bush houses and played games of challenge and competition. We could be wild and apart from adults there and yet within striking distance of security, taking various risks but not too removed from the comfort and shelter of our homes and backyards. The hazards were real to us—skunks, poison ivy, ticks, climbing too high or falling too far, venturing away and perhaps getting lost, coming too close to the choppy waters and being swept away. Like all children, we tested the boundaries of our world, probing and indulging our curiosities and inventiveness. Most of the adults accepted this craving for adventure but rarely endorsed it aloud, usually warning us instead of the dangers of disregarding our fears.

Still, this world of intimacy had its share of somber moments, even terrible ones, which I recall today with an almost paralyzing sadness. Above all else, I remember the death of my father and, soon after, nearly losing my own life as well. Boys and girls lose their parents to premature death, whether by accident, illness, or deliberate design, and yet his death when I was six years old lodged a sense of inexplicable loss in my gut like a deep black hole that I continue to carry around inside of me as like a disaster waiting to happen.

I knew Dad was ill, but this did not register in my young brain as something that could end a life that was central to my existence. No one explained the extent of his illness to me, probably assuming, as adults often do, that young people need to be shielded from the realities of pain and irreversible loss. When Dad was rushed to the hospital one night, it never occurred to me that I would never see him again. When the reality became clear, the intensity of the news was bewildering, and I denied it, looking for some different, more plausible explanation.

Looking back, I believe the only thing that kept me from becoming entirely swallowed up by despondency was the forest—particularly, the company of a wren. I retreated to the forest because it was a good place to be alone. I also secretly hoped that I could wander about and perhaps find Dad again. One time while sitting in the woods, I retreated into a strange fantasy, imagining myself far off in some backcountry a place of deep craters and broken ground and a peculiar dark purple and blue sky above. I followed a tortuous route, being called back only after a long while by a distant, distracting sound. The sound became louder and more insistent and, finally, impossible to ignore.

As my fantasy dissolved, out of the haze emerged a small wren. The tiny bird perched on a low branch no more than a foot from my nose above a thick, dwarfish tree. Its shiny eyes stared at me intently, its small head crowned by a lighter curved stripe, speckled white spots on its brown body. The creature's smallness was at odds with the intensity of its call and its seemingly angry eyes. The bird's song as much as its presence commanded my attention, forcing me to retreat from my sorrow. Its song rose in a loud, aggressive melody, hypnotic and forceful, an ebullient cry from a creature so small it would have fit in the palm of my hand.

Only the most optimistic would think the wren had actually been singing to me, imparting solace. But to my six-year-old brain—and to part of me today—I was convinced that it was. At the time, I did not doubt that the bird was communicating with me and recognized me. Wrens were very much a part of our lives back then, thriving in the forest at the margins of the wild and tame. Each morning, they loudly advertised their presence, sounding at first light with their long lyrical cries and taking possession of the woods as if they owned it. The sound was always shocking when you spied its tiny origin.

Wrens occupied a special place in our family, and not long before this time, one had become an unofficial part of the household. The previous spring, while we were away on vacation, a female wren flew through an open laundry room window and built a nest on top of folded laundry at the bottom of a wicker basket. When we returned, we found her sitting on her unhatched eggs. Most birds confronted by people under such circumstances would have panicked and abandoned their nest, but wrens, bold and nearly fearless, sometimes do not. Also, most people encountering a wild animal in their home would chase it away or worse. But my mother accepted the bird's presence.

Although initially agitated by the sight of my mother, the bird settled down, and Mom soon acted as if a nesting bird in her laundry basket was not an unusual event. We all soon settled into an accommodation. While the wren warmed her eggs, she allowed Mom to do her laundry and us to stare. Eventually, the eggs hatched, and the wren and her mate flew in and out of the window, bringing insects and other fare to their incessantly demanding chicks, and before long the chicks were jumping onto the windowsill and flying out. Soon they disappeared into the forest.

As I leaned against the tree that lonely, disturbing day, staring in utter stillness at the wren, mesmerized by its melodious song and fierce countenance, I wondered whether this bird might be one of the chicks raised in the laundry basket, perhaps returning to help one of those humans who had opted for its life rather than its death. I also remember wondering whether pity could be a solely human possession. What was undeniably real to me was the bird's insistence on my full attention as it sang for what seemed like the longest time. I sat staring back, the creature inches from my face, its flute-like piccolo rising louder but never shrill, reaching a crescendo then tumbling back, one note falling on top of another before reaching bottom and rising again.

The song became unbearable, and I spoke to the bird. Rather than fleeing, the wren became tensely silent as it continued to pay me full and mindful attention. So, I poured my heart out—perhaps more inside my head than aloud—telling the bird of my sufferings and seeking some explanation and validation but, of course, receiving none. Yet I felt relieved, more accepting of the tenuous relation between life and death, of connections that might dissolve my terrible loneliness, comforted by a broader encompassing world that included Dad and myself. This six-year-old even wondered whether the branch, the tree, the soil, the clouds on high, a single species of bird, and a little boy could be bound by some string of substance and time.

As I sat there, I felt myself become another speck in the woods, attuned to its many details and happenings. An ever-widening circle of awareness and connection radiated out, starting with the wren. A vole entered and exited, then a catbird, soon a honeybee, a dragonfly, beetles and ants, scrub oaks and poison ivy, the wind and the sky—all alive and a part of me. Boundaries between life and nonlife dissolved. A garter snake appeared, and I felt fear and an impulse to flee. The wren spied the snake and flew off, making me feel more alone and afraid. But I remained, and after a while, the snake basking in the warm sun became just another part of it all. For the first time since Dad's death, I felt alert and alive, preferring the company of even a snake to the loneliness of the black hole inside me.

I realized then how much I wanted to be with my family. Yet even after returning to the land of humanity, I still visited that special spot in the woods where I had encountered my peculiar communion with the wren. The place became a halfway house for me between human creation and a broader one. I saw in the wren a parallel universe, autonomous yet familiar, a place where kinship could occur despite immense differences.

I have no desire to continue dwelling on my loss, although I must con-clude with what happened next—my particular brush with mortality, an incident of terror that still makes me shudder to this day. Ironi-cally, what occurred stemmed from the well-meaning intentions of those helping me at the time. Walking with me during the full moon follow-ing Dad's death, my uncle pointed out a vague face in the moon that I had never noticed before. He said Dad was looking down on me. The revelation never left me, and the next day I impatiently waited for dark-ness to see my father's face again in the moon and perhaps get closer to him.

I went to bed early, much to everybody's surprise. When it was com-pletely dark, I climbed down the tree outside my window. I made my way to the beach as the full moon was rising above the horizon, orange and magnified by the heat rising from the ground. I stared for a long time before proceeding and then sought the rowboat beneath the pier, used to rescue people who were foolish enough to venture into the dangerous riptide just offshore. I reasoned with the unassailable logic of a six-year-old boy that if I could get close enough, I could even talk to Dad. But we lived where two sounds joined, a place known as the chop because of its almost continuously choppy waters. When the tide and currents were just right, as often occurred during a full moon, the waves became breaking surf, a place that even small skiffs avoided. My little boat soon encoun-tered the chop and gathered speed, unavoidably turning to the northeast despite my best efforts. The water passed quickly underneath the thin hull separating me from the sea. The boat soon slipped out of my control, and I was swept out to sea, helpless and afraid. In the distance, I could see and hear the bell of the green channel buoy, its eerie light blinking like some horrible eye. The wooden boat started to fill as seawater struck the sides and splashed over its sides. The boat swayed and bounced in the surf, terrifying me. The boat slowly filled with water, becoming unbal-anced, its rotation increasing with the swell as I paddled furiously to es-cape the vortex.

The boat twisted more and flipped over. I was in the water, swept by the current, wondering whether, if I drowned, would I join Dad in the sky. Despite my panic, I thought how warm the waters felt. I cried for help, but no one heard, and even in my youth I sensed the hopelessness of it all. A peculiar calm replaced my terror as furious waves passed over me. It had been only seconds, but it felt like forever.

I then saw the blinking light of the buoy as I was carried rapidly to-ward it. I tried angling myself into its sweeping tide, hoping to intercept the great metal float. Some internal compass worked, and after much thrashing it appeared that I just might reach it. The buoy suddenly loomed much closer and larger than I had imagined. Hard and metallic, emerging out of the darkness, it had metal ladders joining a circular rail and walkway that encircled the structure. Sooner than expected, I was thrown against the hard metal surface, the air knocked out of me as I painfully crashed into its side. In blind panic, I somehow grabbed onto a metal rung. Desperately clinging to its side as waters swirled past me as my life hung by a thread of ebbing strength, I used all the power left in me to pull myself closer to the buoy. The tumultuous waters swept past me on both sides. Exhausted, I lingered in relief before gathering strength and then painfully climbing one rung after another until I reached the circular shelf, where I collapsed. I lay there drained and thankful, eventually dropping into a consuming stupor and then sleep. I was soon awakened by the noise of a helicopter and not long after by a flotilla of boats. Mother, discovering my disappearance, had started a search that soon revealed the missing rowboat. The rest was my particular fifteen minutes of fame, followed by the more mundane business of growing up. Dad's death and my close call left some lingering wounds as well as much wisdom. If nothing else, I felt a deeper appreciation of the varied creation that surrounded me and of my rightful place within it. Even for a little boy, it bordered on a kind of serenity.

From Apple Orchards to Shopping Malls: 1966—Late Adolescence

After living in a place where every bird, bush, neighbor, and school chum felt like one extended family, my new world had become quite anonymous. Mom had not wanted to move following Dad's death, but eventually she could no longer deny that a single woman in the 1960s could not find a job in a rural area that would support three kids and pay tuition for one about to go to college. Our house by the shore had become valuable, so Mom sold it, and we moved to the suburbs of the medium-size city where Mom and Dad had lived during college, when she had studied nursing and Dad, law.

I was sad to leave our village, but sixteen-year-old boys are resilient, and moving to the city seemed exciting. Initially, I had no quarrel with our new town, although our neighborhood was distinguished mostly by an absence of distinction, with every house looking like the others and the parallel streets forming a maze worthy of the finest rodent. But the development had its charms, chiefly the large number of children my age and the many activities that ruled most of our days. I was also delighted that some wild places were not far away, despite needing to pass through a jungle of lookalike houses on tiny lots surrounded by a sea of grass and asphalt.

Arriving at the nearby river was more than worth the effort. Much of the river was little more than a 10-foot creek and shallow enough to wade across, but the river also had some deep holes where you could swim and where trout and ducks occasionally gathered. For us kids, the river's constant motion and many kinds of vegetation and critters gave it a personality, like a living thing that adapted but somehow always remained the same. One moment the river was black; the next, blinding sparkles reflected off its surface. Sometimes it was barely audible as it slid over smooth bottom; other times, it cascaded loudly over ledge or the remains of a dam where people once harnessed its fickle power. Apart from us, however, the neighborhood seemed barely aware of the river, although I suppose most recognized its presence in less obvious ways. It certainly lent our ordinary housing development a special quality that most recognized with pride, and the homes closest to the river always sold the quickest and for the highest prices. When a major road was proposed that would have covered a stretch of the river, the neighborhood rose up like a storm, howling and protesting, until the project was killed.

The world that surrounded this little island of wildness included our housing development, some big roads, and a nearby shopping strip astride a large thoroughfare. This road was our great ribbon of commerce, the site of countless convenience stores, mini malls, fast-food restaurants, gas stations, auto dealers, and more. You could find nearly anything there— although never exactly what you wanted—and the employees never seemed to remember and recognize you. Just beyond this main road, a new interstate that had been completed the year before cut through the landscape, indifferent to most natural obstacles and transforming hills and swamps. Few developments had yet been built along the interstate, but rumors flew that great shopping malls were slated to be built next to the town's last remaining farm and one of its largest forests. Both the interstate and the farm were also near the high school I attended.

At the time, the high school consumed most of my thoughts, if for no other reason than that I felt like a misfit there. Its hugeness overwhelmed me. The red brick facade, large white columns, and huge clock tower seemed like a temple from the ancient world, a seat of power that dwarfed the lowly adolescents who occupied it. Yet the building's interior was drab, with dreary halls and rooms lacking color, light, or anything resembling the magnificent exterior. The teachers meant well, and a few instructed with insight and eloquence, but like the students, they seemed numbed by the size and sameness of the school. Its lack of stimulation dominated the architecture and also the pedagogy. Various rules and a prevailing rigidity tried to cap the raging hormones of two thousand teenagers. One day, boiling with anger out of proportion to the provocation that had stirred it, I actually bolted from the school, which set into motion a sequence of events that might have altered the rest of my life.

Escaping from school, I fled northward away from my normal route home and into a woodland, where I hoped I would not be discovered and, presumably, punished. I wandered the forest, eventually becoming hopelessly lost despite my efforts to follow a deer trail and stumble on an old road.

I was unprepared to encounter another person, especially a scowling old man and his dog. By then, I had become so anxious and preoccupied with not shifting my direction yet again that I did not notice them until I was shocked by the sight of a man and his dog staring balefully at me not a hundred feet ahead. I can still see the man's stern look, the border collie motionless yet with its upper lip curling back over canines with a predatory gleam. Their body language clearly communicated that my presence was neither welcome nor legitimate. After watching me squirm for a while, the old man announced that I was trespassing and demanded to know why I was there. I offered clumsy, unconvincing excuses, promised never to return, and pleaded with him not to turn me in. After a long silence, he scolded me about how, if he had been hunting, I might have been shot and then added various other complaints about the state of youth in a world gone awry. Then, after settling his territorial and social issues, the old farmer congratulated me on fleeing the sterile halls of academia and heading into the real world of fields and forests. Most shocking of all, he invited me to join him and his dog on their walk.

Gratefully accepting, I felt like a man saved from the gallows who now was, miraculously, being asked to do what he wanted most. We walked for a long time, the old man's angry scowl soon being replaced by an animated, nonstop recitation about the land and its animals, plants, soils, and history. His knowledge was extraordinary; his intimacy with the land undeniable. His name was Mortimer Richmond, although it would always be for me Mr. Richmond or, as he was more generally known, Farmer Richmond, no matter how close we became. He was then seventy-five years old and had been born and raised on his farm, a member of the sixth generation since his ancestors had settled there in the early nineteenth century. His arthritis caused him to sway, but I soon learned he possessed more stamina than the sixteen-year-old at his side. By the time we arrived at his farmhouse, I was exhausted, yet he showed little sign of fatigue.

To say Farmer Richmond loved the land obscured a deeper, more complicated relationship. He was more like a part of it, an intimate participant of its many rhythms and processes. Although he felt affection for it, he embraced the land with a wider breadth of emotions, including an occasional adversarial stance. His knowledge of the farm reached far beyond matters of mere utility. He delighted in the land's beauty, its secrets, the opportunities it presented for mystery and challenge, and he respected and feared its power. He never grew tired of deciphering the many complexities of its creatures, both great and small. He took pride in feeling in charge but more as steward than as a conqueror. He was a participant who intervened rather than took away and who sought to add richness to what he saw as his extended family. Farmer Richmond regarded himself as chief trafficker in the flow of materials and nutrients that passed through the land like a fountain of living energy. He took possession of the land but always with a sense of duty and a gentleness and respect for its independent birthright.

Perhaps I make Mortimer Richmond sound like a modern druid, a kind of pagan exercising an indiscriminate love for the natural and non-human. In fact, he reveled in manipulating the land and rarely hesitated to, for example, slaughter an animal, wild or domestic, although I never saw him do so wantonly or cruelly. He delighted in hunting, over the years harvesting just about anything legal and edible, including several creatures no longer on the list of game animals. I was initially appalled at this killing, but over time I recognized that for him it represented another entryway through which he became an active, intimate participant with the land rather than an outsider. He never killed unless he consumed his prey, making the creature part of himself, and he never hunted unless he had a reasonable chance of failing. The hunt was always serious and conducted with skill, was never seen as amusement or sport, and was practiced with restraint and never wastefully. For Mortimer Richmond, hunting was sacramental, another way he tied himself to the land and its creatures.

This mentality revealed itself in his relation to deer and ducks but also to domesticated animals, plants, and even soil and water. He rarely hesitated to use, manage, or consume creatures, and he worked at manipulating the land to increase its productivity. But beyond the objectives of security and abundance, he sought a shared, caring relationship with the land and all its life. He saw himself as a colleague more than a controller and sought full membership in the grace of what he called the "land community." Most of all, he sought to impart a more lush, diverse, and resilient world than the one he had inherited.

I owe to Mortimer Richmond much of my abiding interest, knowledge, and emotional attachment to the natural world. At the time, I was not above exploiting his knowledge for my own purposes with surprising effect. My biology skills increased, particularly the ability to use my ears and other senses rather than just my eyes to see and identify all that surrounded me. Farmer Richmond taught me to discern the slightest anomaly in the landscape and to locate my visual prey by recognizing variations in the setting. In doing so, he helped me to experience much more of interest and quality than I would otherwise have encountered. I drank deeply from this stimulation and understanding and emerged ravenous for previously unknown treasures, determined to experience as much as possible before it disappeared in a tenuous world. Given my adolescent shallowness and his gruff ways, I sometimes wonder why we became such steadfast friends, why he took me under his wing at a particularly difficult time in his as well as my own life. Possibly he discerned a kindred spirit in this teenage boy's affinity for nature that reminded him of an earlier version of himself, albeit one needing cultivation and refinement.

He probably enjoyed my unabashed admiration, which was at odds with the increasing hostility he encountered from his two children, a thirty-two-year-old son and thirty-year-old daughter. The children had fallen under the spell of an economic fortune that was being dangled before them by a major shopping center developer who wanted to purchase the farm. Farmer Richmond had already rejected three progressively higher offers for the property. Although he seemed the epicenter of knowledge and wisdom to me, Mortimer Richmond's children considered him a stubborn old man who was standing in the way of the wealth and status that they had never known or thought possible and now desperately wanted.

Originally 350 acres, by the time I met Farmer Richmond, the farm had been reduced to about 200 acres. He had sold lots to people who wanted a rural setting but, after moving there, typically objected to the pungent smell of cow manure in summer, brush burning in spring, and gunfire in the fall. Selling the lots helped the family financially, but the farm rarely earned more than a subsistence income. Farmer Richmond raised dairy cows, but regulations, huge new industrial farms, and a growing distrust of local agriculture marginalized his cattle operation. He shifted to more profitable crops like apples and established a roadside stand, but sales were seasonal, and the apple business also succumbed to factory farming and the consumers' inclination for bright red, perfectly formed apples. The growing relationship between the agribusiness operators and big commercial shopping chains also did not help. Probably his worst mistake economically was refusing to bathe his soil in and subject his animals to a vast array of chemicals, pesticides, growth hormones, antibiotics, and more. He rejected the logic of the new ways of farming that were trumpeted as the triumph of science and technology over nature. He denied both the rhetoric and supposed corroboration, thereby confirming for all, particularly his children, that he was an ornery primitive out of step with progress and the modern world.

Mortimer Richmond was thus perceived as an impediment to prosperity and to the chance that his children craved to escape the pejorative label "swamp Yankee." I am sure they loved and admired their father, having known a lifetime of his keen insight and intelligence, but they resented his stubborn desire to remain a dirt farmer. Their mother had been the family's glue, but their father was more often larger than life and usually away in the fields and forests. So following their mother's death, the children went to college and moved to the city, the first generation in the family to have college educations and live apart from the land. They became urban professionals—the son an accountant and the daughter a medical technician. They were proud of their education, jobs that did not require them to work with their hands, and incomes that were higher than their father ever had earned as a farmer. They occasionally visited the farm but did not find its long, hard labors and economic uncertainty appealing. To them, the farm represented backwardness and oppression—and now, an obstacle to unimaginable wealth and security.

This all became clear to me one Saturday morning when I arrived at the farmhouse. Mr. Richmond had told me to come early so he could show me the rattlesnake den that had miraculously survived in the forest despite the area's extensive development and influx of humanity. He had never told anyone about it before and swore me to secrecy, fearing that if it were found out, there would be a chorus of demands that the snakes be killed.

As I approached the house, I heard angry voices inside. Letting my curiosity get the better of me, I waited silently at the base of the stairs. Farmer Richmond's son was arguing with his father, saying that the farm was worth more money than his father could earn in many lifetimes and that he could use a portion of the sale to buy a bigger, better farm else-where. His daughter then scolded their father, saying that he was being unfair and was preventing them all from having a life of prosperity just so he could indulge his romantic fantasy of an obsolete way of life. She claimed that the world had changed and that it was time for them to move on and enjoy a wealth none of their family had ever known before. Farmer Richmond responded angrily and, after some heated arguing, told his children to leave and never return until they accepted his right to determine the future of the land. That painful family encounter might have provoked his children to conspire with the developer and town officials to sell the land. I later learned that the children actually owned the farm because their parents had transferred the title years before, ironically to avoid taxes that would have forced them to sell the farm.

These byzantine family and financial matters were irrelevant to me at the time. All I wanted to do was romp in the woods with Farmer Rich-mond and help out on the farm. Following his children's departure after the family argument, I was delighted to set out with him in search of the rattlesnake den. As always, he knew every hill, valley, stream, and wet-land, never using a map or compass. He instead invoked memories of particular trees, stonewalls, creeks, and other cues that eventually led him to a nondescript spot in the woods that marked the serpents' den. I was excited but scared at the prospect of confronting creatures that no one else knew remained in our suburban town, and I felt anxious around snakes despite my fascination for all wild things.

The entry to the den was at the base of a great rock tucked into a hol-low almost out of sight. We slipped through the den's small opening, and Farmer Richmond promised it would lead to a much larger cave. I was nearly paralyzed with fear as I peered into that dark hole and probably would have fled if Farmer Richmond had not said that he had been terri-fied when he first discovered the den many years before until he had finally found the courage to enter.

The cave did get much larger after we entered. We made our way to a narrow ledge where we could spy the creatures below. Because it was early spring, the cold-blooded creatures hardly moved, but as my eyes adjusted to the dim light, I began to make out at least ten snakes. They were oblivious to our presence at first, but soon our moving about alerted them. I also suppose the heat of our bodies, more than our sound, aroused their attention. I had read that a rattlesnake's ability to sense temperature allowed it to find a mouse six feet away even if blindfolded and without a sense of smell.

We squeezed into the corner of the overhanging ledge, peering down to the now moving snakes. As minutes passed, it became apparent that they posed little danger to us. A mounting confidence took hold of me as we continued to observe the snakes. Looking back decades later, I recognize the moment as among the most intense of my life. For that totally absorbing and intimate instant, the world stood still, and I was suspended in time and place. Many years later, I still vividly recall the sight and even the smell of the place, its shapes, the quality of the light and air. The memory of it all is permanently seared into my mind. Few experiences since then have provided the clarity, peace, and reverence that I felt that day in the company of the snakes and Farmer Richmond.

For the rest of the year, I continued to roam the woods and margins of our rapidly developing suburb. I had found a new sense of balance, and I carried it around inside me like a treasure. Somehow the experience seemed to have reconciled for me the solitary and the social, the civilized and the primitive, the wild and the tame. I had found my place in my town, and part of me now identified with it.

But this newly discovered calm soon disappeared. Following relentless behind-the-scenes economic and political machinations, the powerful forces arrayed against Mortimer Richmond finally succeeded. Aided by a team of lawyers and officials, his children had sold the property to the developers. When I first heard about it, I ran from school to the farmhouse, bursting in on Farmer Richmond and demanding to know if it was true. He confirmed the sale but seemed less angry than tired and determined to move on. His children had given him a substantial share of the sale price as a golden parachute. He shocked me by announcing that he would move and purchase a new farm in upstate New York, where a modest agricultural economy persisted and farms were available at reasonable prices. In a bewildering few months, Mortimer Richmond departed the town of his ancestors, feeling a profound loss at being physically and spiritually uprooted but seeming relatively cheerful at the prospect of having a new home and life. His children's betrayal was unforgivable to him, however, and father and children never spoke again.

Two days following the sale, the developers' bulldozers descended on the farm and leveled more than 50 acres of forests, fields, and orchards. Soon, the devastated landscape was transformed into access roads and malls—a series of indistinguishable boxes and temples of merchandise decorated by an occasional prisoner shrub or tree. What had been a mosaic of apple blossoms in spring, golden grass in summer, bright leaves in fall, and lingering lavender in winter became oppressive geometric edifices surrounded by asphalt, concrete, and a suffocating homogeneity. The access road to the mall also destroyed the rattlesnake den. I never saw or heard of one again, although perhaps a few clung to survival in some remote hollow.

The destruction of the farm had become my defining moment, closing the door on my particular childhood and home. Nonetheless, I excelled in school, and—aided by some athletic success—I was admitted to a prestigious university on the West Coast. My passion had become being financially successful and independent. Without realizing it, I embarked on a path that one day would transform me into those I had come to loathe. Despite many dead ends over the ensuing years, however, I eventually returned to the wisdom and spirit of Farmer Richmond and the beauty of the land. But that is another story for another time.

Reminiscence of Childhood and the City: 2030 and 2055

It was highly unusual back in 2030 and is still far from common today to encounter a large ungulate or carnivore in or near a city. Even now, the memory unsettles my soul. I was eight years old then, living with my parents and sister in Denver. Our home was in an urban village, a relatively unusual attempt in those days to re-create an old-fashioned neighborhood within the city's core. The village consisted of single-family homes, attached townhouses, and a few multistory apartment buildings, all stitched together by footpaths, small parks, playgrounds, vegetable gardens, a shopping center, a high school, and a lower school. The large streets and parking areas were at the rear of the complex, so people had to navigate the main living and shopping areas by electric cart, bike, or foot. You could see the Rocky Mountains from the complex like some great wall looming in the distance, although my parents said that in previous years the mountains had seemed to vanish into a curtain of polluted air.

You would think a city so populated would offer few places for children to play. But in addition to our backyards, the village also had a number of small parks and paths that led from the village to the city's recently established greenway system. The greenways were trails that linked various parts of the city to one another, to the suburbs, and eventually to agricultural areas and distant wilderness areas. People loved moving about the greenways by bike, foot, and even horseback. One moment you would be close to home, another downtown, next by a shopping center, and with persistence, a national forest. The greenways became so popular that newly constructed or renovated homes along its borders were the most expensive in the city. The village kids were not supposed to venture far into the greenways, and most of the time we were content to play in our backyards and nearby parks. But occasionally, we snuck off to the greenways, often to the one where we had constructed a hideout and tree house in a large cottonwood tree. We worked hard to make our fort more comfortable than our parents could ever imagine, and we planned great battles and trips to distant lands.

One of my great pleasures was meeting Dad once a week for lunch at his office, a fifteen-minute walk from home. I loved his building. Tall and narrow, it rose like a needle, tapering at the top. From a distance, it looked like a forest because of its pyramidal shape, triangular window designs, and trees actually growing on the rooftop. The glass sides had tens of thousands of photocells, which—along with the building's fuel cells— generated most of its electricity. The rooftop included trees, gardens, a pond, sitting areas, meeting places, and two restaurants. The gardens and pond were also connected to the building's heating and cooling system, and the rainwater collected in the pond was used for plumbing and irri- gating the six interior gardens.

Located on every tenth floor, the three-story interior gardens contained plants, aviaries, and butterfly gardens, each representing a different Colo- rado habitat with information about those habitats. Also connected to the building's heating and cooling system, the gardens were places where you could have lunch or just sit. Some of the upper floors on each of the building's four sides also had ledges where peregrine falcons built great nests, raised their young, and hunted pigeons. I could watch the birds all day, particularly when the nests were full or when the adults dive-bombed the pigeons at awesome speeds. The nests helped the once endangered birds, who returned the favor by scaring away songbirds that otherwise would have crashed into the building's glass sides.

We often ate lunch at the office building, but sometimes we ventured to nearby wetlands. Depending on the season, we saw yellow-headed blackbirds, black-necked stilts, avocets, turtles, frogs, fish, dragonflies, cattails, lilies, and more. I recall one time toward the end of winter when we were huddled behind an interpretive display eating our sandwiches while trying to keep warm. Suddenly, we were startled by a loud splash. The critter didn't see us because we had been concealed. But when we looked up, we saw the retreating shape of a sleek gray animal sliding into the water, its sinuous body protruding before disappearing below the sur- face. My first thought was the Loch Ness monster, but Dad exclaimed after a moment's reflection, "I'll be darned. It's an otter!" We saw the animal one more time before it disappeared for good, its cute whiskered face holding a small fish in its mouth.

Practically unknown in the city at the time, otters were thought to avoid swimming under bridges or entering less than pristine waters. But wetland and creek restoration had been going on for some time. The improvement in water quality coupled with a growth in otter populations had led some younger otters to venture into the great metropolis. We were proud of our discovery, although we soon learned that similar sightings had been occurring elsewhere in the city. And it wasn't long before a permanent otter population became part of the Denver scene. People were excited at first, but soon some began to complain that the otters were decimating fish populations. It took some time before people learned to live with the otters while still protecting their property.

The best times on the greenways were the very cold winter days when elk came thundering down from the mountains like a living avalanche, bursting into and through the city on their way to the warmer prairies and wet meadows on the east side of town. Before the greenways, the elk were not able to travel to their historic winter range because of fencing, degraded habitat, and historic overhunting. By the early twenty-first century, however, elk numbers had greatly increased in response to a decline in ranching, an increase in wildlife protection, and ecotourism. All of this would not have brought elk back into the city if not for the greenways, which provided the migratory corridors that were needed to connect the mountains to the plains. The greenways were the great connective tissue that restitched all those open spaces.

Following the greenways completion, few elk used the corridors at first. But when the elk population reached a critical threshold or experienced a harsh winter, the small numbers became a stream, as if some great spigot had been turned on and gushed out tens of thousands of elk. On the first few days, you would see only a lone animal or a small group, but soon a huge mass would appear and advance almost as one across the city. When this occurred, thousands of people turned out to gape, some cheering despite police, fire, and wildlife officials trying to keep them quiet and at a distance. An elk or even a person might occasionally be hurt, but the animals usually passed without incident, parading before kids, adults, television commentators, street merchants, and scientists. They became the stuff of legend, annual celebration, and great pride for the city.

But I will always remember one event above all others. One winter, Dad heard that elk would likely be passing through the city and obtained a permit to occupy a viewing blind in a pine tree preserve at the city's edge. Every day for four days, we arrived early in the bitterly cold mornings hoping to see elk, but nothing happened. On the misty morning of the fifth day, we heard twigs snapping, and soon, barely discernible, ghostlike shapes appeared out of the cold fog, their numbers swelling until the ground nearly shook. The animals' tawny browns and grays, bare heads and flaring spikes, massive bodies and antlers left us in awe. In the weak light, they seemed like apparitions from ancient times, coalescing and dissipating as they passed through our human-dominated landscape.

Then something far more improbable occurred. We had been watching the elk for perhaps an hour. By then, most of the mature males had passed, and the mothers and new calves were following. Suddenly, something bolted from the pines opposite us. At first, it looked like a horse crossing the meadow at full gallop. The elk reacted as if a bomb had exploded, fleeing in every direction, yet one small yearling remained on the ground. The incident had taken seconds but seemed to unfold as if in slow motion. The creature that had streaked from the forest had been fast but hardly graceful and oddly lumbering, at first resembling a horse but lacking that animal's polish and grace. Besides, horses do not run down and pounce on elk. Even my unformed mind sensed that we were in the presence of something wonderful and fearsome. It was the greatest of all land predators, an enormous carnivore of unyielding determination—the great mythical bruin.

"Oh, my God!" Dad cried out. "A griz. But it can't be!"

As far as anybody knew, with the exception of a few hardly believed biologists, grizzly bears were not found anywhere near Denver, and only a small population had been rediscovered and augmented in the San Juan Mountains in the southwestern corner of the state. Occasional grizzly sightings had been reported in Rocky Mountain National Park, not far from Denver, but these were generally unconfirmed and dismissed. Yet this was no apparition. It was probably a young bear who was recently awakened from a deep sleep, hungry who had wandered through the cold mountains, caught the scent of elk, and followed the great herd. It must have been a bear just young and dumb enough not to avoid its ancient archenemy—humans. Maybe it also sensed the diminishing threat from a once lethal species that of late had embraced a new covenant of reverence for the wild, especially for its legendary lord of the mountains.

The young bear stood on its hind feet at Dad's yell, glaring in our direction. It rose perhaps six feet tall, its round, almost humanlike face staring menacingly at us while we gazed back too awed and frightened to flee. An electric arc of conflicting emotions passed between the bear and us like some great indigestible stew—fear, fascination, and possibly mutual respect. We meant the creature no harm, yet Dad assumed an aggressive posture and yelled back at the bear, his first instinct being to protect his young. The bear snorted and growled, his nose flaring. But he soon settled back on all fours and with great strength dragged his prey into the forest, quickly disappearing.

Dad and I felt as though we had just experienced a massive hallucination. We soon told our tale to officials, who were skeptical at first. But following careful investigation and additional sightings, it soon became known that a small grizzly bear population had reestablished itself around Rocky Mountain National Park and adjacent wilderness areas. My young boy's heart had been touched by something miraculous, something beyond amazing that would affect me for the rest of my life. If an eight-year-old can experience a transcendent moment, that was it—and I've carried it around inside me since then. I have reached back during moments of crisis and gathered strength from the memory of the bear. I can pluck the great bruin from the recesses of my mind like a constellation from the sky, retrieving some enduring meaning that somehow mutes whatever anxiety or uncertainty has befallen me.

Even now, as a middle-aged man in 2055, hardly a day passes that I do not recall that instance of inspiration and joy. Today, I awoke stressed by events at work and in the world. I read daily of wanton cruelties and needless destruction, circles of pain radiating from a world of indifference and greed. A pervasive loneliness and self-hatred sometimes seem to have afflicted humanity like a virus that imperils our species. At moments like this, I remember the great bear and gather my dogs for a walk up the mountain near where I live.

When I do this, the city is soon left behind as I follow a path lined with willows along a dry creek bed. Cries of cactus wrens and circling raptors appear to be carried by the wind. I move quickly, driven by the goal of reaching the summit until a mosaic of sensations slows me down. The dogs help, reveling in their curiosities, circling about and encased in a world of smell more than sight, drawn by a multiplicity of plants, rocks, and other signs of life. I begin to open myself to a world of endless detail. At first, I intellectualize, identifying various birds, flowers, and more. I count and classify, drawing pleasure from my growing familiarity and seeming control. But I soon give way to an intense appreciation of wonder, beauty, and discovery. A monarch butterfly alights on a nearby rock, and

I marvel at its orange and black patterns that are so in harmony that they defy the narrow interpretation of mere evolutionary fitness. I am stunned by the miracle of this creature, so flimsy that it seems weightless but able to travel enormous distances. I am awed by its supposedly inconsequential brain, which guides it to distant lands despite weather and terrain.

I finally reach the summit and look back at the city spread across the plain, admiring its immensity and creation. I look up at the clouds and imagine the shape of my childhood bear. I travel with him across the sky, carried by winds connecting me to a world greater than myself. The great bruin never leaves me, always a part of my consciousness. We remain fellow travelers in the grandeur of our lives. And then I am stripped of my self-absorption and self-pity, carried along by this miracle of creation.

I return to my home and office no smarter or skillful but renewed and revived. I have drawn sustenance from the bear and the butterfly, emboldened by their accomplishment. I have become the bear, rising on its hind legs, startled, apprehensive, yet irrevocably tied to those humans who stare back with anxiety but also with reverence and devotion.

10

Children in the Woods

Barry Lopez

When I was a child growing up in the San Fernando Valley in California, a trip into Los Angeles was special. The sensation of movement from a rural area into an urban one was sharp. On one of these charged occasions, walking down a sidewalk with my mother, I stopped suddenly, caught by a pattern of sunlight trapped in a spiraling imperfection in a windowpane. A stranger, an elderly woman in a cloth coat and a dark hat, spoke out spontaneously, saying how remarkable it is that children notice these things.

I have never forgotten the texture of this incident. Whenever I recall it I am moved not so much by any sense of my young self but by a sense of responsibility toward children, knowing how acutely I was affected in that moment by that woman's words. The effect, for all I know, has lasted a lifetime.

Now, years later, I live in a rain forest in western Oregon, on the banks of a mountain river in relatively undisturbed country, surrounded by 150-foot-tall Douglas firs, delicate deer-head orchids, and clearings where wild berries grow. White-footed mice and mule deer, mink and coyote move through here. My wife and I do not have children, but children we know, or children whose parents we are close to, are often here. They always want to go into the woods. And I wonder what to tell them.

In the beginning, years ago, I think I said too much. I spoke with an encyclopedic knowledge of the names of plants or the names of birds passing through in season. Gradually I came to say less. After a while the only words I spoke, beyond answering a question or calling attention quickly to the slight difference between a sprig of red cedar and a sprig of incense cedar, were to elucidate single objects.

I remember once finding a fragment of a raccoon's jaw in an alder thicket. I sat down alongside the two children with me and encouraged them to find out who this was—with only the three teeth still intact in a piece of the animal's maxilla to guide them. The teeth told by their shape and placement what this animal ate. By a kind of visual extrapolation its size became clear. There were other clues, immediately present, which told, with what I could add of climate and terrain, how this animal lived, how its broken jaw came to be lying here. Raccoon, they surmised. And tiny tooth marks along the bone's broken edge told of a mouse's hunger for calcium.

We set the jaw back and went on.

If I had known more about raccoons, finer points of osteology, we might have guessed more: say, whether it was male or female. But what we deduced was all we needed. Hours later, the maxilla, lost behind us in the detritus of the forest floor, continued to effervesce. It was tied faintly to all else we spoke of that afternoon.

In speaking with children who might one day take a permanent interest in natural history—as writers, as scientists, as filmmakers, as anthropologists—I have sensed that an extrapolation from a single fragment of the whole is the most invigorating experience I can share with them. I think children know that nearly anyone can learn the names of things; the impression made on them at this level is fleeting. What takes a lifetime to learn, they comprehend, is the existence and substance of myriad relationships: it is these relationships, not the things themselves, that ultimately hold the human imagination.

The brightest children, it has often struck me, are fascinated by metaphor—with what is shown in the set of relationships bearing on the raccoon, for example, to lie quite beyond the raccoon. In the end, you are trying to make clear to them that everything found at the edge of one's senses—the high note of the winter wren, the thick perfume of propolis that drifts downwind from spring willows, the brightness of wood chips scattered by beaver—that all this fits together. The indestructibility of these associations conveys a sense of permanence that nurtures the heart, that cripples one of the most insidious of human anxieties, the one that says, you do not belong here, you are unnecessary.

Whenever I walk with a child, I think how much I have seen disappear in my own life. What will there be for this person when he is my age? If he senses something ineffable in the landscape, will I know enough to encourage it?—to somehow show him that, yes, when people talk about violent death, spiritual exhilaration, compassion, futility, final causes, they are drawing on forty thousand years of human meditation on *this*— as we embrace Douglas firs, or stand by a river across whose undulating back we skip stones, or dig out a camas bulb, biting down into a taste so much wilder than last night's potatoes.

The most moving look I ever saw from a child in the woods was on a mud bar by the footprints of a heron. We were on our knees, making handprints beside the footprints. You could feel the creek vibrating in the silt and sand. The sun beat down heavily on our hair. Our shoes were soaking wet. The look said: I did not know until now that I needed someone much older to confirm this, the feeling I have of life here. I can now grow older, knowing it need never be lost.

The quickest door to open in the woods for a child is the one that leads to the smallest room, by knowing the name each thing is called. The door that leads to the cathedral is marked by a hesitancy to speak at all, rather to encourage by example a sharpness of the senses. If one speaks it should only be to say, as well as one can, how wonderfully all this fits together, to indicate what a long, fierce peace can derive from this knowledge.

11

Fathers and Sons

Richard Louv

Twenty years ago, on Father's Day, I drove my two boys, Jason and Matthew, then ages eight and two, to a nearby lake. We spent the afternoon walking along the bank. They ran ahead in their life jackets, sometimes fishing, the younger boy with a lead weight on a line tied to the tip of a two-foot rod. More often than not, he dug along the bank for bugs or threw rocks in the water.

Well, fishing isn't about catching fish anyway.

I was using a new fly rod. I did not know the intricacies of fly fishing, but I had discovered the sense of connectedness that fly fishing gives, which is unlike the rituals of high-powered bass fishing, now so high tech, competitive, and loud that it sometimes destroys any sense of connection to nature or to time. Because of this recent interest, I had dug through the utility room that morning until I found a corroded tin canister. I waited until I was on the bank to open the box, which was, for me, a kind of time capsule.

It was filled with large, old tied flies and hand-painted poppers. They had once been used by someone after northern pike or perhaps bass. I carefully removed one of the flies from its fastening and tied it to my line. It looked like a frog with feathers that trailed out behind.

In the mid-1960s in Kansas, my best friend, Pete, and I would often walk over to Red Hoth's house. Red, who was in his sixties, had suffered a stroke in 1952 while fishing and was paralyzed from the neck down except for one arm. Pete visited Red because of compassion. I went for the fishing stories and because, like many kids, I was looking for a father figure.

Red would spin out his stories so vividly that it seemed almost as if we were on some North Woods lake long ago with the early morning mist rising around the boat, his bed.

On one of our last visits, we arrived to find a large tackle box and a set of bamboo fly rods at the foot of Red's bed. He gave all of his old gear, which he loved, to us.

Years passed away. So did Red. Piece by piece, most of this equipment somehow disappeared—except this last tin canister and its contents, which had not been used in decades.

So now I flipped the fly into the water to show my older son, and we watched the feathers transform into kicking legs as it moved through the water. I told my son about Red. It's the small stories that count most, I think. Then I pulled the rod up and made a long, rare, perfect cast, and the frog moved out across the smooth water in a gradual arc, and it fell through time.

Your child can say something to you, just one small thing, and suddenly the universe expands. One evening I walked with Matthew to the library and back. He was about to turn five. I see him then. He wears small, round glasses. He is an impatient person, eager to cut to the chase, a detector of dissembling. He is beginning to connect the dots of the universe.

"Look, Dad," he said. "The moon is a sliver."

We were on a nighttime adventure, a four-year-old's favorite kind of adventure. Walking alone at night with your child is when the truth comes out, like the stars.

"Dad, the moon is really the sun, and it's out all the time," he announced with authority.

I stopped and looked up. I explained to him that the moon is not the sun but is lit by the sun, which is . . . look behind those trees, just over the dark horizon, where we cannot see the sun because the world is curved and round. In that dark, I could feel that Matthew's eyes were big. His breathing had changed. Two crescents of light were reflected in his glasses.

He seemed to accept this version of reality. We walked on for a while, carrying our bags of books.

"Look, Dad, the stars are out."

"Yes, they are."

"Um . . . Dad, . . . I want to tell you something."

"What, Matthew?"

"The stars are following us."

And they were. We moved, they moved. I had not noticed or remembered this phenomenon since I was a child.

In his small voice, Matthew said, "The stars are watching us . . ."

"Yes . . . "

". . . and Dad," he explained, "the stars are fairies."

I did not offer an alternative explanation. His was better than any I could muster. He had cut me loose from the earth.

I wonder if fathers in any other time kept track of what their children taught them in these moments. Our culture has little patience with fathers who dote on moments. Publishers market memory books, in pastels, to mothers: this is when the baby was born, these were my first thoughts, this is when the baby took his or her first step, and this is how I felt in my heart. It seems to be the province of mothers to keep the scrapbooks and records.

I did buy a video camera. But like most fathers, I prefer to stay behind the lens, and that is where I usually end up.

A few months after my father's death, as a kind of lone late-night wake, I pulled out a box of eight-millimeter films. I opened the box and smelled his cigarette smoke. I gingerly removed the gray metal canisters and spooled the film onto the projector, one of his prized possessions.

Clear images moved across the wall—our dog bounding across time, my irritated little brother waving toilet paper, the morning light filling the kitchen, passing clouds carrying the embryos of tornadoes.

All these small moments: my young mother smiling and waving her hand in frustration, my elderly aunt's lumbering Chrysler, my grand-mother in the lacy black dress favored by older women of that time, a friend and I at seven carrying a flag through a field of brittle cornstalks, moving away until only the flag could be seen like the sail of a ship heading out to sea.

In all of this footage I never saw my father.

Only once was there a glimpse, during a backyard picnic as the Missouri wind caught paper plates and Aunt Mary's hairpiece. There, on the concrete wall of the walk-out basement, behind my mother and brother, was the shadow. It was the shape of a man who still had his hair, a silhouetted pompadour. The shadow was holding a camera.

I wish I could see him in these movies. I wish I could see him.

Sometimes I feel that I am connected to the past and the future by mono-filament line.

"I can do it, Dad."

That's the sentence that you wait to hear, I guess, the one that says the boy is growing, starting to separate, and it makes you proud and a little sad.

"I can tie the knot," Jason said, as I handed him a lure. I showed him how but kept part of the information in reserve—for later, I said, when the boat isn't in these waves, but I knew that the real reason was the sadness.

Matthew turned around from his station in the bow and grinned. The sun flashed from his glasses.

A few moments passed. "Would you like to drive the boat?" I asked Jason.

"Sure!" he said. He was wearing his cumbersome child's life jacket, which he detested. He balanced his body low in the boat. All arms and legs, he moved back to sit next to me and took the handle of the engine. He was practicing and succeeding. I was practicing, too, trying to stifle my habitual irritation, trying not to insist that the fishing be perfect, trying to let the boys be boys.

It had been nearly a year since we last fished on this lake. The handle then had vibrated hard in Jason's hand. He had been near tears with frustration. At that age, turning the handle to the right in order to turn the boat left is a difficult abstraction to understand.

Now he knows more about paradox.

He sat up straight. I could sense the new strength he felt in his back and arm. The boat pointed true. He was smiling, hair pushed back by the wind.

A few weeks earlier, my brother and I had flown my mother's body back to Missouri. We had returned to the lake where we grew up, and we went fishing in her honor. My brother joked that he wished that we had brought her to the lake instead of leaving her at the cemetery. He said we could have propped her up and put a rod in her hand. He said this with love and longing.

My rod pulled down. "Cut the engine," I told Jason. He searched for the button. The trout flashed orange. I reached down and hit the button. Jason stood up. "Pull your line in!" I said.

I took a breath. I like to tell people that fishing is not about fishing and that I don't really care if I catch them. The first part is true; the second part is a lie. My father was a sullen fisherman. My mother was incandescent. When my mother lost a fish, the hills were alive with the sounds of cannonballs and missiles, bursts of the artfully profane.

As I wrestled the fish, I accidentally whacked Jason with my elbow. I swore, and we both laughed. Matthew was looking on the wrong side of the boat. "What fish?" he said.

I brought it in, unhooked it, and held it in my hands. Matthew inspected it closely. These days, I usually release fish. To hook and hurt a fish and then to let it go to save it is morally grayer than killing for food, but so it is with paradox.

I stroked its belly and let it go. Stunned, it slowly turned in the water, on its side. "That's not exactly what I had in mind," I said. I reached out for it. "I should have run water through its gills." Just then, it awoke and dived.

We moved down the lake. A year ago, my older son was bored with fishing. Now he had turned serious and was casting accurately with long, smooth arcs.

The sun was low. In a cove at the end of the lake, we got out of the boat and walked through tall grass to where the creek widened into a sandy pool before entering the deep water. Newly hatched tadpoles swam in the pool, and a frog hugged the bottom.

The older boy was suddenly in the water, chasing the frog.

The air was cool and soothing. I looked out across the lake and then back at the pool. In an instant, the younger boy had stripped completely, except for his glasses. He was standing in the creek in water up to his crotch. He let loose a stream of his own and held his hands high and screeched with joy. As the earth turned, I watched my sons, and their beauty amazed me.

A few years ago, I found myself driving toward Ralston, the street where I lived during my most formative years. I went looking for my woods. I didn't find them or at least most of them. Where they had been was now covered with houses, but I could sense where they had been. At one end of the ghost woods was a hand-made sign for a little park called Cap Garvin Park. I got out of the rental car and walked the length of Cap Garvin. A dog was barking somewhere. Some glass shards, a 7-11 Big Gulp carton, and a beer can were lying in the grass. It was just a long field, located at the far end of where the woods had been. A few trees remained near the end of the field.

As I passed under one tree, I remembered walking in the snow there with my father, now dead. He had his old Army coat on and was holding an air pistol, and we were looking for rabbits. I saw the trail of ungraceful tracks across the snow through the trees. Over to the left, a trickle of water ran where the creek used to be. I remembered the bluegills of summer, falling through the ice of this creek one winter, and standing in water up to my waist pawing at the snow-covered bank as my collie looked down.

This part of the field was covered with dandelions.

A few old trees were still there. Up in the branches were the remnants of a tree house built a long time ago. Just four boards, one of them marked with black soot and rusted nails. There had been a small tree house down in this section of the woods, not as big as the triple-decker that my friends and I had built farther up where all the trees were now gone.

I came to the end of the park. It was marked off with barbed wire. Beyond the wire was an old farmhouse, nearly hidden in the trees and brush. There had been a horse down near the swamp, deep in the woods below, and I would go down and stand on a fence to mount it and ride it wherever it chose to go.

From the fence on, the woods were dark and thick. Maybe the swamp was still where the dam had been broken out, where at dusk I had seen, in a blinding flash, a great heron lift on the air up above the old silo that stared with vacant windows out across the swamp—watched the heron lift up into the air and then fade. The dog was gone too, but maybe that swamp and those woods and that silo still existed. Maybe that part of childhood remained. But this was the end of the park. If I had still been a kid, I would have crossed the barbed wire and gone exploring. But now I am an adult.

It was good to know that the best part of my childhood was still safe. I turned and walked back to the car and, as I passed the sign, I thought: Here's to Cap Garvin, whoever you are.

One day, Jason announced that there was one more thing he wanted to do before school started. As we left the dock, we felt the cool air coming up from the water. Fishing air feels and smells like no other air. It cools your face and gets in under your shirt, and everything is left behind—all work, all worries, all the static of the city.

"Remember last time?" asked Jason as he let his line out behind the boat. I did. Here we had seen a strange sight. At the end of the lake, there was a valley—violet hills, green pastures, scattered cattle, and a little river running through the willows—that seemed to recede from view as we approached. "The closer we get, the farther away it seems," I had said to him. His eyes had grown wide. The light had turned red and begun to fade. We had turned back.

"This time, I'd like to go find the mystery valley," said Jason.

So just after dawn, we headed straight for the endless arm and the valley at the end. It took a long time to get there. As we approached, Jason said with awe, "It's like Africa."

The foothills looked like pink sheets plucked up by invisible fingers, and a stream ran between them and out of another century, meandering slow as Sunday morning through willows and cottonwoods, oozing eventually through a marsh and into the lake. "Look!" said Jason. Ahead, we saw the fields of mustard grass and cattle and two white egrets standing tall, lifting their feet in slow motion, watching the surface of the water.

We moved through the shallows and into the stream. Running the outboard slowly, I slid the boat between drowning bushes. Minnows shot ahead and to each side. The air closed in.

Jason's job was to watch for stumps and hidden obstructions below the surface. He knelt on the front seat and leaned over.

"Dad, a log. . . . Dad, an . . . alligator!"

He straightened up, eyes wide. "I thought it was a log, but then the log moved forward real quick and ate a minnow." He said the thing was as long as the boat or almost as long.

Probably a big catfish or carp, I told him. "Water magnifies. But then again it could be . . ."

Pause. ". . . the monster of mystery valley."

Jason rolled his eyes. Nine-year-olds do a lot of eye-rolling. But I could tell that part of him believed in the possibility and that he was pleased.

I recalled a similar morning on the Lake of the Ozarks. It is one of my earliest memories. I looked up at the sky as my father and mother loaded rods and tackle boxes into the boat and saw a sun so swollen that it seemed to fill half the sky. It was an optical illusion, I'm sure, but to this day, part of my mind still believes that on certain magical days the sun approaches us like an eye at the other end of a microscope.

Jason and I moved forward, got stuck a couple times, and poled out with an oar. And far up the stream, where the air grew silent, we banked the boat and got out. I wanted to see what was in the line of trees; perhaps it was a deeper channel. So we headed across a mushy field of high weeds through drifting clouds of green, newly hatched flies. Our feet sank down now, six inches below the surface, then more.

At the edge of the trees was a shallow pool of muddy water where something moved beneath the surface. As we approached, a phalanx of panicked life charged away from us, churning the water. We waded on beneath the trees, where the light was coming down in a kind of sunfall through the branches, and then we stood, awestruck in the silence. As far as we could see was what appeared to be a field of glowing, green snow. We reached down and scooped up fistfuls of duckweed, each plant with the delicacy of miniature clover. Both of us, I think, stopped breathing for a moment and stood there for a long time looking out across that scene, and finally we let out our breath.

After a while, we headed back to the brown pool and knelt in the water. "Feel around," I said, moving my hands in the muck below the surface.

"Dad, yuck."

"Really, do it." I felt something moving and came up with it in my hand—a squirming, fat bullfrog tadpole.

Jason, excited and proud, caught one, too.

We made our way back to the boat, and Jason climbed in. I took my rod from the boat and waded along the stream, pulling the boat behind me. I saw a flash of color and a good-sized bass hit my fly just below the surface. And I hooted and hollered and fell sideways into the stream. Jason pointed. He could see an even bigger fish following the one on my line. A few minutes later, I held the bass in the water and stroked its belly, and we watched it slowly swim away.

I made a wish—that when Jason reached my age, he would still believe in the monster of mystery valley and that he would know that sometimes the closer you are to a place, the farther away it can become. We turned the boat and moved back down the stream. Jason again scouted the shadows in the water, watching for danger until he could no longer see the bottom, and the valley disappeared.

After a heavy snow, my father and I trudged through the drifts, up the road to a hill that sloped down through the woods. It was a precarious slide. The afternoon was achingly cold. I can still feel the stabs of blowing ice on my cheeks.

I recall hurdling down that hill, head first on the sled, clutching the shoulders of his army coat, which I loved for its smell and its sturdiness (I wore it at college). Today, I can feel the bumps and the dips of that hill, hear the slice of the runners, and see the trees flying by, and I recall both of us laughing as we lifted into the air, came back to the earth, and then left it one more time. We were alone on that hill, and we were together.

12

Moving through the Landscape of Healing

Stephen J. Lyons

A cold, northern Idaho September arrives with crisp, dry air from the Arctic when I take my twelve-year-old daughter to see the Canada geese camped at Spring Valley Reservoir. It is our last day together this week. Tonight she will go back to her mother and stepfather, who live in the nearby town of Deary. In the back of my car are Rose's clothes and shoes, a stuffed lamb, and a small velvet pillow filled with a pocket of fragrant mugwort given to her, as a baby, with a guarantee of sweet dreams.

I have never felt comfortable with these comings and goings. Joint custody compresses our time together into half a life. On the drive we are quieter than usual. It is safer to simply look out the windows and let protection come to us through the rapid images of fields and forests. How many times can you have your heart broken? Healing will continue today, I reassure myself as we bounce over the washboard county roads, and that healing will take place within the landscape. Maybe even redemption will occur. I do not know what Rose expects.

By the time we arrive at the lake, the restless geese have moved on. Instead, a flock of black coots occupies our investigative powers. We get out the red, well-traveled western-region edition of *Audubon Society Field Guide to North American Birds* and quickly turn to the section "Duck-like Birds." Absentmindedly, Rose keeps chanting, "black body, white beak" while she turns the slick pages past colorful pictures of buffleheads, shovelers, and lesser and greater scaups. This is the happiest work I can imagine. I look out the window, past her gold hair dissolving in the autumn colors that float beneath the ducks, and I shiver when I think of the snow to come. I am not ready for six months of Idaho frost and cold. I am not prepared for the darkness that presses down at four o'clock in the afternoon. But all my life I have not been prepared for anything that has happened.

I think back to last Memorial Day and a bird-watching tour we took at the Malheur Field Station, in the desert country of eastern Oregon. On the trip, we identified more than seventy birds, Rose jotting down their names in pencil on a page of yellow legal paper as we passed the binoculars back and forth. With more seasoned birders, we spent twelve hours a day driving around and learning how to see the obvious. It was then, at the odd, halfway age of thirty-five, that I learned the sweet, teasing song of a marsh wren and the subtle difference between a swift and a swallow. Rose said a graceful trumpeter swan landing on the Donner Und Blitzen River was her favorite sighting. We saw so much that weekend, from drumming sage grouse in the early morning, to nests with great horned owlets in downy perplexity; from a surprise whip-poor-will, concealed like a small stump, to thirty white-faced ibises in the late afternoon, waves of heat rising beneath their wings. Hundreds of white pelicans—their bills sporting the distinctive triangular bump on their upper mandible that appears only during breeding season—caught the early light from the east one morning. I have never been to Africa's Serengeti National Park, but this is how I would have imagined it—filled from horizon to horizon with wildlife.

American avocets and coots, willets, flashy western tanagers, long-billed curlews, black-necked stilts, and cinnamon teals covered the wetlands of the 185,000-acre national wildlife refuge during our stay. There was so much color, movement, and raw spring life in that vast American desert that I felt we were nineteenth-century overland pioneers or Native Americans, and the land was still empty and yearning.

How do we know where to lead our children? All I knew then—as I do now on this bright fall Sunday in our familiar Idaho stomping grounds of tamarack, white pine, and bleached basalt—is that to feel our lives again it's necessary to take Rose and me from our relative town comfort to an unpredictable landscape of open sage and paintbrush. That Memorial Day, we had birds for sky and the wetlands for imagination. I want Rose to see it all before the deserts become housing tracts and the lakes turn to sterile mud, but I don't tell her this reason. Such discoveries are personal.

When I was seventeen, immortal, with a life stretched out in long, lazy patches of slow afternoons of large clouds shadowing red southwestern mesas, I gave myself to the desert. I learned the powerful magnitude of simply being quiet, and how to slow my breath to match the rhythm of rocks. I crushed juniper berries between my palms and rubbed sage into my hair. A single day lasted beyond the rigid boundaries of time. Arizona,

New Mexico, Utah, and Colorado all merged into one magical back yard, beckoning, promising, and delivering the answers to all my biggest questions. Political borders of county and state meant nothing. The great Shiprock near Four Corners became a comforting beacon in the desert's endless sea. The Los Animas River really was the river of lost souls. The La Plata Mountains meant home and the warmth of friendships and autumn potlucks. And the Apache Reservation was where I heard a mountain lion scream the neighborhood dogs into silence—an experience I have never wanted to recover from. Lost in the privilege of youth, I didn't know how fleeting those moments would become.

But like all true love that endures, it took time. I spent my very first night camping alone in an abandoned cowboy camp, tucked under a redrock overhang in Canyonlands National Park. I was eighteen and frightened, filled with more than my share of self-doubt and anxiety, the noise of hometown Chicago still echoing through my attempted calm. On that long February night, piñon pines held the dry rattle of wind and a great horned owl kept me from resting comfortably in my sleeping bag. I was scared, scared of myself, my youth, my past, frightened of being placed among these great cliffs that resembled strange gargoyles and griffins that would outlive *me*. When I awoke the next morning from an hour's restless sleep, something had changed forever. Something at the core of who I've become today here in Idaho. As a parent. As a man. I was initiated into a world I knew nothing about. And it continues every time I step out my door and feel the first rush of breeze.

We move on to the cattails along the shore, where Rose shows me how to find shampoo hidden within the long, green stalks. I am amazed she knows this trick of stripping the cattail to reveal a sticky, clear goop. Sold for an expensive price, she says, then adds a warning: "The rest of the cattail is poisonous." We have reversed roles: this day I am the student and she is the teacher. "If you're lost in the wilderness, at least you can have clean hair." Although Rose has taught me much in the last twelve years, the lesson has never been so formal and direct. She exudes wisdom in a new way. Ten minutes ago, on the drive up here, she was quiet and sulky. But not anymore. Not outside.

We still have wild, renegade apples to pick this afternoon. With timeless regularity, the abandoned, gnarled fruit trees of northern Idaho blossom, fill, and empty without the interruption of human care. Ghost fruit. Neglected gene pools of edible apples, pears, and plums—varieties lost long ago in the hybrid shuffle of agribusiness—lie at the feet of these survivors, collecting angry, starving yellow jackets in the fall and the occasional opportunistic black bear. "Grandfather Trees," Rose once would call them, like the eighty-year-old mountain maple she would climb and swing from in the back yard at the small house of her first years. Runaway fruit is always the sweetest and snappiest, with antique tastes that even the cleverest food scientist cannot duplicate. Yet. I'm sure somewhere, someone is working on it. It is estimated that only 10 percent of the original varieties of American apples are left. Rose and I seek them out like detectives on a top-secret mission.

We have our favorite trees of other varieties, too, including the pear tree in the alley just across the street from the Moscow Public Library, and the two creaking chestnut trees in our front yard that dump their shiny load onto the street in October. As with our blackberry gleanings in the summer, it seems the choicest fruit is always the most inaccessible. In the case of the ancient tree we find, the biggest apples are guarded by two-inch thorns and hang in the upper reaches. Once again the bears have beaten us to the more accessible apples. The surrounding brown grass is matted and the lower tree limbs stripped to their green skin. Delicacy has never been a bear's virtue when it comes to eating.

I stand on my tiptoes to hit the bigger apples with a stick, and Rose runs around the tree to catch them. Because her gums are tender from her braces, I bite off chunks to give her. It reminds me of feeding her when she was a baby. There are no words for this moment, only the warmth we give each other: the unspoken support between father and daughter. The unconditional nurturing. I'm not foolish enough to disregard what this means, and I wonder what Rose will remember of these years when it has been just the two of us, what will stick to her memory. And what she'll give back to me later. Decades from now, when she eats an apple, will remembrances of this day surface as she takes her first bite?

It was almost a year ago that we made the journey back to my mother's house in Illinois. From the vantage point of 30,000 feet above ground, I showed Rose the Bitterroot Mountains, Yellowstone, Great Falls, Montana, and the Missouri River, curving and coiling upon itself. When we crossed the Mississippi somewhere over Wisconsin, I thought back to all the times I crossed that great river as a kid, riding the Union Pacific's Empire Builder out of Chicago's Union Station to my grandparents' home in Cedar Rapids, Iowa, and how that crossing seemed important to me, stepping over a boundary and out of my child's life, and how I desperately longed to ride the train past Iowa, and my waiting grandparents, west, to those towns with romantic names like Cheyenne, Denver, Whitefish, and Coeur d'Alene. At Rose's age, all I had were those names and a well-developed imagination that easily took over on those many times when reality fell short. I had never seen snow-capped mountain peaks, or rivers that weren't muddy. With its gentle motion on tracks and ties, that crossing of a great bridge was always more than enough to lift my spirit, and to carry me away.

As Rose and I waited for our flight that morning, a voice on the airport intercom urged passengers to board a plane for Detroit. The final plea said, "We are closing the door on Detroit," as if the hinges turned perfectly, the lock clicked, and everyone who did not make the boarding faced a formidable door behind which were the automobile factories of Detroit. Rose understood the silliness of such a statement. She looked at me with a slight raising of her eyebrows. That's all it takes for understanding to pass between us. I can say the word *Yellowstone* and she will nod—a tribute to an early summer camping trip when we were chased by a bull moose and failed at cooking popcorn over an open fire. Or I can say *thimbleberry* and our hands will twitch with the memory of crimson-stained fingers, and our lips tingle as we remember the tart taste of early-autumn fruit.

We sit in the quick closing of twilight, crunching apples, and I think of all the husks of abandoned homesteads in this area. Because the rolling Palouse fields resemble ocean waves, the disappearing farms take on the appearance of half-sunk ships. The same principles of atrophy apply. First the raucous winter storms strip the paint off the walls of the houses and outbuildings. Structures take on the ballast of wind. Foundations shift and crack and begin to feel the weight of time pulling them into the welcoming soil. Pack rats come back on board for the final journey, building nests of oat straw and cottonwood leaves. The thin line between inside and outside dissolves with each passing season until one day it is extinguished. Not in time that is black and white, but simply exhausted into another world. The farm returns to the earth, where it belongs. Where we all belong. But the daffodils and tulips still surface each spring; the small orchard so bravely planted still endures with pink blossoms and the simple magic of fruit; and the asparagus along the ditches remains tender, sweet, and stoic.

There's more. Now and then in these Palouse fields, you'll run across a pie-sized horseshoe from the era of horse farming, when neighbors gathered together to harvest the wheat with big teams of Belgians and Shires, when hard-earned sleep came from *physical* exhaustion and the community granges were the reward, with music and dance and the enticement of courtship. I like to think those farmers felt this was enough.

But I know now that here, in the shadows of abandoned homesteads and burgeoning cities, it's not. We always want more. We can't help ourselves. A lost horseshoe is the tip of remembering, the bridge between the fantasies of history and the realities of the present. Dig any deeper in the dark, wet western soil and you might not come back. And you would not be the first to disappear.

These are the moments I am moving in. As I get older, I lean more and more toward these small pockets of the obvious and the mysterious that rise from the landscape, surround my memories, and enhance a sense of possibilities. This is also where I am leading my daughter during the short years of our time together. Here, in the dense forests of northern Idaho, is where we'll make our stand. I want to unravel a thread in Rose: the thread of understanding, strength, sympathy, action, and change. The thread that weaves the fabric of humanity.

When I am an old man, with my memories replacing my future, I will remember this day and draw out its sweetness like water from a sponge: fall colors reflecting off the lake; first bite of apple; and my daughter—her spirit strong, steady, still curious—and our enduring friendship.

We toss our apple cores aside with the hopes that raccoons and badgers will benefit, then drive on and watch the first stars emerge in the darkest part of the sky—toward Montana and the eastern horizon. In a few short miles, Rose will join her mother and stepfather and be wrapped in the warm quilt of her extended family. And I will return to town, driving the slower back roads, listening for the faint cries of geese, gently guiding us with the grace of flight, as we make our journey home in the night.

13

Belonging on the Land

David Mas Masumoto

The land belongs to those who own it, work it or use it. Or no one?

In the Sixth Grade

In 1966, while in the sixth grade at Del Rey Elementary School, I sat next to Jessie Alvarado. We had what, I later learned, was a symbiotic relationship. We'd cheat on tests together—he'd open a book so I could read the needed information, and then he copied my response. I provided the answers, he took the risks.

But that was before they told me he was Mexican and I was Japanese. Our cultures were different they said; he ate tortillas and I ate rice at home. We each had "our own thing" and belonged in different worlds despite both living in this small farm community just south of Fresno, California.

That was before they told me that my family was the farmers, and his family was the farm workers. We owned the land; he came to work for us. Nature rewarded us differently. While we talked about profits, Jessie's family spoke of hard-earned wages. We worked in all four seasons in our fields, he came to labor seasonally. My family would pass on the land to the next generation. His family's dream was for the next generation to get out of the fields. We were supposed to be on opposite sides, even though we both sweated and itched the same each summer as we picked peaches in one-hundred-degree heat.

That was before they told me he was poor and I was rich. It made me feel guilty yet confused as a kid growing up. I guess his brother's Chevy Impala wasn't as good as my brother's '58 Ford with a V-8 engine. Or during lunch, I learned that no one wanted my peanut butter and jelly sandwiches when lots of the other kids had fat burritos kept warm by wrapping them in aluminum foil. Or how we all wore hand-me-downs from our older brothers, and I remember once when a very poor boy in the second grade had to wear a blouse from his older sister. Jessie and the other kids were cruel and viciously teased him until he ran home crying.

That was before an early spring frost hit our vineyards in late March and we lost over half our grape crop. I remember Jessie's father coming by to check on us the next morning, slowly walking out into the fields with my father. They both stood and silently watched the sun rise over the fragile shoots, now frozen and blackened by the frigid temperatures. Jessie's father pawed the ground with his feet, knowing he'd have to look for other work. Dad shook his head, figuring he'd still have to work to keep the vines thriving, knowing there'd be no pay for his labor, and he'd have to work for free the rest of the year. We seemed a whole lot poorer at that moment.

Was I supposed to feel sorry for Jessie? Wasn't nature supposed to be fair and democratic? I wonder what they have told Jessie since the sixth grade when we cheated together, and what stories we have left behind.

White Ashes

At a Buddhist funeral, we chant a passage about white ashes. We may live a full life, yet no matter what, in the morning we have radiant health, and in the evening we are nothing more than white ashes.

I'm a third-generation Japanese American farmer but am quite sure my lineage in agriculture dates back centuries. The Masumotos are from a solid peasant stock, rice farmers without even a hint of samurai blood. I'm proud of that fact.

My grandparents journeyed from Japan to farm in California. They spoke Japanese instead of English or Spanish or German. They were Buddhists instead of Protestants, Catholics, or Jews. They came in 1898 and 1917 instead of the late 1700s or early 1800s. They sailed east instead of west, yet their voyage was similar to those of hundreds of thousands of other immigrants who crossed an ocean to the land of opportunity. They hoped to farm. They wanted land.

On the west coast of North America, Asian immigrants found the beginning of a new continent, not the end. Traditions had yet to become firmly entrenched, and, if anything, the West had a tradition of conquest and change. Ownership of land became the first step in carving a place in this landscape, controlling nature an essential step in controlling one's destiny.

My grandfathers left little behind in Japan, both second sons of peasant farmers, they had no claim to family rice plots. Yet in California they
discovered Alien Lands Laws of 1913 and 1920 that prevented "Orien-
tals" from land purchases, singling out the immigrants from Asia and
condemning a generation to life as laborers. But they stayed, working the
fields for strangers. Some Japanese Americans saved and purchased land
by forming an American company or waiting until they had children
and buying the land in the name of the second generation, the Nisei—
Americans by birth. Most, though, waited until their Nisei children
were grown and working so they could pool their labor and buy a place
together as family. They sacrificed so the next generation could have
opportunity.

Dad explained the advantages of land ownership. "It's American!" he
claimed. "You keep all the profits." But I knew him better. He also meant
you had a place of your own, a place the family could plant roots. A piece
of the earth with time—he'd work one season, gradually improving the
soils, replanting grape vines or peach trees, with the intention of returning the next year and the year after that. Owning your own farm meant
you had "next years."

My family were quiet folk, preferring to communicate through their
actions than their words. I was born in the fifties and only learned of their
lives through an occasional story.

Once, during a dreadfully hot day in the summer, with daytime read-
ings of 105 degrees and low temperatures that never dropped below 70
degrees, Dad told me a story of our family during the Great Depression.
"We knew nature very well," he said, "almost too well." He explained
that the family were farm workers, laboring in the fields, living in shacks,
constantly exposed to the elements, feeling each minute change in weather.
In the heat of summer the family would sleep outside, on a low wooden
platform my grandfather built, staring up at the stars. "You could hear a
breeze rustle the grape leaves," Dad explained. "The sound makes you
feel cool." Life was hard but they knew their lands and how to work and
live with nature.

Dad then revealed to me another side of nature, this time human nature. For the first few years of his education, he jumped from school to
school, the family moving from field to field, working and leasing different pieces of land. Profits were thin for everyone in the 1930s. Japanese
Americans had it rougher. He explained: "Had to rent on a 50/50 percent agreement with owners. Others got at least a 60/40 split, the ones

working the land got the bigger share like it should be. But Japanese didn't have option, they couldn't own land. We were still good farmers though, took care of places. Not a whole lot of choices."

The Masumotos eventually found a place to rent on Manning Avenue just outside a small town called Selma (about ten miles southeast of Fresno, California). The fields were productive, with grapes that were dried into raisins. Despite the meager earnings, they leased the same place for years. They could "stay put for a while," although Dad said they still hoped for their own place. "If it was ours, we'd do a lot better 'cuz we could plow back the profits into the land, like adding manure after harvest, build up the soil for better crops. For the future, years down the road," Dad said.

The Masumotos were optimistic by 1940. My uncle George, the oldest son, had finished high school and was working full time in the fields. Dad, the second son, would finish soon and there were two other younger boys old enough to help during the summer harvest season. Together, as a family, they started saving money despite half their income going for rent. They began to pull together and pool resources, until they could afford a place they could call their own. All plans changed in the fall of 1941.

Uncle George was drafted into the army, the oldest son left to serve his country. The family kept farming, still planning for a future on the land, until December 7, when Japan bombed Pearl Harbor. Overnight, everything changed and was turned upside down. My family was suddenly considered the enemy. Dreams of the land—forging a relationship with nature, working with her bounty—were shattered and lost. By the late summer of 1942 the United States government commanded all persons of Japanese ancestry to be evacuated from the West Coast and imprisoned in relocation camps located in desolated areas of the country. The Masumotos were exiled to Gila River Relocation Center, in the high deserts south of Phoenix. But the farm we were renting stayed behind; so did the harvest of 1942.

They were given weeks to pack up and leave. Even on rented land, they had gradually accumulated various household goods, which had to be sold, given away, or left behind. Desperate emergency sales were held, buyers knowing well the sellers had to part with their possessions. Uncle George, the eldest son, now in the army, had just purchased a new car. Gone, sold for half the price. Clothes, kitchen goods, farm tools—pennies were exchanged for them.

But the biggest concern was the grape crop of 1942. Military orders decreed that by mid-August, all Japanese Americans were to be herded on trains to depart for unknown destinations. No one knew when or if they'd return. But grapes would need to be picked in September and dried into raisins. A year's worth of labor harvested in a month, a year's worth of hope and work bundled into a single moment each year. It was the calendar of farming, part of the rhythm of working with nature.

My grandfather and grandmother had immigrated from Japan and never learned English. As the August deadline neared, Jiichan/Grandpa Masumoto grew nervous about the vines he had pruned, irrigated, and fertilized. He and Baachan/Grandma Masumoto had "made" the crop. Only harvest was needed, the most rewarding time of the year.

The Caucasian widow who owned the land was worried too. Not over the departing "Japs" but rather who would pick the grapes and manage them as they dried in the sun into raisins? She was scared. With thousands of Japanese Americans leaving, a cheap source of labor would be lost: vineyards could lay unpicked, harvests lost. The Fresno County Farm Bureau had issued a resolution calling on the government to delay evacuation at least until the grapes were picked. Then the Japanese aliens could be hauled off, the crop safely in.

So Dad had to do the negotiating. He'd talk with the widow. She didn't say much. He'd try to explain the situation with his folks, already traumatized by the sudden orders to leave. "How can this happen in America?" Jiichan whispered.

Without warning, Dad was informed that the widow had found a tenant. An "Okie" would take over the ranch and harvest the grapes. Stories circulated in the farming community: because of the war and the potential opportunity for food demands, the price of raisins could double from a year before. In 1940 raisins sold for $56 a ton. They'd be worth over $100 in 1942. The depression was ending for farmers and landowners.

(Raisins prices indeed soared during the war, boosted by government support and the reduction of imports, especially of sugar and sweeteners. From the decade of the thirties, when prices hovered between $39–60 a ton, prices per ton rocketed to $109 in 1942, $157 in 1943, $194 in 1944, $195 in 1945, and a high of $309 in 1946, the year Japanese Americans began to trickle back to the San Joaquin Valley, released from their wartime prisons.)

The "Okie" had a demand though—he wanted a place to live with his family. So the landlord "kicked us out," Dad said. "Hell, we'd be leaving

in two weeks—maybe forever. Bur the owner told us to get out now."
Dad managed to negotiate a settlement; for the year's worth of work the
Masumotos would receive $25 per acre or about $12 a ton for the crop.
The owner and the new renter would split the profits from that bitter
harvest. "No wonder the 'Okie' wanted to move in so fast. All he had to
do was pick the damn grapes and count his profits for a month of work,"
Dad fumed.

My grandparents were hurt. This was the landlord they had been with
for years. Dad grew angry. He felt that at least nature—bad weather,
spring frosts, hail storms, rain on the raisins—was democratic. It didn't
matter the color of your skin or your religion or where your family came
from. But human nature was worse, it left scars that would not heal.

My family was homeless. A sixty-year-old immigrant and his fifty-
year-old wife were once again aliens in a land they had called home for
thirty years. A number-one son caught in the United States Army, Uncle
George wrote: "After Pearl Harbor, they didn't know what to do with us.
Finished basic training but they wouldn't issue us guns to keep training.
No one knew what to do with us."

On a neighboring farm, across the street, the Nakayamas, another
Japanese American family, prepared for departure. But their landlord
was a good man. He had heard of my family's situation and felt awkward; he allowed the Masumotos to stay in his barn for those final two
weeks. He even gave a ride to the Masumotos to the train station where
they were to report. He was a good neighbor.

So to this barn the family dragged their few suitcases and packed
boxes, all tagged "No. 40551." What couldn't fit or be carried, they
would have to leave behind.

But Dad would not go quietly. He was not the reserved father whom I
came to know later—the man who could silently watch a rainstorm dev-
astate a crop or slowly shake his head as he felt a wicked summer wind
topple peach trees and batter nectarines a few days from harvest. This
humble man who fought with nature, knowing well who would ultimately win, responding the next day by walking his fields with a passion
to start work over again. Dad didn't leave quietly.

As he vacated the house, he smashed every dish and cup they owned
rather than leave them. He broke every piece of furniture they had bought
or Jiichan had made, including the family's "summer platform" and
tossed them into a pile. Then he burned them. The flames danced into the
evening sky and glowed in the night's darkness. They would be used by
no one. All he'd leave behind was white ashes.

Bitter Melon

"Let's eat," Francis said.

Marcy, my wife, and I weren't expecting supper. We had dropped in to chat with Francis, a Nisei woman in her sixties, recently widowed. Even though their farm was miles from ours, we still considered them neighbors. Her late husband, who had died in the early 1990s, and Dad had known each other for decades—together they had learned to farm through good times and mostly bad. More than once I heard the silence they shared after a rainstorm or freeze, two farmers standing next to each other staring into empty fields. Our families became friends for generations and now Marcy and I were paying a visit to see how she was coping alone.

We sat around a polished cherry-wood dining table the couple must have used daily. The finish had faded in two spots at the corner of the table; the natural, lighter grain matched where elbows and place settings must have rested. I believed I was seated where her late husband had sat.

Parts of the room were immaculate, free from clutter and dust. In other areas—a bookshelf near the phone, the counter beneath the china cabinet—sat piles of papers, stray envelopes, old magazines, and Japanese newspapers. I was surprised by the clutter because whenever I drove into their yard, their vegetable garden was pristine. Cucumbers were neatly tied up a lattice, tomatoes were staked and grew upright, squash plants flourished with huge leaves that dominated one corner. Clusters of bright flowers grew, rows of bulbs along one edge, even wildflowers scattered along the fencerow. The soil was damp but not muddy. Weeds grew only in a few places and didn't compete for nutrients—they looked as if they too had been planted. I was reminded of a joke the late husband had once told me. "Work ethic," he said. "My folks worried so much about me growing up the right way, I swear they planted weeds to make sure I always had enough work to keep me busy."

From the kitchen, Marcy carried three water glasses filled with ice and small bunches of dark purple currant grapes floating in them.

"What's this?" I asked.

Through a small window that connected the kitchen to the dining room, Francis poked her head and answered, "We've had them for years but even after retiring and selling the place, he still took care of that one outside row, right next to the garden." She pulled her head back into the kitchen and continued. We leaned forward and turned our ears toward the kitchen. "I once saw in a gourmet food magazine, a place setting with crystal glasses and sparkling water filled with currants—they called them "Black Corinths" but you know they were just fresh currants floating in the water. Well I always wanted to try something fancy like that! I don't think Herb would have minded. He actually smiled when I talked about the idea."

Herb was a quiet man and very hard working. He had a grin, even when I passed by in my truck and he was at the end of a row, leaning on his shovel, using the excuse of a neighborly wave with a dip of the head to take a brief break from his work.

But he'd smile, wave, and dip his head. In my rearview mirror I could see his gray work shirt was soaked with sweat, a deep stain across his chest and along the spine. Maybe the gesture made him feel a little cooler, help to tolerate the heat and accept the daily tests of nature.

At the table, Francis opened three of the serving dishes and we watched steam escape out of them. Two were filled with zucchini, one appeared to be fried in butter and the other steamed. The third bowl was filled with hot corn on the cob.

She smiled and announced, "From his garden." Francis spooned out the zucchini and a huge gob plopped onto my plate. "Personally I like mine microwaved, keeps it as natural as possible," she whispered. "Help yourself to the corn, picked it this morning."

"How you doing with the garden?" I asked.

"Two hours in the morning, two in the evening," she answered. "It's a lot more work when you're by yourself. Much more than I thought. I never realized how much we did together. I'm exhausted."

She smiled gently, her lips tight but grinning and showing no teeth. I poked at a cob and set it on my plate.

Francis said, "Go ahead, taste it. Tell me how sweet it is. Really how sweet."

I bit into it, knowing I'd agree with her. But I was surprised. I couldn't help but raise my eyebrows. It was sweet, very sweet. The natural taste exploded in my mouth.

Marcy's bite seemed just as pleasantly surprising. "My god, you can eat this for dessert," Marcy mumbled with her mouth full. Francis glowed.

"The hardest part is the watering. I tried keeping all these little notes taped on clocks and doors, telling me when to start or shut off a hose. He had so many different furrows and raised plots. No one knew how he kept it all on schedule."

Marcy and I devoured the food and looked up for more. Francis smiled and brought out a chilled platter with thin slices of some type of yellow melon. We eagerly grabbed for the fruit with our hands and bit into the flesh. My left eye squeezed closed, and my lips puckered. Francis giggled out loud.

"He used to trick us too." Her voice dropped as low as it could, mimicking Herb's soft voice. "It's not all sweet like candy."

"What is this?" Marcy asked.

"I think it's a type of Chinese melon. He was trying to breed them for years but no one knows if this was what he sought. I think he just wanted to leave behind a taste, a different flavor.

I sucked on my tongue and swallowed.

"Wait a while," Francis advised. "It'll start tasting better, sort of bittersweet."

14

A Field Guide to Western Birds

Kathleen Dean Moore

My son reads field guides at the breakfast table, leaning over his bowl and scooping cereal into his mouth while he scans the color plates of banded snakes or studies the pawprints of cats in snow. He will study the same set of drawings for long minutes, absorbing the differences between stingrays and sharks. Or he will read a field guide late into the night, cover to cover, as if it were a novel—taking sides with the predators, imagining himself part of each small plot, turning pages all the way to the end, then rereading the first page and dropping the book on the floor. Field guides lie in heaps under his bed—*A Field Guide to Western Birds, Shells of the Pacific Coast and Hawaii, A Field Guide to Western Reptiles and Amphibians, The Pacific Coast Fishes*, and now, *The Field Guide to Eastern Birds*, a gift for high school graduation.

Most of the field guides are small, clothbound books, about the color of dried moss. We call the books by their authors' names, as if they were our grandfathers. "Should we bring Peterson?" we ask. "Somebody remember to pick up Murie before we go." The covers are worn, the fabric corners ground into the cardboard as if someone had taken sandpaper to them. The pages are stiff and wrinkled—*The Field Guide to Rocks and Minerals* carried ten feet by a flash flood, *North American Mammals* left on a rock in the snow. In our *Field Guide to Western Birds*, the pages describing ducks are smudged with black streaks, because when you sit at the edge of a marsh late in the evening while ducks whistle in and drop onto the pond with the sound of a canoe paddle pulling water, midges swarm to the pages of the bird book, their bodies small and soft as ashes. If you brush them away, they smear across the page.

Pintail. *Anas acuta*. Male Pintails are slender white-breasted ducks with slim necks, quite different in cut from other ducks of ponds and marshes. They have long, needle-pointed tails. . . . Habitat: Marshes, prairies, grainfields, fresh ponds, lakes, salt bays.

—Roger Tory Peterson, *A Field Guide to Western Birds*

Some of the books on my shelf—the fern book, the lichen book, the *Field Guide to Ponds and Streams*—had been my mother's. She was a person who exulted in natural facts, who greeted frogs as old friends and rejoiced to find in the forest something she had known only as a picture in a book. The first mayapple in spring, a glimpse of Scorpio crawling claw over claw into the sky above darkened mountains, the first sighting of a vermilion flycatcher—any of these would fill her with what Joseph Wood Krutch called "the joy we cannot analyze." "*Imagine* living in the same world as the scissor-tailed flycatcher," she would say. *Imagine.* The word always sounded as if it were throwing open its arms. A painted bunting. A blue skink. Elephant flowers, with pink elephant heads spiraling up a stalk in a high mountain meadow. Marshes full of skunk cabbage, smelling like lemonade. If these things can exist, then nothing is impossible. "That's the ticket," she would say.

Among my mother's things, I found a bird book that my son had written for her when he was four. On the first page, he had printed, "LOVE JON," except that he spelled it NOJ and there was a smiley face cradled in the curve of the J. He had drawn a dozen birds with large-scale swoops of a marking pen he held in his fist. Then he brought the drawings to me and told me what words to write. *The Two-Sets-of-Wings Bird and the Hundred-Sets-of-Wings Bird. The big one is trying to swoop down on the little one and he is trying to sneak away. He has four legs.*

Page after page, the birds line up: The Tufted Striped Hawk. The Sharp-toothed Duck. The Rocket Turkey Hawk. The Tufted Pelican-Pelican. The Tiny Sandpiper. All the waterbirds stand on sturdy stalklike legs. But the hawks! Legs shoot out behind diving hawks like exhaust from rockets, or they string out taut as piano wire, or trail under the birds like the crumpled legs of a dead crane fly. All the birds look as though they have on yellow boots, and some of the boots seem to be on fire. The joy we cannot analyze.

I once asked my son what it is about field guides. It's like a dream coming true, he had said. You read about a bird, say, and for years you hold it in your mind. It's an image, a drawing, length and wingspan—that's it. A picture in your mind. But all the time you think, Maybe someday I will see that really. The real thing. And then, someday, you do. And what was just an idea, it comes true. Like a wish.

The fern book has my mother's signature on the title page and, be-tween pages 109 and 110 (LADY FERN *Athyrium filix-femina*), the tip of a fern frond, folded back on itself and pressed flat and dry. Her field book of ponds and streams was published in 1930, when she would have been seventeen. I open the book to the first plate, a softly washed water-color of a stream and its little life, all overlaid by a piece of tissue paper on which the plants and animals are sketched in ink and number-coded to a list. *Winter life in a brook: a section through swift flowing shallows. 1, stonefly; 2, water cress; 3, alga; 4, sponge gemmules; 5, caddis worm; 6, planarian; . . . 10, dusky salamander.*

I haven't looked at this page in—how many?—fifteen years, and still I recognize the overhanging willows, the glint on the water, the feathery gills of the salamander. I turn to figure 18, a diagram of all the things that live on the underside of a lily pad—the eggs of a whirligig beetle, dragon-fly larvae. I remember watching my mother take Jon by the hand and wade knee-deep into a marsh, rejoicing to see a dragonfly split up the back and crawl out of its shuck, bent and damp. With a plastic bucket, they dredged for water boatmen and fairy shrimp. I leaf on through the book and by the time I get to bryozoans, *clustered on the surface of large masses of jelly which . . . hang from twigs,* I have to close the book to keep from being swamped by all the memories.

Spring peeper (*Hyla crucifer*). Spring peepers cling to dead grassblades by the pond-side uttering their shrill peeping, one of the earliest calls of spring in the ponds and marshes. They begin to sing in March, when the spotted salamander is laying its eggs, and continue through May. After that they scatter through swamps and meadows and are only occasionally seen.
—Ann Morgan, *Field Book of Ponds and Streams*

Lessons from my father are woven into the dichotomous keys at the beginning of every field guide. He was a taxonomist in his professional life and had a taxonomist's view of the world. *Are the plants free-floating on still water, or are they not? Are the stems jointed and hollow, or are they not? Are the leaves entire, or are they variously divided?* And so it goes, in sets of disjunctive syllogisms. Every creature in the whole of the natural world, every scaled or furry or slimish, beetle-backed, high-flying, zero- to hundred-legged creature of night skies or ocean bottoms or mountain sunlight, can be identified in twenty questions, if you get the questions right. *Is it now or has it ever been alive, or not? If living, is it animal, or something else? If an animal, warm-blooded or cold?*

One step at a time. Twenty discriminations. "So how many kinds of things are there in the world?" I once asked my father. He pulled his slide rule out of its sheath and computed two to the twentieth power. "One million forty-eight thousand five hundred and seventy-six," he said.

A few years ago, my father gave his grandchildren a special legacy—a hand lens on a leather thong and the logic of the dichotomous key. I remember the exact day. Arriving at our house after a cross-country flight, he immediately changed into jeans and pulled the *Handbook of North-western Plants* out of his suitcase. He called for his granddaughter. He called for his grandson and a flower. Then, step by step, he slowly keyed out the flower. This or that. This or that. This or that, until everyone was convinced beyond any doubt that this was an *Ipomopsis aggregata*. Then, reaching out his arms, he pulled the children close to him and each of them in turn keyed out the flower, then another, until he was sure they could do it right.

A gift of rationality. A faith in order. Gratitude for the glory and beauty of a natural world that allows itself to be arranged by reason. A cause for great rejoicing: to wake up every morning knowing that whatever you encounter in the natural world will yield to Linnaeus's two-name scheme, genus and species, a scheme based on the premise that order constrains the violent world of natural creation, that everything in the world relates in predictable ways to everything else. There are no freaks. No miracles. A family for everyone, even *Ursus horribilis:* the terrible bear. A genus, a genesis, a genius. Within that, a specification—a species.

This fact, my father said, should make us tremble with wonder every day of our lives. You can't take the planet for granted; it could all be otherwise. There must be worlds spinning on the far side of Jupiter where field guides are futile, where nothing is this or that, but rather nothing at all or everything at once. Imagine a simple world where everything is one kind of thing, evenly distributed, like red cinders blown out of a red cinder cone onto an even plain, so when the wind blows across the roughness, it plays a single endless note. Cinders and one sound—nothing more. Imagine a planet where no two things are ever the same and there are infinitely many things, a planet where you could not play twenty questions because there are no dichotomies, no regularities, no repeated patterns: one of each, and nothing like anything else. Or imagine a world where chaos never yielded to creation, a world forever unsorted, spinning in the glare that is all light combined. These are worlds that rationality cannot conquer.

So the great miracle is not that conditions on earth permit life to evolve, my father told us, but that conditions on earth permit field guides.

Carry a field guide out of the library, out through the old cross-and-bible front door, across the mowed lawn and into the field, the open country, to the edge of the marsh and to the edge of the sea, to the edge of the night sky, to the edge, and then into the wilderness, where—even there—a book will tell you how to make sense of what you encounter.

6A. Adults with protruding upper jaw teeth—felt by stroking tip of salamander's snout from below, while holding its mouth closed; toes often with squarish tips. Climbing Salamanders, Pl. 6.
6B. Teeth rarely protrude; toe tips round. Woodland Salamanders, Pl. 5.
—Robert Stebbins, *A Field Guide to Western Reptiles and Amphibians*

Most days, I feel safe and comfortable in the rational world my father described, but sometimes it makes me restless, and I turn back toward my mother. When we were growing up, my sisters and I would often come across a flower we didn't know. "What is this?" we would ask. My father would touch the flower gently under its chin. "Some *Ranunculus*," he would answer. A short pause while he studied the sky over the mountains. "*Ranunculus glaberrimus.*" A chorus of boos from his children. "The real name! What is the real name?" "That is the real name," he would insist, but my mother knew better. "It's a buttercup," she would say, and give my father a dirty look, and we would be satisfied. Buttercup was exactly right. Although we would accuse my father of making up gibberish-ranunculish names to suit himself, we never doubted the names my mother gave, no matter how improbable or flamboyant they were—pussytoes, morning glories, whimbrels and whippoorwills, farewell-to-spring, love-lies-bleeding, and the fiery searcher.

Does the world match the capacities of our minds, or do our poor minds limit what is possible for us to know about the world? Maybe our minds do the best they can, capturing what is slow, wounded, common, but missing the best part. The possibility of something beyond human capacity to see makes me wild with frustration, like a dog racing back and forth in front of a closed door, scratching, sniffing air that comes through the crack at the bottom. What is out there that is invisible because it does not match our categories? What exists beyond the visible spectrum, beyond the audible range, outside binomial nomenclature, so glorious that it would blind us, blow out our senses, knock us to the ground?

Fiery Searcher "Caterpillar Hunter" (*Calosoma scrutator*). Description: Black beetle with dark greenish gold on sides of head and prothorax. Bluish luster on femora. Elytra edged with gold. Reddish hair inside curved middle tibiae. Habitat: Gardens, crop fields, and open woods.

—*The Audubon Society Field Guide to North American Insects and Spiders*

It is important to me that my children can distinguish a vulture from a golden eagle by the cant of its wings. It reassures me to know that they can recognize the evening call of robins and the morning call of doves, that they know from its tracks whether a rabbit is coming or going, that they always know which way is west. I want them to go out into a rational world where order gives them pleasure and comfort, but also an improbable world, wild with sound and extravagant with color, where there is always a chance they will find something rare and very beautiful, something that is not in the book.

15

At Home with Belonging

Danyelle O'Hara

Part 1: Land, Stories, and Belonging

Some years ago, I was an observer at a conference on African American land loss. My employer at the time provided organizational support to southern grassroots groups, and the conference host was one of our clients. The conference brought attention to the precipitous decline of black-owned land in the United States over the past century and provided a forum for landowners and former landowners to share their experiences, learn about available legal and technical assistance, develop strategies for land retention, and organize to obtain better governmental support for farming and other land-based economic strategies.

Outside of the conference sessions, I shared meals and conversations with the conference participants. Many were elderly black southerners who spoke movingly about their land—how hard they, their parents, or their grandparents had worked to acquire it, how persistently they had fought to hold onto it, and how much it hurt to lose it. I was mesmerized by the stories and the emotion that filled them but even more by the sense of belonging that they made me feel. This was startling to me because, in general, I don't expect to belong. My father made a career as a naval officer, and our family had moved to five towns in three different states by the time I was six. I'm adaptable, I make new friends easily and stay in touch with old ones, I get along competently in most situations, but I'm not necessarily someone who feels like she belongs. I bloom where I'm planted, sometimes even with deep roots, but I don't see myself as a native species.

Moreover, I am a second-generation black northerner who was nearly thirty years old before I ever traveled to the South. To claim belonging based on feelings about stories I was hearing for the first time seemed presumptuous. Like most African Americans, I have family relationships that bridge me to the South. But my parents divorced when I was young, and I did most of my growing up with only tenuous connections to my father's side of the family, the side that remained most connected to the South. They were family but not really familiar.

Although I didn't fully understand the sense of belonging I felt through the stories, I itched to be an active participant in the conference rather than an observer. I left full of excitement to learn about land and its significance to me, to forge a connection to it, and to develop a new narrative about my family as southerners. I considered contacting my father's family to learn about the land in Arkansas that I had heard they still owned. I thought about traveling to the family home site with my then one-year-old, Jonah, so that I could pass the gift of land connection onto him. I imagined myself digging around in the county courthouse records, walking the land with Jonah in the baby backpack, and chewing the fat with neighbors who remembered my grandfather and his family.

I wasn't too deep into my back-to-the-land revelry when it became clear that uncovering my roots in southern land would mean much more than MapQuesting an address in Arkansas and driving to it. It would mean more, even, than arriving at that place and feeling a physical and emotional bond with it. Connecting with the land would involve navigating my way to and through family, most of whom I didn't know well or from whom I was essentially estranged. Beyond reckoning with family, beyond finding and traveling to a physical location, reconnecting with land as a black person in the United States would entail an even larger journey to understanding the commonly held assumptions—my own and others'—about my place in this country, about belonging as an African American.

In her essay "Earthbound," bell hooks equates relationship with land and nature, particularly for African Americans, with a deepened understanding of who we are as humans, our power relative to nature, and the fallacy of white supremacy that infuses American culture. In the past, hooks states, when most blacks lived in the rural South, there was a grounded understanding of the black self and the white self: "[Southern black folks], whether they were impoverished or not, knew firsthand that white supremacy, with its systemic dehumanization of blackness, was not a form of absolute power." Urbanization and capitalist and consumer culture have not only separated blacks from the land but, as hooks points out, alienated us from the reality that "even when the land was owned by white oppressors . . . it was the earth itself that protected exploited Black folks from dehumanization," resulting in a sustained and internalized myth that the dominant white culture is all-powerful.

According to hooks, the self-knowledge relative to others that emerges through a connection with land and nature is critical for blacks to claim a rightful place in America and American history. This is something of a paradox for a population that left southern land in an exodus in search of economic opportunity and a safe haven from racial hatred. For many, southern land was perceived as a location of violence. In *The Souls of Black Folk*, W. E. B. Dubois describes this perception, as voiced by a black man in southern Georgia in the early 1900s: "'This land was a living Hell,' said a ragged, brown, and grave-faced man to me. . . . 'I've seen niggers drop dead in the furrow, but they were kicked aside, and the plough never stopped.'"

Following the conference, I sought to heed hooks's call for black folks to "collectively renew our relationship with our agrarian roots." First, however, a more immediate exploration was required for me to understand my relationship with the region that held those roots. Not only did distance of geography and two generations separate me from the South, but a mental image sustained a broad gulf between the region and me. Clearing the path to my agrarian roots in the South entailed delving into what that "living Hell" was.

Part 2: A Black Woman and the South

Tenuous as my ties were to my paternal family, I always knew that despite my grandparents' adulthood move to Detroit in the late 1930s, they were southerners first and foremost. They were from Arkansas and spoke frequently about their youths there—my grandfather's in a small town called Fordyce and my grandmother's in Hope. My grandfather's two siblings also moved to Detroit, but my grandmother's nine siblings all stayed in Hope, and my grandparents drove south regularly to visit them. Throughout my childhood, I received letters from my grandmother in her wobbly arthritic handwriting updating me on aunts and uncles I had never met and could never keep straight.

My grandparents' connection to Arkansas and the South didn't filter down to me. I never had much interest in it, and it's probably fair to say that I never visited the South until my late twenties largely because I had avoided it. My avoidance was unarticulated and unexamined but grounded in assumptions that the South was a violent, unsafe, and inhospitable place for black people. I grew up in the 1970s and 1980s, and media stories that felt antirural, antipoor, and antiblack were probably a key source for my impressions. But I had no direct lived experiences to substantiate my assumptions other than a fear in the pit of my stomach whenever the dark, poor, deprived, and dangerous landscapes emerged in my mind's South.

I spent nearly a decade working in some of the poorest countries and communities in sub-Saharan Africa—places that rivaled the poorest and most deprived communities of the American South. However, I never found Africa threatening, even places that were reputedly dangerous for Westerners. Although I took care, I perceived nothing personal in the danger other than the reality that as a Westerner, I had many more re-sources and privileges than most Africans. In the American South, my impression was that danger would be specific to me, a black person who was despised for the color of my skin, not for what I had. My deeply rooted preconceptions remained in place, even when marriage brought me to North Carolina after returning from Africa. I wrote in my journal constantly about the unsettling familiarity of the rural places I visited and the pain I sensed. Some of my perceptions about the South were rooted in the real-time poverty I witnessed and the racism I experienced, but many were "just a feeling."

I didn't seek to explore my feelings about the South until I was in my early thirties and read Evelyn White's essay "Black Women and the Wilderness." In this essay, White reflects on and analyzes her emotions about the outdoors, which she both is attracted to and fears. White understands her fears as being tightly interwoven with a "genetic mem-ory of ancestors hunted down and preyed upon in rural settings." Al-though she seeks to connect with and find peace in wild settings, "I imagine myself in the [wilderness] as my forebears were—exposed, vul-nerable, and unprotected—a target of cruelty and hate."

White's essay has slowly affected my thinking and understanding. On a basic level, as a distance runner and avid hiker, biker, and swimmer, I simply couldn't relate to White's fear of the outdoors. I also thought the piece could be misread to confirm and exacerbate white environmentalist stereotypes about people of color who were disconnected from nature. My professional life has been spent working in or in partnerships with environmental conservation organizations in which I am usually the lone or among very few nonadministrative persons of color. Many environ-mental groups have made attempts at increasing senior staff diversity, but the results have been limited. Rather than understanding failure as a need for deeper efforts to support youth of color in developing career pursuits, address structurally rooted discrimination in workplace culture, policies, and practices, and perhaps reframe the focus of environmentalism, many environmentalists see failure in diversity efforts as evidence that people of color lack interest in the environment. One common argument is that people of color are largely urban and disconnected from the environment. This ignores the reality that most white people working in environmental organizations are also urban. Given my own love of the outdoors and my own professional choices, I have found such stereotypes blind and self-serving, and I was frustrated that White's essay seemed to confirm the status quo.

As I began reading more deeply into my life for the relevance of White's message, I understood the obvious: White's "wilderness" was my "South." In the same way that White's direct (or "real-time") experiences in nature were interrupted by her "genetic" memories of ancestors and other blacks who had suffered in the wilderness, I was unable to experience the southern landscapes in which I lived and traveled separate from cultural memory. My cultural memories were of the terror that those landscapes and ones like them had held for black people throughout the United States' history. Instead of being awestruck by the beauty of the deep forests and rivers crisscrossing southern Alabama and northern Mississippi, I was preoccupied with mental images of limp bodies hanging from trees near riverbanks, swinging to the tune of "Strange Fruit." Only when I explicitly named my cultural memories and acknowledged the terror they held for me was I able to begin separating them from my direct experience.

Intermingled with these memories were other, more recent experiences and memories of the South that were not my own but that influenced and shaped my perceptions. I knew that although my grandparents retained their southern identities, they bore the scars of growing up black in Arkansas in the 1920s and 1930s. As I pondered my relationship to the South, I yearned to ask my grandparents about those seldom-mentioned scars and, more generally, about Arkansas. My grandmother had died years ago, and my grandfather soon after I attended the land-loss conference. To explore my questions, I contacted my grandfather's brother, my Uncle Rowe, to ask him about his relationship with Arkansas.

The indicator that I was out of touch with Uncle Rowe was that he wasn't even listed in my address book. I sheepishly called my older brother, who had stayed in contact with our paternal relatives, for my uncle's number. I imagined Uncle Rowe would find it strange to receive a call out of the blue from a long lost niece, but if he did, he didn't let on.

He greeted me as if we had talked the afternoon before—not full of sur-prise and excitement but happy to hear from me. I was embarrassed that I hadn't bothered to stay in touch and suddenly felt silly wanting to talk about land and my epiphanies. But after I updated Uncle Rowe on my family and he filled me in on the weather in Detroit and the highlights of his physical condition, there was nothing to do but to move onto the purpose of the call.

When I asked him about land in his family and what it meant to him, my uncle was silent and thoughtful. I sensed he wanted to take seriously my questions about the meaning of land, home, his ties, and his sense of belonging, even if he had no idea where they were coming from. Finally, he said, "They all gone, baby. Back in the thirties and forties, they either moved north like us or out to California. The jobs they had for us back in those days weren't no jobs. If blacks wanted to work back then, all they could do is go to the farm and pick a hundred pounds of cotton for a dollar." I could imagine him shaking his head on the other end of the phone line: "Girl, there weren't no jobs for us. What kind of 'home' you goan call that when you can't make a living and white folks is hell bent on keeping things that way? And from what I hear tell, things ain't changed much." He added, kind of as a refrain, "No, there weren't no jobs, so we all had to leave."

He was quiet for a little while and then added, "Those that was still there, those that decided to make their life there, they dead, baby. They almost all dead now. Ain't no reason to go back. I don't know why Ridgell and May Franklin [my grandfather and aunt] kept that land. I can't keep up with what I got here, why'm I goan try to keep up with that stuff down there? Anyway, the old house burned down, you know? It's been over ten years. Any memories I had is gone. If I had some ties, they about gone now."

In the same way that cultural memories affected my real-time experi-ences with and of the South, my conversation with my Uncle Rowe clari-fied how the experiences of my immediate elders had also formed and influenced my understanding of the South. These memories inherited from my family shouldn't dictate my responses and actions, but they should inform them. As Lauret Savoy suggests in her unpublished essay "Properties of Desire," the United States' past acts of violence against whole groups of people and against the land are present in our everyday, and only when we acknowledge our history can we truly engage with one another about who we are as Americans and fully participate in creating our country as we want it to be: "Justice in the present asks us to remember historical injustices and to recognize how they continue to shape identities, inequities, and social structures by which we live."

Part 3: Land, Stories, and Alienation

I once attended a gathering at which participants were asked to share stories about their connections to land. Participants told about visiting a grandfather's cabin in the Virginia woods, spending summers on a farm in New England, family camping trips, and postcollege Outward Bound experiences. One person shared a story about how a particular piece of land surfaced painful childhood memories around betrayal. Not one person situated their experiences of land in the broader context of the United States' history, the history of land stolen and destroyed, or the history of people maimed, killed, forcefully relocated, imprisoned, and enslaved on the land.

I was the only person of color in the group and found myself unable to answer the question. I felt a certain trauma even considering it. I couldn't trace my land connection to a piece of real estate or any particular event, happy or sad, in my life. I felt alienated by my inability to match the group norm with a story that was uplifting or at least personal. In that moment, all that surfaced for me was my connection to the people brought to the United States against their will, forced to work the land, and dehumanized to justify the system. To consider my relationship to land through a private or personal lens would have been to void us—the land and myself—of our history.

I feared that my silence confirmed my lack of attachment to land, which made me feel humiliation. This I took as additional evidence of my separation and of white environmentalists' claims that people of color, certainly black people, don't care about nature and are disconnected from it. To try to make sense of this, I decided that disunion was a product of the tragedy of the black experience as second-class citizens—that we do not belong here and that the only attachment African Americans can claim to land in the United States is through our trauma.

For a long time, I stalled in this understanding. I tried accepting that I had no real connection to land and that my main relationship was to trauma. But if this was true, then the joy I experienced in my life didn't make sense. A life framed only through a lens of trauma was one-dimensional and didn't square with the fullness and depth that I knew my life to hold. Over time, I have come to understand that my relationship to land in the United States is, in fact, deep. The pain I might experience in response to a question about my connection to it is an indicator of that depth, not disconnection. In *The Souls of Black Folk*, W. E. B. Dubois said about land in the South, "How curious a land is this, how full of untold story, of tragedy and laughter, and the rich legacy of human life; shadowed with a tragic past, and big with future promise!" Although my inherited memories of land—the stories, tragedies, laughter, and legacies—are not the whole of my experience, I can't fully understand my direct experiences, no matter how joyful, without them.

If this is the case for me, it also must be true for my white counterparts. United States history is not mine or people of color's history alone. The histories of genocide, land theft, slavery, relocation, internment camps, persistent poverty, and the list goes on are the collective histories of American people. They are stories that lie beneath all of our experiences on this land. An honest dialogue about history underlies the ways that we choose to engage with one another about land, which is implicit in our discourse about belonging. Dominant culture in the United States conceives of land largely as a private good, but this frame obscures the communal resource and experience that land is, regardless of the laws and notions that govern it. It also obscures the basic fact that land is where our lives and our histories unfold and that those histories are intertwined and interdependent.

My experience at the land gathering left me wondering why I was the only person in that group remembering and holding the pain, terror, and sadness part of our collective history with land. I don't have an answer for this, but Wendell Berry's awakening (in *The Hidden Wound*) to his own responsibility with respect to race and racism joins Lauret Savoy in offering an explanation for why American history must be acknowledged and held in full by all of us: "If the white man has inflicted the wound of racism upon Black men, the cost has been that he would receive the mirror image of that wound into himself. As the master, or as member of the dominant race, he has felt little compulsion to acknowledge it or speak of it; the more painful it has grown the more deeply he has hidden it within himself. But the wound is there, and it is a profound disorder, as great a damage in his mind as it is in his society."

Part 4: At Home with Belonging

My six-year-old daughter, Marjanne, told me the other day that because of her skin color, she doesn't belong. Her exact words were, "I'm brown, and I don't fit here." "Here" is Oklahoma, where we have made our lives for the past two and a half years. Her comment took my breath away, but not because it surprised me. It shouldn't. Her nine-year-old brother, Jonah, has been noting and naming racial differences and stratification since he was three and a half and we lived in North Carolina. What took my breath away is the fact that at forty-two, I'm still pondering the same race and place issues as Marjanne. What I could offer Marjanne is that something may be missing for her in Oklahoma but that nothing is missing in her or about her. Marjanne's sense that something doesn't fit is about what's lacking in our American story.

As a parent, I want the work I've done acknowledging the fullness of my connection to land to make a difference in others' willingness and ability to take responsibility for what it means to be American. But a decision on my part to claim my place doesn't signify the end of experiences like the one I had following the 2008 elections, when two young white men in a speeding pickup truck bellowed out to a black friend and me, "*We hate Obama!*" It won't change the fact that my six- and nine-year-olds, because of their skin color, understand more about privilege and oppression in the United States than the average middle-aged white person. What has changed is my willingness to accept and embrace a sense of belonging if I feel it. I know now that the stories at the land-loss conference all those years ago evoked a sense of familiarity and belonging because the people telling the stories let the land hold the breadth of their experiences—the good and bad, joyful and painful. Such honesty created a safe space for me to be with the breadth of my own experiences, lived and remembered.

What has also changed for me is a reengagement with the sense of enthusiasm I felt leaving the land-loss conference to see where in the South and elsewhere my family's path leads me. It's a zig-zagging path. My great-great-great-great-grandparents were born as slaves in Wilcox County, Alabama, and after emancipation created a home for themselves in Fordyce, Arkansas. My grandparents moved to Detroit but maintained their sense of belonging in Arkansas, and my Uncle Rowe left the South and created a place for himself in Detroit. My parents were born and raised in Detroit and brought my siblings and me "home" to Detroit, regardless of where we were stationed by the military. For the past thirty-one years, including a large part of my own childhood, my mother has created her home on a ranch in Bridger, Montana.

Detroit, Wilcox County, Hope, Fordyce, Bridger: my family's places on this continent are many, including, my children will learn, North Carolina, Oklahoma, and anywhere else we live. Our inheritance is the knowledge that we can define belonging for ourselves. bell hooks says that this knowledge will come through direct connection to land and nature. I think that for those of us finding our paths to land, nature, or whatever holds truth, connection, and belonging can also come through the journey.

Note

1. In 1910, the number of farm acres owned by African American farmers reached a peak of over 15 million acres, nearly all of which were in the South, largely Mississippi, Alabama, and the Carolinas. Today that number has dropped to about 3.4 million, with black land ownership declining at three times the rate of white ownership. African Americans have lost land through a variety of means—tax sales, partition sales, land sales to non-African Americans, limited access to legal counsel, forceful land takings, discrimination by public and private institutions, and failure of the U.S. Department of Agriculture and the land grant complex to provide adequate resources to small farmers. Janice Dyer, C. Bailey, and Nhuong Van Tran, "Ownership Characteristics of Heir Property in a Black Belt County: A Quantitative Approach," *Southern Rural Sociology* 24(2) (2009): 192–217.

16

Animal Allies

Brenda Peterson

"My imaginary friend really lived once," the teenage girl began, head bent, her fingers twisting her long red hair. She stood in the circle of other adolescents gathered in my Seattle Arts and Lectures storytelling class at the summer Seattle Academy. Here were kids from all over the city—every color and class, all strangers one to another. Over the next two weeks we would become a fierce tribe, telling our own and our tribe's story. Our first assignment was to introduce our imaginary friends from childhood. This shy fourteen-year-old girl, Sarah, had struck me on the first day because she always sat next to me, as if under my wing, and though her freckles and stylish clothes suggested she was a popular girl, her demeanor showed the detachment of someone deeply preoccupied. She never met my eye, nor did she join in the first few days of storytelling when the ten boys and four girls were regaling one another with futuristic characters called Shiva and Darshon, Masters of the Universe. So far the story lines we'd imagined were more Pac-Man than drama. After the first two days I counted a legion of characters killed off in intergalactic battle. The settings for all these stories portrayed the earth as an environmental wasteland, a ruined shell hardly shelter to anything animal or human. One of the girls called herself Nero the White Wolf and wandered the blackened tundra howling her powerful despair; another girl was a unicorn whose horn always told the truth. All the stories were full of plagues and nuclear wars—even though this is the generation that has witnessed the fall of the Berlin Wall, the end of the Cold War. Their imaginations have been shaped by a childhood story line that anticipates the end of this world.

After three days of stories set on an earth besieged by disease and barren of nature, I made a rule: No more characters or animals could die this first week. I asked if someone might imagine a living world, one that survives even our species.

It was on this third day of group storytelling that Sarah jumped into the circle and told her story:

"My imaginary friend is called Angel now because she's in heaven, but her real name was Katie," Sarah began. "She was my best friend from fourth to tenth grade. She had freckles like me and brown hair and more boyfriends—sometimes five at a time—because Katie said, 'I *like* to be confused!' She was a real sister too and we used to say we'd be friends for life. . . ." Sarah stopped, gave me a furtive glance and then gulped in a great breath of air like someone drowning, about to go down. Her eyes fixed inward, her voice dropped to a monotone. "Then one day last year, Katie and I were walking home from school and a red sports car came up behind us. Someone yelled, 'Hey, Katie!' She turned . . . and he blew her head off. A bullet grazed my skull, too, and I blacked out. When I woke up, Katie was gone, dead forever." Sarah stopped, stared down at her feet and murmured in that same terrible monotone, "Cops never found her murderer, case is closed."

All the kids shifted and took a deep breath, although Sarah herself was barely breathing at all. "Let's take some time to write," I told the kids and put on a cello concerto for them to listen to while they wrote. As they did their assignment, the kids glanced over surreptitiously at Sarah, who sat staring at her hands in her lap.

I did not know what to do with her story; she had offered it to a group of kids she had known but three days. It explained her self-imposed exile during lunch hours and while waiting for the bus. All I knew was that she'd brought this most important story of her life into the circle of story-tellers and it could not be ignored as if *she* were a case to be closed. This story lived in her, would define and shape her young life. Because she had given it to us, we needed to witness and receive—and perhaps tell it back to her in the ancient tradition of tribal call and response.

"Listen," I told the group as the cello faded and they looked up from their work. "We're going to talk story the way they used to long ago when people sat around at night in circles just like this one. That was a time when we still listened to animals and trees and didn't think ourselves so alone in this world. Now we're going to carry out jungle justice and find Katie's killer. We'll call him before our tribe. All right? Who wants to begin the story?"

All the Shivas and Darshons and Masters of the Universe volunteered to be heroes on this quest. Nero the White Wolf asked to be a scout. Unicorn, with her truth-saying horn, was declared judge. Another character joined the hunt: Fish, whose translucent belly was a shining "soul mirror" that could reveal one's true nature to anyone who looked into it.

A fierce commander of this hunt was Rat, whose army of computerized comrades could read brain waves and call down lightning lasers as weapons. Rat began the questioning and performed the early detective work. Katie, speaking from beyond the earth, as Sarah put it, gave us other facts. We learned that two weeks before Katie's murder, one of her boyfriends was shot outside a restaurant by a man in the same red car—another drive-by death. So Sarah had not only seen her best friend killed at her side, but she had also walked out into a parking lot to find Katie leaning over her boyfriend's body. For Sarah, it had been two murders by age thirteen.

With the help of our myriad computer-character legions we determined that the murderer was a man named Carlos, a drug lord who used local gangs to deal cocaine. At a party Carlos has misinterpreted Katie's videotaping her friends dancing as witnessing a big drug deal. For that, Rat said, "This dude decides Katie's got to go down. So yo, man, he offs her without a second thought."

Bad dude, indeed, this Carlos. And who was going to play Carlos now that all the tribe knew his crime? I took on the role, and as I told my story I felt my face hardening into a contempt that carried me far away from these young pursuers, deep into the Amazon jungle where Rat and his own computer armies couldn't follow, where all their space-age equipment had to be shed until there was only hand-to-hand simple fate.

In the Amazon, the kids changed without effort, in an easy shape-shifting to their animal selves. Suddenly there were no more Masters of the Universe with intergalactic weapons—there was instead Jaguar and Snake, Fish and Pink Dolphin. There was powerful claw and all-knowing serpent, there was Fish who could grow big and small, and a dolphin whose sonar saw past the skin. We were now a tribe of animals, pawing, running, invisible in our jungle, eyes shining in the night, seeing Carlos as he canoed the mighty river, laughing because he did not know he had animals tracking him.

All through the story, I'd kept my eye on Sarah who played the role of her dead friend. The detachment I'd first seen in her was in fact the deadness Sarah carried, the violence that had hollowed her out inside, the friend who haunted her imagination. But now her face was alive, responding to each animal's report of tracking Carlos. She hung on the words, looking suddenly very young, like a small girl eagerly awaiting her turn to enter the circling jump rope.

"I'm getting away from you," I said, snarling as I'd imagined Carlos would. I paddled my canoe and gave a harsh laugh, "I'll escape, easy!"

"No!" Sarah shouted. "Let *me* tell it!"

"Tell it!" her tribe shouted.

"Well, Carlos only thinks he's escaping," Sarah smiled, waving her hands. "He's escaped from so many he's harmed before. But I call out 'FISH!' And Fish comes. He swims alongside the canoe and grows bigger, bigger until at last Carlos turns and sees this HUGE river monster swimming right alongside him and that man is afraid because suddenly Fish turns his belly up to Carlos's face. Fish forces him to look into that soul mirror. Carlos *sees* everyone he's ever killed and all the people who loved them and got left behind. And Carlos sees Katie and me and what he's done to us. He sees everything and he knows his soul is black. And he really doesn't want to die now because he knows then he'll stare into his soul mirror forever. But Fish makes him keep looking until Carlos starts screaming he's sorry, he's so sorry. Then . . . Fish *eats* him!"

The animals roared and cawed and congratulated Sarah for calling Fish to mirror a murderer's soul before taking jungle justice. Class had ended, but no one wanted to leave. We wanted to stay in our jungle, stay within our animals—and so we did. I asked them to close their eyes and call their animals to accompany them home. I told them that some South American tribes believe that when you are born, an animal is born with you. This animal protects and lives alongside you even if it's far away in an Amazon jungle—it came into the world at the same time you did. And, I told them, it dies with you to guide you back into the spirit world.

The kids decided to go home and make animal masks, returning the next day wearing the faces of their chosen animal. When they came into class the next day it was as if we never left the Amazon. Someone dimmed the lights, there were drawings everywhere of jaguars and chimps and snakes. Elaborate masks had replaced the Masters of the Universe who began this tribal journey. We sat behind our masks in a circle with the lights low and there was an acute, alert energy running between us, as eyes met behind animal faces.

I realize that I, who grew up in the forest wild, who first memorized the earth with my hands, have every reason to feel this familiar animal resonance. But many of these teenagers have barely been in the woods; in fact, many inner city kids are *afraid* of nature. They would not willingly sign up for an Outward Bound program or backpacking trek; they don't think about recycling in a world they believe already ruined and in their imaginations abandoned for intergalactic nomad futures. These kids are not environmentalists who worry about saving nature. And yet, when imagining an Amazon forest too thick for weapons to penetrate, too primitive for their futuristic Pac-Man battles, they return instinctively to their animal selves. These are animals they have only seen in zoos or on television, yet there is a profound identification, an ease of inhabiting another species that portends great hope for our own species's survival. Not because nature is "out there" to be saved or sanctioned, but because nature is *in* them. The ancient, green world has never left us though we have long ago left the forest.

What happens when we call upon our inner landscape to connect with the living rainforests still left in the natural world? I believe our imagination can be as mutually nurturing as an umbilical cord between our bodies and the planet. As we told our Amazon stories over the next week of class, gathered in a circle of animal masks, we could feel the rainforest growing in that sterile classroom. Lights low, surrounded by serpents, the jaguar clan, the elephants, I'd as often hear growls, hisses, and howls as words. Between this little classroom and the vast Amazon rainforest stretched a fine thread of story that grew thicker each day, capable of carrying our jungle meditations.

When Elephant stood in the circle and said simply, "My kind are dying out," there was outrage from the other animals.

"We'll stop those poachers!" cried Rat and Chimp. "We'll call Jaguar clan to protect you." And they did.

This protection is of a kind that reaches the other side of the world. Children's imagination is a primal force, just as strong as lobbying efforts and boycotts and endangered species acts. When children claim another species as not only their imaginary friend, but also as the animal within them—their ally—doesn't that change the outer world?

This class believes it to be so. They may be young, but their memories and alliances with the animals are very old. By telling their own animal stories they are practicing ecology at its most profound and healing level. Story as ecology—it's so simple, something we've forgotten. In our environmental wars the emphasis has been on saving species, not *becoming* them. We've fallen into an environmental fundamentalism that calls down hellfire and brimstone on the evil polluters and self-righteously struts about protecting other species as if we are gods who can save their souls.

But the animals' souls are not in our hands. Only our own souls are within our ken. It is our own spiritual relationship to animals that must evolve. Any change begins with imagining ourselves in a new way. And who has preserved their imaginations as a natural resource most deeply? Not adults, who so often have strip-mined their dreams and imagination for material dross. Those who sit behind the wheel of a Jaguar have probably forgotten the wild, black cat that first ran with them as children. Imagination is relegated to nighttime dreams, which are then dismissed in favor of "the real world." But children, like some adults, know that the real world stretches farther than what we can see—that's why they shift easily between visions of our tribal past and our future worlds. The limits of the adult world are there for these teenagers, but they still have a foot in the vast inner magic of childhood. It is this magical connection I called upon when I asked the kids to do the Dance of the Animals.

The day of the big dance I awoke with a sharp pain at my right eye. Seems my Siamese, who has always slept draped around my head, had stretched and his claw caught the corner of my eye. In the mirror I saw a two-inch scratch streaking from my eye like jungle make-up or a primitive face-painting. "The mark of the wildcat," the kids pronounced it when I walked into the dimly lit room to be met by a circle of familiar creatures. Never in ten years had my Siamese scratched my face. I took it as a sign that the dance began in his animal dream.

I put on my cobra mask and hissed a greeting to Chimp, Rat, Jaguar, and Unicorn. Keen eyes tracked me from behind colorful masks. I held up my rain stick which was also our talking stick and called the creatures one by one into the circle. "Sister Snake!" I called. "Begin the dance!"

Slowly, in rhythm to the deep, bell-like beat of my Northwest Native drum, each animal entered the circle and soon the dance sounded like this: Boom, step, twirl, and slither and stalk and snarl and chirp and caw, caw. Glide, glow, growl, and whistle and howl and shriek and trill and hiss, hiss. Each dance was distinct—from the undulating serpent on his belly, to the dainty high hoofing of Unicorn, from the syncopated stomps of Chimp on all-fours to Rat's covert jitterbug behind the stalking half-dark Jaguar. We danced, and the humid, lush jungle filled this room.

In that story line stretching between us and the Amazon, we connected with those animals and their spirits. And in return, we were complete—with animals as soul mirrors. We remembered who we were, by allowing the animals inside us to survive.

The dance is not over as long as we have our animal partners. When the kids left our last class, they still wore their masks fiercely. I was told that even on the bus they stayed deep in their animal character. I like to imagine those strong, young animals out there now in this wider jungle. I believe that Rat will survive the inner-city gangs; that Chimp will find his characteristic comedy even as his parents deal with divorce; I hope that Unicorn will always remember her mystical truth-telling horn. And as for Sarah who joined the Jaguar clan, elected as the first girl-leader over much mutinous boy-growling—Sarah knows the darkness she stalks and the nightmares that stalk her. She has animal eyes to see, to find even a murderer. Taking her catlike, graceful leave, she handed me a poem she'd written; it said "Now I can see in the dark" and was signed "Jaguar— Future Poet."

17

Grandmother, Grizzlies, and God

Brenda Peterson

Montana, 1959

The makeshift garage in Missoula, Montana, in which my parents and ten or so other families met for church service might as well have been a tiny ark. Its old wooden rafters held us together in a vast Western "wilderness, an ancient sea bottom of wide prairie lands with no other Southern Baptists. I was nine years old, but to this day I remember the musty, sweet-mash smell of horse or chicken feed and the engine oil that stained the cement floor under our folding chairs. Staring at the oil spill patterns in this garage floor, since there were no windows, I'd concentrate on the birdsongs outside—any natural sound to escape the sermons, which were always too loud and frightening.

Every time I did tune in to the minister's Bible stories, something terrible was happening to humans or animals: Adam and Eve cast out of their Garden and God's wise serpent condemned to crawl on its belly, demon-possessed pigs stampeding off a cliff, Abraham raising a knife over his own son and slaughtering a ram instead. It was strong stuff for a child whose imagination had first imprinted on animals.

The problem with those Bible stories was that they felt so vivid and visceral, so dangerous to children and other animals. I well remembered crawling, serpent-like, on my first forest floor, where sharp pine needles pricked my skin and palms. What if, like that admonished Biblical serpent, or the one my own father had killed, I was never allowed to walk upright? And when I imagined Isaac trembling naked under his father's upraised knife, it was a terrible mixture of relief and remorse to hear the bleating of the ram, which I knew would have its throat slit for my sake. Hadn't I watched beautiful deer leap in the woods and later seen their skinless bodies hang in the shed awaiting our appetites? Everyone in the Old Testament seemed to be at war with God the Father, with offending armies, with themselves and Satan, and with the other animals.

There was one salvation for me in that Montana garage-church. It was not the fundamentalist religion—although my parents expected that soon I might offer myself up at the minister's weekly invitation to be saved; it was a fur coat and the first sermon I ever truly loved. Mrs. Ashworth was an elderly churchwoman whose husband had died in a hunting accident; some said she was a wealthy widow, for she wore real gold-hoop earrings and expensive rouge, which made her look like an old gypsy. But what people envied most was her cavernous bearskin coat. It was huge as a mountain man and she joked that it was like wearing her husband to church. It didn't seem strange to me that Mrs. Ashworth equated her thick, black bearskin coat with a lifelong mate. I'd seen pictures in her wallet of her husband and he did look like a bear, with luxurious tufts of black hair from the top of his head to his fuzzy arms. My own father wasn't as furry as Mr. Ashworth, but then my father limited his hunting to moose, elk, and the like. Maybe to hunt a bear, I reasoned with my child's logic, a man had to somehow be recognized as bear-kin. Then the bear would let the man close enough to shoot or wrestle or embrace in a bear attack.

My father had long ago taught me what to do if I met a bear in the woods: raise myself up to my full child's height, wave my hands above my head to look taller and fiercer, and scream out, "I'm a human being! I'm a predator, too. I'm as big as you!" Sometimes when we camped or hiked we'd tie silverware to our mess kits and that percussive clang and clatter let the bears know it was our turn on the trail.

One year, camping in Glacier National Park with my grandmother, we'd had our first close grizzly bear encounter. My three siblings and I had seen grizzlies only at Forest Service dumps, where we'd watched from a safe distance. But the past winter had been especially cold and the ravenous bears coming out of hibernation coincided with our spring camping.

That May morning while my parents and Uncle Clark were hunting for kindling to start a breakfast fire, Grandmother Elsie laid out a picnic table with fresh bread, thick bacon, campfire skillet–blackened scrambled eggs, and her famous homemade apple butter. Grandmother's apple butter, along with her recipes for Wolverman's relish, chowchow chopped pickles, black-walnut divinity, and cherry fudge, was her finest legacy. My grandfather even had a word for Grandmother's culinary delights: "larrapin" he called these delicious foods. And we did lap up Grandmother's cooking, especially the luscious, darkly sweet and tart apple butter, which had the slow consistency of molasses with succulent chunks of bright apple flesh and skin.

This homemade jam brought us kids to the wooden picnic table more surely than any breakfast call, for although we were all finicky eaters, we followed our noses to Grandmother's apple butter the moment we heard the whoosh and pop of the Bell jar wax break open. Other noses must have quivered at the scent of such a sweet treasure, too, because while we kids were saying grace with our eyes open, heads bowed over the apple butter, I saw a big blurry shape out of the corner of one eye: a gigantic grizzly bear was raised up on hind legs and lumbering toward us while we said grace.

Not one of us did what we had been so carefully taught by our forester-hunter father. At least we did not cower. We froze like possum in the glare of flashlights, standing absolutely still in the presence of such absolute animal power. This grizzly was so splendid in his reddish-black shaggy fur and paws the size of my little brother's head. We were more awestruck than afraid. Our paralysis was as ancient as if our reptilian brains had memorized this image: giant bears hovering over barely human beings. There was no talking to this creature, no bargaining or boisterous argument about sharing top predator status. We were in thrall and insignificant to this big bear. Eerily human-like, he walked on strong back legs toward our table. He did not roar, perhaps appreciating our sudden silence while Grandmother continued grace. I remember clearly being impressed by the bear's black, sniffing nose raised high with a surprising delicacy, as if this bear, too, understood the joy of homemade jam.

I also remember the familiarity and fascination I felt for this grizzly's great body. I'd slept as a child with Smokey Bear and still had a collection of stuffed animals in my bed. As my father later rose through the ranks to at last become chief of the U.S. Forest Service, people would give him Smokey Bear memorabilia—from hats to carvings to a huge painting of Smokey Bear with a shovel in one giant paw and a Bible upraised in the other. In this painting, Smokey wore blue overalls, belt, and hat as in all the official Forest Service posters, but his face was the familiar, round, half-bear, half-human face of my own father.

That morning in Glacier National Forest as a grizzly lumbered toward Grandmother's apple butter, it did not seem odd to feel complete reverence. Smokey had lived in my crib, in my first forest, and now he was coming to breakfast when we called him by saying grace. That was my child's logic, and it made more sense than trying to pretend I was as tall and as fierce as this gigantic grizzly hovering above us. It was my grandmother who lifted her head after a firm "Amen" arid shook her finger defiantly at the bear.

"You! Shoooo!" she yelled at him as if he were one of her grandchildren stealing her apple butter. Grandmother was so possessive of her recipe that she hadn't even passed it on to my mother. She was darned if she would share her jam with a bear. "Shooo, shooo, shooo!" With each admonishment, Grandmother flapped her flowered apron at the bear. She was about half the size of the grizzly, but her fierceness was impressive. "This is my last batch of apple butter," she argued with the bear, "and it's not going to be gobbled down by any big bear! Go on with you now! Git!"

I closed my eyes then, expecting the bear to decapitate my grandmother with one massive blow from those paws whose claws seemed huge as rakes. Poised over my grandmother and her jam, the grizzly gave one last, almost longing sniff and then, with a huge harrumph and sigh, turned around and fell down on all fours. The grizzly did not run away, but strolled pigeon-toed nearby and shook his massive head back and forth. I wondered if we had hurt the grizzly's feelings by not sharing our sweets.

None of us, including my grandmother, felt endangered in the presence of that mighty grizzly, who now slowly lumbered a distance from our picnic table. In fact, we didn't say much about it, just dived into the apple butter with our own animal hunger. It wasn't until Uncle Clark came back, waving his arms and telling us to hide under the picnic table from the grizzly, that it occurred to us we were in grave danger.

"You can bet that bear didn't get my apple butter, by gum." Grandmother came the closest to swearing that I'd ever witnessed.

Uncle Clark stared at his mother in disbelief, then turned pale as we told him about grandmother's flapping apron. He quickly packed us into the station wagon so fast we didn't get to finish eating. As we waited in the car for my parents to return, I looked back and saw several grizzlies turn the picnic table upside down, licking the wood where I'd spilled some jam. I was very pleased to see that the bears had at least gotten a taste of Grandmother's glory.

Later in that Glacier Park trip, we pulled up to another campground at night and saw grizzly bears banging trash can lids against trees and crushing the metal containers like soda-pop cans. It was very dark, and when my mother saw the grizzlies she complained of a migraine, so

I had to sleep in the tent with my father while all around bears crashed through the forest.

"They won't eat much," my father joked. "Just as long as we keep all the food in the car and not the tent." All day he'd been teasing me about eating M&M's on camping trips. "The bears will sniff that sweet chocolate smeared all over your mouth and they'll chew your lips off," he warned me.

Now I *was* frightened of bears, and I suppose that had been my father's intention—to instill a little terror in his children, who during the breakfast incident had seemed much too open and curious about these other creatures. "It's *good* to be afraid of bears," he'd said. "Smokey Bear is different. He's tame. These grizzlies are *wild* animals and they'd just as soon tear your heart out as look at you." He said this so cheerfully, I knew he was happy to have taught us healthy fear. "Sometimes people who don't know any better worship animals," he'd say. "Why, just until recently in Japan people were worshipping monkeys. And in India they have sacred cows and elephants."

This did not seem to me like such a wrongheaded instinct. If wonder and reverence inspired human worship, what child wouldn't feel a spiritual instinct toward such animal power? Awe and terror of an animal's divinity were absolutely real to me as I lay awake at night in the tent while the monster-shadows of grizzlies danced in silhouette around our campfire. My father snored contentedly in his sleeping bag while I lay wide awake worried about my lips being chewed off by a grizzly who smelled the sweet, telltale scent of M&M's.

I wanted to wake my father and ask, *Did Smokey ever attack children who ate chocolate? Why didn't we ever say grace to thank the animals we ate for supper for our survival?* I did wake my father up, but not with these questions. I awakened him after watching those grizzlies rear up on their hind legs and move together in bear embraces like giant dance partners. These bears had no interest in me. They were caught up in something bigger than me, maybe even bigger than themselves. Even I, who had been raised in a Southern Baptist Church that forswore dancing and drinking—even I recognized what my early primate ancestors must have witnessed when they came upon bears dancing in the woods.

Here was some kind of ceremony, maybe even an animal way of worship. The grizzlies were no longer banging trashcans, they were raising their shaggy heads and paws as if to greet the tall, ancient trees. They were circling around each other making pleasurable snorts and harrumphs like some kind of bear-song or celebration. I recognized a power and primitive joy that I rarely saw in humans, even in church when they sang the fast, military songs of salvation. I'd witnessed my mother's capacity for this rapture when she played her ragtime piano; I'd seen my father actually leap and shout when he'd brought down a stately elk on a hunting trip; and I'd seen siblings and friends my age do circle dances in snow or autumn leaves out of sheer pleasure. But I'd never seen animal ecstasy of this magnitude before and I will never forget its growling, physical happiness.

"Dad, do you think a bear would really kill us while we were praying?" I whispered. "Don't you think the bear would know we were talking to God?"

My father tossed about in his sleeping bag and unzipped it as if he were burning alive. This was exactly the kind of question he loathed. He never enjoyed philosophical dialogues, preferring the practical and reasonable realms of what he called "good horse sense." "Listen, you don't waste time wondering what's on a grizzly's mind! If you are bowing your head or you go down on your knees—it doesn't matter if you're praying or scared stiff—the grizzly will think you're dead and come investigate what he believes another animal has killed and left for him. But if you stand up and wave your hands and scream out that you're a human and his equal, he'll think twice before he attacks. Now, that's that. Go to sleep."

"But I'm not as big as a bear. I'm not his equal no matter how much I flap my arms. Grandma could do it because she's bigger and besides, it was her last batch of apple butter. Even a bear could understand that."

"Bears are not as smart as human beings," my father said wearily. "They don't have minds and souls like you and I. They're just animals and we have to respect them. But that's it. Don't go giving them what belongs to human beings."

"If animals don't have souls," I asked, "why do you put a slice of apple and a pine sprig in the dead doe's mouth after you've killed her for us? Isn't that so the deer can find her way back to earth in afterlife?"

My exasperated father threw up his arms. "Oh, honey, don't attach any spiritual significance to it. It's just something I learned from my own father and some other hunters I grew up with. More like respect."

I was very confused, as usual, whenever my father told me things that seemed at odds with his actions. Like the way he hoarded his animal skins as if they were more precious than money. Every Christmas Eve we were given carefully measured-out pieces of deer or elk skin to make moccasins for the New Year. And he never parted with his animal trophies, which adorned every fireplace like shrines in every one of our houses. In fact, the only falling out my father ever had with a friend was over a magnificent pair of moose antlers that one of his hunting buddies tried to claim for his own mantel. If this behavior didn't show some signs of spiritual practice and worship in my father, what did? Certainly not his calm and practical calculations of the church budgets or the chores of pulpit and finance committees that his status as deacon required of him.

Unlike my mother, who played the church organ and piano like a crazed saint—her upbeat tempo and enthusiasm so high-spirited they'd had to put potted plants in front of her to keep her zeal from distracting the whole church—I'd never seen my father inspired by church service or a minister's sermons. He never sang out "Hallelujah" or "Amen, brother!" like some of the other fundamentalists. The only time I'd ever seen my father really guffaw or give out belly-laughs was telling his hunting-buddy stories, and the only times I ever saw him truly happy and caught up in something obviously greater than himself was first when he was in the forest and later when he'd come home from the office and tend to his Tennessee Walker horses. The first time I'd seen my father cry was when his mother passed away. Decades later in Virginia, my father would weep for the second time when his favorite filly—the one he'd helped midwife—lay down in the snowy pasture and couldn't stand up again. My father would weep when he told me how he'd pleaded with Starlight to get up on her trembling legs, and when he saw she couldn't anymore because of her degenerative spinal disease, he'd called the vet and put her down because she was already so far down on the frozen ground.

But that night in Glacier National Park my father's favorite filly had not died; she had not yet even been born. That night I would ask the question that decades later I would know enough not to ask when Starlight died: "Do you think animals go to heaven? When you kill animals, Daddy, don't they go to heaven with us?"

"They go to sleep," he mumbled grumpily by way of giving up this midnight conversation. "Bears don't go to heaven. But they do hibernate in the winter and then in the spring they keep us awake nights with all this racket. They're not dancing, they're not in heaven. They're just—well, maybe they're playing, like you do." He reached over a paw to pat me on the head, then said groggily, "You go to sleep now. That would be some kind of heaven for me."

18

Parents without Children: Confessions of a Favorite Uncle

Robert Michael Pyle

In my father's latter working years, single and still involved with my younger brother's well-being, he joined an organization called Parents Without Partners. He wasn't the first single parent in my family. All my grandparents, both his folks and my mother's, had been divorced in the 1920s, when broken families were rare. After my own parents divorced when I was ten, I lived with my father at first and then with my mother through junior high and high school. Unpartnered parenting was the norm in my family long before it became a common social pattern. I don't know whether that fractured background has anything to do with the fact that of my parents' four offspring, only one has had children of his own. For my part, I have come to think of myself as a parent without children.

Not that I made a conscious decision not to reproduce. On the contrary, I imagined bringing forth children who would benefit from what I had learned from my own scattered but diverse family. Of course, I envisioned children made much in my own mold, living rich childhoods bathed in nature, allowing me to relive my own early enchantments but with specific improvements—such as an intact family.

Nor have I lacked the circumstances for potential parenthood. Thrice blessed in marriage, I found in the first union that our ages, economics, college, and jobs militated against early childbearing. Far-flung travel, career hopes, and financial uncertainty put off pregnancy in my second marriage. Our irresolution saved me from perpetuating the family pattern for a third generation, and the great women involved went on to become mothers of great children. When Thea and I married, we too considered procreating, but she already had children and quite rightly wasn't sure she wanted to do it all over again just as her life was opening out. My reasons, by then largely sensual and sentimental, were insufficient for creating a new life with an ambivalent partner while in the midst of an overstuffed, uninsured, half-spent life.

So I cannot say that my lack of biological children was the clear result of an ethical decision not to reproduce, such as the one announced by conservation writer Stephanie Mills in her famous 1969 college commencement speech at Mills College. Even so, influenced (like Stephanie) by Paul Ehrlich's *Population Bomb*, I decided that none of us had any business doing more than replacing ourselves. I admire Paul and Ann Ehrlich's symbolic withholding of baby presents after the second child, and as they do, I believe that our estate is at urgent risk, in Waylon Jennings's words, "under the weight of the whole human race." So I felt fine, as a citizen of the ecosystem, having kept my genes to myself.

Still, a shade of regret must chill most of the childless from time to time. To see one's genes, mixmastered through meiosis with those of your loved one, expressed in the eyes and face and mind and toes of a baby; to experience the unmatched exultation that parents must feel when their own children jump into their arms for a hug or onto their laps for a story; to aid another life as only a parent can—these are large and real desires only poorly mitigated by the relief of not exposing one more child to the modern malaise or oneself to the fears and heartbreak that go along with the joys of parenthood. Yet no one remotely open to the immatures of the species can remain aloof from their gifts, their needs, their futures. So while largely reconciled to my role as one of this world's uncles, I find myself asking from time to time not only what I gain as a parent without children but what I can give to young I have not helped to conceive.

When I am afield with kids, on butterfly walks or hikes with their folks or just knocking about where families are likely to be encountered, I frequently receive a kind compliment from the adults. It used to go, "You'll be a great parent." As my beard became increasingly grizzled, the subjective gradually took over: "you'd make a great dad." Well, maybe and maybe not. If I were top-drawer dad material, making children might have been a higher priority than the things I have done instead. I think that what these parents are really reacting to is not only my genuine interest in their children and how they perceive the natural world but also the freshness that I, as a nonparent, can bring to the enterprise of taking in the world with children. In fact, my appetite for teaching and learning with kids is pretty finite; they wear me out. But in modest spurts, as ranger, teacher, friend, uncle, and finally stepfather and grandfather, I have been privileged to go afield with many other people's kids, giving their parents a little relief from the constant questions while giving the young 'uns the benefit of my unjaded enthusiasm. It should go without saying that, up to a point (when I can go home, kidless), the pleasure has been mine.

This has been especially true of my own blood kin. I have one niece, Heather, and one nephew, Michael. Their father, my older brother, Tom, once told me that he could not imagine my ever settling down to have children. "Then it's a good thing *you* have," I told him. And it is true. Tom and Mary furnished these great kids for all of us, is how my other brother and sister and I see it. Geography limits our visits, but whenever I can, I take full advantage of my collateral kids. When Heather and I walked up and down her neighborhood streets in Colorado Springs looking for the serpentoid caterpillars of two-tailed tiger swallowtails on green ash shade trees, and when she wrote to tell me about the black swallowtail larvae whose mothers had found the dill in her garden, I felt every bit of the buzz that parents must experience when passing on the details of the world beyond the back door, in any culture. When Mike accompanied me to a National Wildlife Federation Conservation Summit (a family natural history camp where I was teaching), broadening the bounds of his universe by a bit, I knew something of the sense of continuity that the elders know in passing on the secrets of the vision quest. I flatter myself that they will remember these days too; and as I watched them complete their formal educations, Heather in landscape architecture and Michael in the arts, I liked to think I made a contribution to these important people— small, but different from the daily donations their parents make to their lives. And when Heather married Pete and had children of her own, I became a great-uncle. When Grant and Jarrod showed me around their special fort, a cool crevice among pink granite boulders on the family cabin site north of Pikes Peak, I was able to tell them how their dad and I made do with dens among dirt mounds and cottonwood thickets beside a ditch on the high plains.

I have never heard of a culture in which uncles and aunts are not accorded important roles in child development. These roles extend to highly stylized and vital kinship patterns in certain clan systems, as any perusal of Franz Boas or Margaret Mead shows. Such a function goes well beyond the genetics of actual siblings of the parents. The ability to perform an avuncular part in the lives of the next generation lies in all of us who, free of the demands of parenthood ourselves, have the leisure, the energy, the experience, and the desire to influence positively the lives of other people's children. This fact was driven home to me by the entries for an essay contest sponsored recently by my rural Grange. The subject was community and rural life, and we were looking for personal responses.

Some of the most striking essays came from boys whose fathers, uncles, and their bachelor friends had apprenticed them in the ways of logging, fishing, hunting, and country life and from two girls who spoke fondly of the women in their church who had provided a circle of aunties to pass on the stories, skills, and lifeways of their Finnish immigrant community. Reading these loving, earnest pieces, I felt as if I'd stepped back in time, but these were contemporary kids with computers and cars. Their ways of life might change as old livelihoods pass, and they might leave, but they will remember their grown-up guides when their own chance comes.

No one should be surprised that childless adults bring much that is good to the world by virtue of their freedom from parental responsibility and their concomitant energy, expendable income, and time. Many of our finest artists, writers, and social activists have borne great works from their intellects instead of children from their loins. The greater surprise is that many other creative persons have done both. Yet scarcely a generation has passed since young couples who chose not to bear children got nothing but grief, not only from parents eager for grandchildren but from society at large. This is still true in communities and creeds where childbearing is next to godliness or where family planning is suspect. But by now, when reproduction as a virtue in itself has become distinctly questionable in ecological terms and same-sex marriage is increasingly accepted as a love option in a world that desperately needs more love more than more people, the choice not to replace oneself can be seen as heroic rather than anomalous.

Opportunities for expression, personal development, and social participation clearly arise from the relative freedom that childlessness affords. Beyond these, I find myself asking what are the *responsibilities* of the nonparent? Aside from the obvious answers of providing relief, assistance, and moral support to the sainted parents, the best thing we can do (it seems to me) is to serve as vessels for the transmission of wisdom. While this role is terribly important in every area of civil and cultural life, it is nowhere more timely than in the passing on of natural lore. Books, TV, Twitter, Google Earth, environmental ed. classes, and family vacations in national parks are all very fine. But there is no substitute for an elder who has been out there, knows a thing or two from direct experience, and is willing to share hard-earned knowledge with receptive and curious young minds.

Among the people who served this role in my life, I picture a spinster teacher or two, some gifted gardeners and bachelor lepidopterists, and my Great-aunt Helen, who was a sturdy five foot six in pants and pumps, with high cheekbones hoisting her bright smile, and an intelligent forehead broad beneath the gray nimbus of her perm. Of course, my mentors included my parents and grandparents, den mothers, the fathers of friends, teachers, and other reproducers. But of the ones who really had time for me, not a few had no children of their own—like Aunt Helen.

I don't see such people as nonparents but as parents without children. Smart phones may be wonderfully interactive, but they are not interactive with the *world*. Not, in any case, as Aunt Helen was. Whenever she took me into the Front Range west of Denver to explore granite chasms, up to heavenly Boreas Pass that once had been "ours," or just across from her Seventeenth Avenue apartment into Denver's City Park, I had her full attention. I had the benefit of her knowledge, experience, history, wit, and lore, freely offered up as perhaps only the dead-end elders can do. In this way, the dead end of mere genetics was short-circuited. I carry something of Aunt Helen and her all-encompassing love of the universe just as certainly as if it had been balled up in a double-dominant allele and passed to me in traditional gametic union, as it was from her sister, my grandmother Grace.

In *The Geography of Childhood*, the book he coauthored with Gary Nabhan, Steven Trimble wrote, "As parents, our job is to pay attention, to create possibilities—to be careful matchmakers between our children and the earth." I agree abundantly and would add that perhaps our job as parents without children is to augment those possibilities in ways that mothers and fathers might less easily be able to do by the very nature of their demanding role and sacrifice.

I have found, for example, that children sometimes show a special receptiveness toward grown-ups other than their parents. As novel personages free of the disciplinarian's burden, we may have open access to a child's enthusiasm that his or her parent might be denied. Three times one spring, young Tyler came along on my butterfly classes. Robert, his father, was his good buddy, and he participated as well. I wouldn't think to butt into their outdoor idyll together. Yet the different dynamic Tyler forged with me—precisely because I wasn't his father—brought something to the forays that each of us could appreciate. When, too few years later, Tyler found himself in Fallujah as a Marine, catching some sanity along with the few butterflies in the compound with a hand-fashioned net, and later, home safe, pursuing further studies and a career in wildlife, I like to imagine that his butterfly-uncle had helped him out a little bit.

This power of the nonparent is an evanescent quality that wears thin with familiarity, but it can be a marvelous entrée while it lasts—the stock in trade of nannies, aunties, and favorite uncles everywhere. Friends acting in loco parentis, if only momentarily, can help prevent "parent burnout." When Thea and I went afield with our friends Ed and Cathy, we borrowed Gavin long enough to give his parents time to key out a plant or poke about while we enjoyed the lad's fascination with a frog or a swallowtail. Something was exchanged, all around. Now, working on the oyster beds of Willapa Bay, Gavin might recall those days outdoors with family friends from time to time.

Contemporary recombinations of old family patterns permit many variations on the standard types of adult role models. In addition to a growing array of avuncular sorts, children nowadays often have access to more than four grandparents, and the child without at least one stepparent is becoming the exception. I had a stepmother when they were rare outside fairy tales. Stressed by the usual fault lines that mixed families often suffer, ours was not an altogether happy blend. But Pat and her family had a cabin in Crested Butte, Colorado, where they routinely took cool vacations from the flatlands. Suddenly I found myself pitched into a big family with its own rituals and was shy and resentful at first. But Pat's dad, a white-haired, genial teacher, made a new grandpa for me, and her several sisters furnished a flock of friendly and encouraging aunts. That flowery mountain paradise happened to be situated near the Rocky Mountain Biological Laboratory. Out fishing with Dad one day, I drifted off with my butterfly net and by chance met university lepidopterists who were to become major mentors for life. In spite of my attitude, I came out much richer in adult guides for having been a stepkid.

Twenty-five years ago, the question of stepparents came to have immediate meaning to me again, as I became one. When Thea and I were married, Tom and Dory came to live with us, giving me a crack at parenting after all. At the wedding, I read a sonnet for my new family. As John Donne insisted, "He is a fool which cannot make one sonnet, and he is mad which makes two." So I wrote one, celebrating this gift that came to me whole cloth deep in middle age. One line read, "Having no children, I'll not be childless."

They already had a good dad, so Tom and Dory did not need another. Since I did not have to try to become their father, I was free to be a different kind of adult in their lives. We hunted tree frogs for their terrarium and poked among ruins of old cannery villages above the Columbia. They too came to National Wildlife Summits with us for several years in several states, once involving an 8,000-mile cross-country trek by train. Though they came from a family that was already oriented to the out-of-doors, I was able to furnish some experiences they might not otherwise have enjoyed.

These days, visiting Tom in his Mexican village home or looking over Dory's shoulder as she juggles motherhood and career in Portland, I am guilty of a parent's pride. The sentiment of my sonnet was borne out richly. And now they have brought their own kids into the mix. A recent Fourth of July expedition to Mount St. Helens included Tom and Iliana's children, David and Cristina, just before they moved to Jalisco, and Dory and Jeb's little boy, Francis. At the meadow where we picnicked, I put nets into their hands, and we all chased off after summer ringlets, Francis scrambling gamely through the grass and thistles to keep up with his older cousins. When they all come to our old Swedish homestead together, and we throw Frisbees for our stepdogs and have snowball fights with snowball-bush flowerheads in June or rake up and leap into leaf piles in the fall, I am every bit as thrilled as Thea to be their grandparent. Step-grandchildren don't give a darn about genetics when it comes to love, a lap, and a book—or a butterfly net out-of-doors. It's all just more grandparents to them and more fun. The fact that we without children can yet have grandchildren is a grace note in our lives and, I hope, in the lives of those children abundantly blessed with elders.

The trend toward what used to be called "barren unions" can only accelerate, as acceptance of alternative lifestyles and human population pressures rise. More couples will decide that they prefer the rewards of life without offspring or that they cannot afford to raise children. Others, like Stephanie Mills, will declare their unwillingness to further populate the planet, still others will decline to introduce children to such a world as this, no matter how much they would like to be parents. Yet this must not be seen as an unmitigated tragedy. As the uncles and aunties of the world increase, so meaningful contact grows between children and adults other than their parents, enriching lives all around. We may finally come to see unions that produce no young as anything but barren. For same-sex couples and unmated individuals who may be denied some traditional satisfactions, the rewards from coparenting the young of the species will become more and more profound.

Frustration of the biological imperative to breed need not (and for our ultimate survival, must not) be a baleful thing. We can be progenitors outside the genetic loop, ancestors who have escaped the helix—parents without children. Though we may never join the great biological parade, we walk alongside, at our own pace, responsible yet for young lives beyond our own.

19

Raising Silas

Janisse Ray

Between West Green and Broxton, Georgia, a giant cedar tree alone covers a corner of Lone Hill Methodist Church Cemetery like a misshapen green archangel. It is the national champion of Southern red cedars.

The tree is a forest unto itself. Beneath its branches is deep cool. Resurrection fern, growing hairlike on sun-touched limbs and along much of the trunk, withers in drought but after a rain revives, each fern leaf vibrantly green and erect. Walking up to the cedar is like coming side-on to a wooly mammoth. Where the fern does not grow, the tree is finely shaggy in the habit of ancient cedars. Some of its limbs touch the ground, and the tree covers close to 100 feet. Tribes of animals could live in the tree, oak snakes and squirrels and cedar waxwings. And although the tree is full of life, it lives among the dead. I wanted Silas to see it.

Silas and I spent three days in Tallahassee, where we used to live. For two days, nine-year-old Silas played with buddies while I worked freelance for a magazine there, and the third day, New Year's, we visited friends.

In three days, Silas watched a total of six movies. He played hour upon hour of computer games and celebrated his friend's birthday at a video game restaurant for young people. New Year's Eve, he and three of his young friends had a slumber party and stayed up until 2 a.m., the first time ever I went to bed before him. He used his twelve-dollar savings to buy two new action figures.

When it came time to drive the four hours home, back to Georgia, he was jumping with neighborhood kids on my friend's trampoline. "I'm not going," he said flatly. I kept loading the truck, strategizing. On the farm we have nature, slow in its revealing, and solitude. How could those compete with a neighborhood of children? Should we stay another night?

I looked up once from organizing the truck—we'd bought supplies we couldn't get in Baxley—to see a neighbor boy named Derek, three years older, push Silas down on the trampoline. When Silas rose, protesting, the boy tripped him.

"Silas," I called, straightening out of the truck, "you're welcome to fight back." The children instantly snapped their attention toward me. Had I said what they thought they heard?

"You're welcome to whip his butt," I called. The children looked at me, wide eyed and solemn, trying to understand.

"I don't believe in violence," I said, "but I don't think anybody should push someone else around."

"Mom," Silas said in a don't-be-ridiculous voice. "I couldn't beat him. He's bigger than me."

"Maybe not," I said, "but you're welcome to try."

I went back in for a bag, and when I emerged, my ridiculous suggestion had somehow worked to ease the bullying. Another child, Kevin, whom Silas had known since he was a baby, had challenged Silas in fun and they were tangled good-naturedly on the trampoline, Kevin on top.

"Hump him, hump him," said a bigger girl, pushing Kevin's butt up and down.

Those words made Kevin mad, and he went at Silas with fury, locking his head and forcing it repeatedly forward into the canvas. I thought he'd break Silas's neck.

"Silas, time to go," I called calmly. "Tell everybody good-bye."

This time he didn't hesitate.

Their world, my world. This boy, my son. I so wanted him to be a child of stars and dirt, not jiggering images of aliens and laser guns. Town life was enticing, with its toy stores and theaters and malls. Among those: four-lane highways, intense development, crime, high rent, traffic, people moving fast. To think in terms of city versus country, pitting lifestyles rather than social mores, is illogical, but I have a childhood mapped out for Silas that doesn't revolve around electronic entertainment and a culture hyped on sex and money. Still, I know child rearing is more complex than that.

I remembered a night back in Georgia, after school let out for the Christmas holiday.

"Who can I ask to come over tomorrow?" Silas asked from a full bathtub.

"Chris?"

"He won't come." Chris didn't like to leave his family room with its two TVs, both going, one hooked to a movie and the other to Nintendo.

"Jesse?"

"No way."

Jesse bored Silas. His Christmas present was a Bible, and even at nine he was very devout. "He does everything I tell him to," Silas said. "There's never anything he decides to do."

"Seth?"

"He hits me and doesn't stop when I say 'Stop.' "

Once I was talking to Sandy West, an octogenarian friend who lives on Ossabaw Island, off the coast of Georgia, about young people growing up now. Ossabaw is undeveloped; Sandy inherited the island and sold it to the state at a reduced cost in order to preserve it forever. For all her life Sandy has shared an entire wild, glorious barren island with osprey, alligator, and wild hog. She worries that because of overpopulation, our young people will never know privacy, that they will always have to be entertained. Sandy worries that fewer young people know the smell of a book or the feel of one. "I feel about books as if I were a drunk," she said. But the real tragedy by far, Sandy believes, is their loss of a relationship with the natural world.

"They have never known total darkness or total stillness," she said.

Sometimes in the country I think I am depriving Silas, saying no too often, trying to push back something bigger than all of us, something that has brainwashed us. I am the mother with one finger in the dike, holding back glitz and materialism and sex hype. The tribe is gone—Silas has no swarm of cousins (there are two), no great-grandmother rocking by the fireplace. What we trade to live on the farm is a soccer team, art lessons, the coffee shop in Montana where we ordered hot cocoa and cranberry bagels after school, snowboarding, skate parks, festivals, natural history museums.

One day Silas went home after school with his friend Clint while I paddled Ebenezer Creek near Savannah with friends. I saw prothonotary warblers, solitary sandpipers, coots, white ibises, great egrets, little blue herons. A few cypresses were so big we could back our kayaks inside to take pictures. I glimpsed the tail of a snake as it disappeared into a hollow tupelo, and where we stopped for lunch, a tiny treefrog with peach and green markings. Afterward, when I picked up Silas early evening, he began to cry.

"I don't want to go home," he said.

"Baby, it's a school day tomorrow. You can't spend the night with a friend on a school night."

"I mean I don't want to go at all," he wept. "I don't like that house. It's too big and lonely and just me and you there."

"I know," I said.

"It's time to leave here."

"What do you mean?"

"It's time to leave Georgia. I want to go back to Missoula, or Tallahassee, or anywhere. I mean, I want to leave tomorrow."

"We can't do that."

"And you never do anything with me. You pitched the baseball until I hit it and then you left. You're always doing something else."

"I'm sorry. I'm busy a lot."

"I don't even mind leaving my friends here. I just want to go. You can't imagine the fun I have with my dad in Vermont. They don't have the rules like here." He didn't mean his father's house, he meant the place in general, that the people there had fewer rules.

"Honey, what are you needing that you don't have here?" I asked this question thinking that maybe something in particular was wrong, and I could go out of my way to fix that. Did he need more friends? Different friends? Did he need soccer? We could drive to Savannah, if that's what it took to find a soccer league.

"What's wrong with it here?" I asked again.

Through his tears, he said a line astounding in its profundity, a sentence I turned over and over in my mind. "Here there is no imagination," he said. I remembered it vividly the next summer when I heard Barry Lopez say, "Fundamentalism in any form is the sign of a failed imagination."

I don't dare wonder aloud whether we can make it, whether I will be able to piece an existence for him—before he is grown, his childhood gone—where the world is whole and in tune with the essence of life. But I will not give up.

I took a different route home from Tallahassee, up through Douglas, so I could pass Lone Hill Cemetery. As we rode along, we exchanged a candy called an atomic fireball back and forth. When the ball of candy got too spicy for Silas, he handed it to me, and I sucked on it awhile. Sometimes we had to hold it in our fingers.

Near Pavo, we passed a plowed cornfield that looked as if it were covered by a black wool blanket—but then the edge of the blanket lifted into the air. It was a throng of birds—thousands of red-winged blackbirds. We pulled off the road. A rafter at a time, the birds rose, flew across the highway, then rebounded, stringing between two fields. Shifting, they shaped themselves into shimmering optical illusions, like the changing patterns of a computer screensaver. At one point they arched over us like an umbrella or a mosquito net. It was an exaltation of birds. They pivoted and hovered and sifted, their red wing-patches flashing in the gray day.

"Come home," they sang.

The day was almost done when we reached the cemetery. "Why are you stopping here?" Silas asked.

"To show you that tree over there. Let's walk over."

"Walk all the way over there?"

"Yeah. Four miles is a long way to walk," I teased. The tree was not 100 feet away, across rows of graves. A sign in the cemetery proclaimed, "Thou Shalt Not Litter."

"Mom, why are you always bringing me to graveyards?"

"I'm showing you a tree. This is a national champion red cedar. It's the biggest red cedar tree in the entire country. Look at this. Some of its limbs touch the ground. See this one limb here? The biggest cedar tree I've ever seen was as big as this *limb*."

"Ssssshhh," Silas said. "I hear something."

I hushed. Silas, wearing my big denim coat, looked back over his shoulder. Evening was coming on, the temperature dropping.

"Leaf rattling," I said, and continued. "Here are the graves of an entire family buried beneath the tree. Look at their death dates."

I passed from grave to grave, kneeling at the headstones to feel the weathered granite. The gravestones, though darkened by weather and moss, were yet readable. February 23, 1870, February 19, February 26, February 18.

Intent on the gravestones, I was subtracting in my head to figure out the tragic sequence of events. The silence of the story never fails to tear at me, wanting to be told. "This is the father. He died first. This is the mother beside him. Here's a six-year-old, and an eighteen-year-old."

"Listen," Silas said, turned away. He listened. Then abruptly, "Mama, let's go."

"OK," I said, and twisted back to the tree. "You're a grand old cedar," I said to it.

"Why's it so big?" Silas said, as I paused with my hand on the trunk. "Like, fertilizer?"

"I think it holds the grief of that family. Did you see how they died within days of each other? They died in an epidemic. Yellow fever, someone said."

Silas and I clasped hands as we zigzagged slowly through the graves, back to the warmth of the truck and the remaining hour home.

"Back there I kept hearing noises," he said. "From all directions."

I lowered my voice, said sotto voce, "We better get out of here." I was teasing him. We were in the truck now, cranking up, and safe.

"Mama, don't talk about spirits anymore," he said. "It makes me scared." Upon admitting his panic, he started to cry.

"It's because you believe in them," I said. "I believe in them, too, but they don't scare me."

"Don't talk about it," he said.

"Look at the moon!" Silas yelled when we turned the dirt corner of the farm. It was a gold sickle dangling over the bottomless head that feeds Ten Mile Creek, the road like a slowly closing gate that clicked shut behind us when I pulled into the driveway and cut the engine.

The minute we opened the truck door, our ecstatic unpedigreed dogs were all over us. The headlights showed they'd chewed up more plastic toys and brought deer bones to the yard while we'd been gone. The house was frigid, our breath white.

I unloaded our bags. On his own, Silas wadded newspaper in the fireplace and layered pinecones across strips of fat pine. He struck a match and pretty soon had a warm fire brightening and softening the icy living room.

I was looking at the Christmas tree, still up, and thinking of the evening Silas and I erected it. We had gone walking across the pasture into our own spare woods, looking for a tree, but the pines had longish needles, and they didn't branch. Many-branching was what we needed. So we brought the saw and drove riverward, looking along fencerows and highway right-of-ways, where young trees were doomed, until we ended up where thick electric lines from the nuclear plant cross the county. It was near dark and hunting season had started, so we didn't want to go into the woods. At the edge of the Georgia Power swath, growing hugged into a thirty-foot pine, we found a lovely double-trunked cedar about six feet tall. We took one trunk with only a few strokes of the saw.

We set it in a bucket of rocks filled with water and hung our modest ornaments on it. The room was cold. We made hot cocoa and worked by the fire, then brought our sleeping bags, and before we slept I read aloud for an hour from *The Wind in the Willows.*

There is an unmistakable feeling you get when a day or an evening is perfect. Sometimes it's perfect for one person and not the other, but there's a certain feeling when it's perfect for all present. Silas and I have the same ideas about a good day, and we appreciate one when it comes along. Most days are good, but only a few are perfect. That evening was perfect.

Now, more than a week later, we lounged in front of the fire and the tree again, shelling pecans and talking, until the clock headed toward eleven. Silas rescued a coal-red nail from the embers with a pair of pliers and experimented with it, drilling holes through a plastic milk jug, playing that he was a blacksmith. Before we came here, he wouldn't strike a match, afraid of getting burned. We heated cocoa, and before bed I read more of *The Wind in the Willows.*

The next morning, I looked out across the hoary fields at the tender, rosy light of new day. When I am away, I cannot imagine this place, nor guard it intact in my mind, but when I gaze upon it, I almost choke with love for it. That winter day, the only thing holding up the woodshed was the yen of my heart to see it there another day. The line of grapevines was a tangle of brown sinew since the leaves had loosened their attachments and drifted away. Behind the log outbuildings, the pasture grass stretched frostily to the woods.

Here are the tools Silas needs, I thought. *Fire will make a grown man out of him—the sun's fire, igniting the moon's fire, becoming his fire.*

20

Grandma's *Bawena*

Enrique Salmon

The dark creases and lines on my Grandma's face deepened as she smiled at my eagerness to learn about plant medicine. To my young mind, she seemed the perfect Grandma. Her white hair contrasted with her dark brown skin. The brightness of the sun deepened the wrinkles and creases on her face. She cooked the best cactus fruit jam. She always had cookies around when I came to visit. And she seemed to know everything about the land.

One day in our yard that was dotted with herbs and fruit trees, I watched her bend over to pick a sprig of *bawena*—spearmint—and hold it out for me to smell. Her old faded cotton dress with the flower print outlined her frail eighty-year-old frame. Her full set of teeth glistened as she smiled, watching me enjoy the scent. Then in a voice made scratchy from smoking, she explained, "That is what *bawena* does to your stomach. It makes it smile." I cannot forget the many times when my Grandma or mother rescued my upset stomach with some hot tea of *bawena*. Always, after just one cup, my insides would begin to smile again, ready for more food that I probably shouldn't eat.

I understand now what my Grandma and mother, as well as my grandfather and other family members, were teaching me. They introduced me not only to plant knowledge but also to a frame through which I place myself into my environment and universe. I learned the names of plants, their uses, and their place in Rarámuri culture, philosophy, and cosmology. I understood them to be relatives and living beings with emotions and lives of their own. I learned that they are part of my life as well and that I should always care for them. In short, my family led me into the way of being a Rarámuri—a human being who walks well in the sun.

My grandparents' souls now rest in the Milky Way with the other Rarámuri spirits who have departed this earth. But their lessons live on in my memory. I recall my Grandma's smiling face and her short shuffling gait. If I am ill and drinking a steaming mug of *bawena*, I hear her scratchy voice, describing the uses of other plants from our yard and the land.

The plant knowledge I learned from my family was one aspect of a trove of culturally accumulated ecological knowledge. When my relatives introduced me to individual plants, they also introduced my kinship to the plants and to the land from where they and we emerged. They were introducing me to other relatives. Through this way of knowing, especially with regard to kinship, I realized a comfort and a sense of security that I was bound to everything around me in a reciprocal relationship.

The richest memories of my family are associated with plants. I frequently remember the seasonings my grandmother, mother, and aunts lovingly added to our meals. Epazote, cilantro, salvia, yerba buena, and chile pequin embodied the mural of flavors expressed on the table. These foods were eaten at home but were also central figures at fiestas, weddings, and other gatherings. I recall the many plant-related lessons in my Grandma's herb house. It was a latticed structure filled with hanging dried and living plants. The roof was no longer visible through the layers of vines that draped over the eaves to the ground. On hot days, the interior would be nearly ten degrees cooler than outside. Inside, Grandma ground her herbs for cooking and for medicines on an old *metate*. I would often visit her and enjoy the many scents and aromas. It was during these times that she told me about the lives of plants and their characteristics. She described the relationships plants had with each other. She taught me that the plants were not only plants but were people, too. Some were Rarámuri, while others were Apaches and non-Indians.

When I was older, my grandfather introduced me to plants while we shooed away crows and other critters from the corn, beans, and chilis growing in his large garden. We would sit in the shade under his fruit trees, whittling and enjoying the outside while Grandfather retold short bits of traditional knowledge. From many of my immediate relatives, I gained scores of plant knowledge. It is difficult now to brew a cup of some medicinal herb for myself or for my children without picturing the specific time someone in my family introduced me to that particular remedy.

In most cases, I consumed the remedies as a result of something I should not have eaten. My cousins and I were erstwhile urban wildcrafters. We roamed our communities in constant search of something to do while taking advantage of all the available and free plants to munch. We sucked on a succulent grass with yellow flowers we called lemon grass. Its juices resembled the tartness of real lemons. We found bushes full of red, juicy, and semisweet berries and filled ourselves to capacity. These and other plant foods became our emergency stores for short treks that we imagined were epic adventures. Eventually, we encountered a plant we should not have eaten. Fortunately for us, we were related to wonderful and forgiving herbalists who could come to our stomachs' rescue.

Today, as an ethnobotanist, I realize that plants are one of the many ingredients from nature that are the rudimentary materials of human metaphors, stories, mental spaces, cultural models, language, thought, and traditional ecological knowledge. Humans contemplate their landscape and attempt to express what is seen. Our expressions rely on cultural models that embody unique representations of place and relationships. The representations are verbally expressed in metaphors and prototypes and nonverbally expressed in mental spaces of the local environment. The metaphors and prototypes color the language and discourse and become part of the cultural history that describes how the place was created, how the people arrived, and how the people should sustain their niche in this place. Language and mental operations encode the centuries-old ways of conserving the land and the plants, ensuring the survival of nature and the survival of the culture.

The names for plants are markers of our cultural sensitivity to the ecology of the land and to how our culture has embodied that ecological knowledge into our cognitive workings. In addition, cultural references to plant locations, the best sites for plant harvesting, and cultural history add further evidence of how ecological practices have been shaped by the bioregion.

Traditional ecological knowledge provides a basis for understanding culture and for understanding the influence the bioregion has on the history, social organization, and religious and aesthetic components of culture. From methods of land management to the application of plant medicines, from understanding the properties of small habitat ecologies to the reflection of ecology in their language, they demonstrate a way of knowing that recognizes that their actions as humans affect the entire ecosystem. Divorced from its bioregion, culture loses meaning. The interplay between the people, their minds, and the plants can be revealed only by taking the bioregion into consideration. In this work, the elements of plants, landscape, language, and culture merge. They can exist as separate entities but will coalesce into a kincentric unity.

The Rarámuri homeland is the southeastern flank of the Sierra Madres of Chihuahua, Mexico. For centuries, we have maintained a direct connection and relationship with a rugged mountain range that is perceived as the spine of the earth. In many ways, the mountain range is also the spine of our culture. The land shapes our lives. It is a place where human ecological interactions unfold daily.

These interactions are expressed in the language of the place. The Rarámuri speak of the land as the place of nurturing—*gawi wachi. Gawi* refers to the mountain ridge. *Wa* means to ripen and to help one reach maturity. *Chi* is a derivative of place and a noun ending. Ecological issues dominate our everyday existence. This is because the land is thought of as a kindred relative. The land is an important element in a bioregion filled with interconnecting niches, one of which the Rarámuri occupy.

In *Yellow Woman and Beauty of the Spirit*, Leslie Marmon Silko elegantly expresses how indigenous people in North America know that life is viable only when humans view their surroundings as kin. Their mutual roles are essential to their survival. To many indigenous people, this awareness unfolds after years of listening to and recalling stories from elders about the land. Silko, who is from Laguna pueblo, notes, "I carried with me the feeling I'd acquired from listening to the old stories, that the land all around me was teeming with creatures that were related to human beings and to me."

Silko says that human beings must maintain a complex relationship with "the surrounding natural world if they hope to survive in [it]." To Silko, humans could not have "emerged into this world without the aid of antelope and badger." The sustained living in the arid region of the Southwest could not have been viable without the recognition that humans are "sisters and brothers to the badger, antelope, clay, yucca, and sun." It was not until they reached this recognition that the Laguna people could "emerge."

In simplistic ecological terms, the earth exists as a functioning unit that can be reduced to smaller, self-contained entities referred to as *ecosystems*—self-sufficient communities of interacting organisms and their abiotic environments. Interactions are the commerce of ecosystem functioning. Without the correct mix of essential elements, the ecosystem would collapse. The elements are comprised of the animals, plants, fungi, insects, soil compositions, and chemicals unique to the system. Indigenous cultures of North America include human communities in their cultural equations of interacting ecosystems as one aspect of the complexity of life. The cognitive model of nature among the indigenous people of North America is founded on the perception of the natural elements of land, animals, insects, and plants as relatives. To indigenous people, humans are at an equal standing with the rest of the natural world with whom they are kindred. In addition, indigenous people believe that the complex interactions that result from this relationship enhance and preserve the ecosystem. Indigenous kincentricity with the natural world can also be viewed as an indigenous kincentric ecology.

The Rarámuri believe that we live interdependently with all forms of life. Our spiritual, physical, social, and mental health depends on the ability to live harmoniously with the natural world. Indigenous identity, language, land base, beliefs, and history are personifications of culture that regulate and manifest the health of the human and natural worlds. It is understood that a person who harms the natural world also harms himself.

History, identity, language, land base, and beliefs connect, secure, and regulate the human and nature relationship. Rarámuri history does not remain in a linear past. History is continuous and, more important, contextual. Cultural history includes the origins of humans and nature. Like many cultures, our origins are a result of relationships to animals, plants, and all nature. The Abenaki believe they were created from ash trees. The Lenape tell that humans sprang from a great tree. The Mayans believe they came from corn. The Hopi owe their emergence into this world to a spider, a spruce tree, a pine, and a stalk of reed that were used as ladders through the *sipapu* into the fourth world.

The concepts of identity and language are connected to Rarámuri concepts of self. Words shape thought. Thought is an expression of spirit. Both humans and other life forms are essentially spirit and matter, and both are manifestations of the interdependency of humans and nature. Self-identity is a result of a developed relationship to the environment as it is perceived by the culture. Cultural perception, language, and thought are related to both the land and cultural histories.

To the Rarámuri, beliefs form and explain the relationship. Beliefs help people recognize their links to the natural world and their responsibility to ensure its survival. People are not truly connected to the natural world or to their culture if they do not maintain physical, social, spiritual, and mental health. Together they form the breath of life—*iwigara*. Breath is the matter and energy that the Rarámuri believe moves in all living things. Maintaining a balanced and pure human breath also ensures the purity and health of the breath of the natural world.

With the awareness that one's breath is shared by all surrounding life, that one's cultural emergence was possibly caused by some of the life forms around one's environment, and that one is responsible for a mutual survival, it becomes apparent that all life is related to you. Nature shares a kinship with you and with all humans, as does a family or tribe. A reciprocal relationship has been fostered with the realization that humans affect nature and nature affects humans. This awareness influences Rarámuri interactions with the environment. These interactions and cultural practices of living within a place are manifestations of kincentric ecology. This kincentric awareness fosters a standing metaphor among the Rarámuri that perceives plants as people.

Plant-related expressions encountered in discourse and in ceremonial songs concerning agriculture and plants as humans also reveal those same relationships unfolding into the heart of Rarámuri kincentricity and the cultural application of traditional ecological knowledge. What emerges is that in ceremonial songs kincentricity precipitates from the Rarámuri metaphor that plants are people. The concrete concept of people is mapped onto the more abstract one of plants that can breathe, play, maintain family relationships, and have emotions. With this realization, plants are as important to the Rarámuri as are our nonplant relatives. There is little distinction between our world and that of nonhumans. We all share the same breath. I am the mint tea, the *bawena*, that Grandma used to offer to sooth my ailing.

21

Mountain Music I

Scott Russell Sanders

On a June morning high in the Rocky Mountains of Colorado, snowy peaks rose before me like the promise of a world without grief. A creek brim full of meltwater roiled along to my left, and to my right an aspen grove shimmered with new leaves. Bluebirds darted in and out of holes in the aspen trunks, and butterflies flickered beside every puddle, tasting the succulent mud. Sun glazed the new grass and licked a silver sheen along the boughs of pines.

With all of that to look at, I gazed instead at my son's broad back as he stalked away from me up the trail. Sweat had darkened his gray T-shirt in patches the color of bruises. His shoulders were stiff with anger that would weight his tongue and keep his face turned from me for hours. Anger also made him quicken his stride, gear after gear, until I could no longer keep up. I had forty-nine years on my legs and heart and lungs, while Jesse had only seventeen on his. My left foot ached from old bone breaks and my right knee creaked from recent surgery. Used to breathing among the low, muggy hills of Indiana, I was gasping up here in the alpine air, a mile and a half above sea level. Jesse would not stop, would not even slow down unless I asked; and I was in no mood to ask. So I slumped against a boulder beside the trail and let him rush on ahead.

This day, our first full one in Rocky Mountain National Park, had started out well. I woke at first light, soothed by the roar of a river foaming along one edge of the campground, and looked out from our tent to find half a dozen elk, all cows and calves, grazing so close by that I could see the gleam of their teeth. Just beyond the elk, a pair of ground squirrels loafed at the lip of their burrow, noses twitching. Beyond the squirrels, a ponderosa pine, backlit by sunrise, caught the wind in its ragged limbs. The sky was a blue slate marked only by the curving flight of swallows.

Up to that point, and for several hours more, the day was equally unblemished. Jesse slept on while I sipped coffee and studied maps and soaked in the early light. We made our plans over breakfast without squabbling: walk to Bridal Veil Falls in the morning, raft on the Cache la Poudre River in the afternoon, return to camp in the evening to get ready for backpacking up into Wild Basin the next day. Tomorrow we would be heavily laden, but today we carried only water and snacks, and I felt buoyant as we hiked along Cow Creek toward the waterfall. We talked easily the whole way, joking and teasing, more like good friends than like father and son. Yet even as we sat at the base of the falls, our shoulders touching, the mist of Bridal Veil cooling our skin, we remained father and son, locked in a struggle that I could only partly understand.

For the previous year or so, no matter how long our spells of serenity, Jesse and I had kept falling into quarrels, like victims of malaria breaking out in fever. We might be talking about soccer or supper, about the car keys or the news, and suddenly our voices would begin to clash like swords. I had proposed this trip to the mountains in hopes of discovering the source of that strife. Of course I knew that teenage sons and their fathers are expected to fight, yet I sensed there was a grievance between us that ran deeper than the usual vexations. Jesse was troubled by more than a desire to run his own life, and I was troubled by more than the pain of letting him go. I wished to track our anger to its lair, to find where it hid and fed and grew, and then, if I could not slay the demon, at least I could drag it into the light and call it by name.

The peace between us held until we turned back from the waterfall and began discussing where to camp the following night. Jesse wanted to push on up to Thunder Lake, near eleven thousand feet, and pitch our tent on snow. I wanted to stop a thousand feet lower and sleep on dry dirt.

"We're not equipped for snow," I told him.

"Sure we are. Why do you think I bought a new sleeping bag? Why did I call ahead to reserve snowshoes?"

I suggested that we could hike up from a lower campsite and snow-shoe to his heart's content.

He loosed a snort of disgust. "I can't believe you're wimping out on me, Dad."

"I'm just being sensible."

"You're wimping out. I came here to see the backcountry, and all you want to do is poke around the foothills."

"This isn't wild enough for you?" I waved my arms at the view. "What do you need—avalanches and grizzlies?"

Just then, as we rounded a bend, an elderly couple came shuffling toward us, hunched over walking sticks, white hair jutting from beneath their straw hats. They were followed by three toddling children, each rigged out with tiny backpack and canteen. Jesse and I stood aside to let them pass, returning nods to their cheery hellos.

After they had trooped by, Jesse muttered, "We're in the wilds, huh, Dad? That's why the trail's full of grandparents and kids." Then he quickened his pace until the damp blond curls that dangled below his billed cap were slapping against his neck.

"Is this how it's going to be?" I called after him. "You're going to spoil the trip because I won't agree to camp on snow?"

He turned and glared at me. "You're the one who's spoiling it, you and your hang-ups. You always ruin everything."

With that, he swung his face away and lengthened his stride and rushed on ahead. I watched his rigid shoulders and the bruise-colored patches on the back of his T-shirt until he disappeared beyond a rise. That was when I gave up on chasing him, slumped against a boulder, and sucked at the thin air. Butterflies dallied around my boots and hawks kited on the breeze, but they might have been blips on a screen, and the whole panorama of snowy peaks and shimmering aspens and shining pines might have been cut from cardboard, for all the feeling they stirred in me.

The rocks that give these mountains their name are ancient, nearly a third as old as the earth, but the Rockies themselves are new, having been lifted up only six or seven million years ago, and they were utterly new to me, for I had never seen them before except from airplanes. I had been yearning toward them since I was Jesse's age, had been learning about their natural and human history, the surge of stone and gouge of glaciers, the wandering of hunters and wolves. Drawn to these mountains from the rumpled quilt of fields and forests in the hill country of the Ohio Valley, I was primed for splendor. And yet now that I was here I felt blinkered and numb.

What we call landscape is a stretch of earth overlaid with memory, expectation, and thought. Land is everything that is actually *there*, independent of us; landscape is what we allow in through the doors of perception. My own doors had slammed shut. My quarrel with Jesse changed nothing about the Rockies, but changed everything in my experience of the place. What had seemed glorious and vibrant when we set out that morning now seemed bleak and bare. It was as though anger had drilled a hole in the world and leached the color away.

I was still simmering when I caught up with Jesse at the trail head, where he was leaning against our rented car, arms crossed over his chest, head sunk forward in a sullen pose I knew all too well, eyes hidden beneath the frayed bill of his cap. Having to wait for me to unlock the car had no doubt reminded him of another gripe: I carried the only set of keys. Because he was too young to be covered by the rental company's insurance, I would not let him drive. He had fumed about my decision, interpreting it as proof that I mistrusted him, still thought of him as a child. That earlier scuffle had petered out with him grumbling, "Stupid, stupid. I knew this would happen. Why did I come out here? Why?"

The arguments all ran together, playing over and over in my head as we jounced, too fast, along a rutted gravel road toward the highway. The tires whumped and the small engine whined up hills and down, but the silence inside the car was louder. We had two hours of driving to our rendezvous spot for the rafting trip, and I knew that Jesse could easily clamp his jaw shut for that long, and longer. I glanced over at him from time to time, looking for any sign of detente. His eyes were glass.

We drove. In the depths of Big Thompson Canyon, where the road swerved along a frothy river between sheer rockface and spindly guard-rail, I could bear the silence no longer. "So what are my hang-ups?" I demanded. "How do I ruin everything?"

"You don't want to know," he said.

"I want to know. What is it about me that grates on you?"

I do not pretend to recall the exact words we hurled at one another after my challenge, but I remember the tone and thrust of them, and here is how they have stayed with me:

"You wouldn't understand," he said.

"Try me."

He cut a look at me, shrugged, then stared back through the windshield. "You're just so out of touch."

"With what?"

"With my whole world. You hate everything that's fun. You hate television and movies and video games. You hate my music."

"I like some of your music. I just don't like it loud."

"You hate advertising," he said quickly, rolling now. "You hate billboards and lotteries and developers and logging companies and big corporations. You hate snowmobiles and jet skis. You hate malls and fashions and cars."

"You're still on my case because I won't buy a Jeep?" I said, harking back to another old argument.

"Forget Jeeps. You look at any car and all you think is pollution, traffic, roadside crap. You say fast-food's poisoning our bodies and TV's poisoning our minds. You think the Internet is just another scam for selling stuff. You think business is a conspiracy to rape the earth."

"None of that bothers you?"

"Of course it does. But that's the *world*. That's where we've got to live. It's not going to go away just because you don't approve. What's the good of spitting on it?"

"I don't spit on it. I grieve over it."

He was still for a moment, then resumed quietly. "What's the good of grieving if you can't change anything?"

"Who says you can't change anything?"

"*You* do. Maybe not with your mouth, but with your eyes." Jesse rubbed his own eyes, and the words came out muffled through his cupped palms. "Your view of things is totally dark. It bums me out. You make me feel the planet's dying and people are to blame and nothing can be done about it. There's no room for hope. Maybe you can get by without hope, but I can't. I've got a lot of living still to do. I have to believe there's a way we can get out of this mess. Otherwise what's the point? Why study, why work—why do anything if it's all going to hell?"

That sounded unfair to me, a caricature of my views, and I thought of many sharp replies; yet there was too much truth and too much hurt in what he said for me to fire back an answer. Had I really deprived my son of hope? Was this the deeper grievance—that I had passed on to him, so young, my anguish over the world? Was this what lurked between us, driving us apart, the demon called despair?

"You're right," I finally told him. "Life's meaningless without hope. But I think you're wrong to say I've given up."

"It seems that way to me. As if you think we're doomed."

"No, buddy, I don't think we're doomed. It's just that nearly everything I care about is under assault."

"See, that's what I mean. You're so worried about the fate of the earth, you can't enjoy anything. We come to these mountains and you bring the shadows with you. You've got me seeing nothing but darkness."

Stunned by the force of his words, I could not speak. If my gloom cast a shadow over Creation for my son, then I had failed him. What remedy could there be for such a betrayal?

Through all the shouting and then talking and then the painful hush, our car hugged the swerving road, yet I cannot remember steering. I cannot remember seeing the stony canyon, the white mane of the Big

Thompson whipping along beside us, the oncoming traffic. Somehow we survived our sashay with the river and cruised into a zone of burger joints and car-care emporiums and trinket shops. I realized how often, how relentlessly, I had groused about just this sort of "commercial dreck," and how futile my complaints must have seemed to Jesse.

He was caught between a chorus of voices telling him that the universe was made for us—that the earth is an inexhaustible warehouse, that consumption is the goal of life, that money is the road to delight—and the stubborn voice of his father saying none of this is so. If his father was right, then much of what humans babble every day—in ads and editorials, in sitcoms and song lyrics, in thrillers and market reports and teenage gab—is a monstrous lie. Far more likely that his father was wrong, deluded, perhaps even mad.

We observed an unofficial truce for the rest of the way to the gas station north of Fort Collins, where we met the rafting crew at noon. There had been record rains and snowfall in the Rockies for the previous three months, so every brook and river tumbling down from the mountains was frenzied and fast. When local people heard that we meant to raft the Cache la Poudre in this rough season they frowned and advised against it, recounting stories of broken legs, crushed skulls, deaths. Seeing that we were determined to go, they urged us to settle for the shorter trip that joined the river below the canyon, where the water spread out and calmed down. But Jesse had his heart set on taking the wildest ride available, so we had signed up for the twelve-mile trip through the boulder-strewn canyon.

I was relieved to see that the crowd of twenty or so waiting at the rendezvous point included scrawny kids and rotund parents. If the outfitters were willing to haul such passengers, how risky could the journey be? The sky-blue rafts, stacked on trailers behind yellow vans, looked indestructible. The guides seemed edgy, however, as they told us what to do if we were flung into the river, how to survive a tumble over rocks, how to get out from under a flipped raft, how to drag a flailing comrade back on board.

Jesse stood off by himself and listened to these dire instructions with a sober face. I could see him preparing, gaze focused inward, lips tight, the way he concentrated before taking his place in goal at a soccer game.

When the time came for us to board the vans, he and I turned out to be the only customers for the canyon run; all the others, the reedy kids and puffing parents, were going on the tamer trip. Our raft would be filled out by three sinewy young men, students at Colorado State who were being paid to risk their necks: a guide with a year's experience and two trainees.

The water in Poudre Canyon looked murderous, all spume and standing waves and suckholes and rips. Every cascade, every low bridge, every jumble of boulders reminded the guides of some disaster which they rehearsed with gusto. It was part of their job to crank up the thrill, I knew that, but I also knew from talking with friends that most of the tales were true.

At the launching spot, Jesse and I wriggled into our black wet-suits, cinched tight the orange flotation vests, buckled on white helmets. The sight of my son in that armor sent a blade of anxiety through me again. What if he got hurt? Lord God, what if he were killed?

"Hey, Dad," Jesse called, hoisting a paddle in his fist, "you remember how to use one of these?"

"Seems like I remember teaching *you*," I called back.

He flashed me a grin, the first sign of communion since we had sat with shoulders touching in the mist of Bridal Veil Falls. That one look restored me to my senses, and I felt suddenly the dazzle of sunlight, heard the river's rumble and the fluting of birds, smelled pine sap and wet stone.

One of the trainees, a lithe wisecracker named Harry, would guide our run. "If it gets quiet in back," he announced, "that means I've fallen in and somebody else better take over."

We clambered into the raft—Jesse and I up front, the veteran guide and the other trainee in the middle, Harry in the stern. Each of us hooked one foot under a loop sewn into the rubbery floor, jammed the other foot under a thwart. Before we hit the first rapids, Harry made us practice synchronizing our strokes as he hollered, "Back paddle! Forward paddle! Stop! Left turn! Right turn!" The only other command, he explained, was "Jump!" Hearing that, the paddlers on the side away from some looming boulder or snag were to heave themselves *toward* the obstruction, in order to keep the raft from flipping.

"I know it sounds crazy," said Harry. "But it works. And remember: from now on, if you hear fear in my voice, it's real."

Fear was all I felt over the next few minutes, a bit for myself and a lot for Jesse, as we struck white water and the raft began to buck. Waves slammed against the bow, spray flew, stone whizzed by. A bridge swelled ahead of us, water boiling under the low arches, and Harry shouted, "Duck!" then steered us between the lethal pilings and out the other side into more rapids, where he yelled, "Left turn! Dig hard! Harder!"

He kept barking orders, and soon I was too busy paddling to feel anything except my own muscles pulling against the great writhing muscle of the river. I breathed in as much water as air. The raft spun and dipped and leapt with ungainly grace, sliding through narrow flumes, gliding over rocks, kissing cliffs and bouncing away, yielding to the grip of the current and springing free. Gradually I sank into my body.

The land blurred past. Sandstone bluffs rose steeply along one shore, then the other, then both—hundreds of feet of rock pinching the sky high above into a ribbon of blue. Here and there a terrace opened, revealing a scatter of junipers and scrub cedars, yet before I could spy what else might be growing there it jerked away out of sight. I could tell only that this was dry country, harsh and spare, with dirt the color of scrap iron and gouged by erosion. Every time I tried to fix on a detail, on bird or flower or stone, a shout from Harry yanked me back to the swing of the paddle.

The point of our bucking ride, I realized, was not to *see* the canyon but to survive it. The river was our bronco, our bull, and the land through which it flowed was no more present to us than the rodeo's dusty arena to a whirling cowboy. Haste hid the country, dissolved the landscape, as surely as anger or despair ever did.

"Forward paddle!" Harry shouted. "Give me all you've got! We're coming to the Widow-Maker! Let's hope we come out alive!"

The flooded Poudre, surging through its crooked canyon, was a string of emergencies, each one christened with an ominous name. In a lull between rapids I glanced over at Jesse, and he was beaming. His helmet seemed to strain from the expansive pressure of his smile. I laughed aloud to see him. When he was little I could summon that look of unmixed delight into his face merely by coming home, opening my arms, and calling, "Where's my boy?" In his teenage years, the look had become rare, and it hardly ever had anything to do with me.

"Jump!" Harry shouted.

Before I could react, Jesse lunged at me and landed heavily, and the raft bulged over a boulder, nearly tipping, then righted itself and plunged on downstream.

"Good job!" Harry crowed. "That was a close one."

Jesse scrambled back to his post. "You okay?" he asked.

"Sure," I answered. "How about you?"

"Great," he said. "Fantastic."

For the remaining two hours of our romp down the Poudre I kept stealing glances at Jesse, who paddled as though his life truly depended on how hard he pulled. His face shone with joy, and my own joy was kindled from seeing it.

This is an old habit of mine, the watching and weighing of my son's experience. Since his birth I have enveloped him in a cloud of thought. How's he doing? I wonder. Is he hungry? Hurting? Tired? Is he grumpy or glad? Like so many other exchanges between parent and child, this concern flows mainly one way; Jesse does not surround *me* with thought. On the contrary, with each passing year he pays less and less attention to me, except when he needs something, and then he bristles at being reminded of his dependence. That's natural, mostly, although teenage scorn for parents also gets a boost from popular culture. My own father had to die before I thought seriously about what he might have needed or wanted or suffered. If Jesse has children of his own one day, no doubt he will brood on them as I have brooded on him for these seventeen years. Meanwhile, his growing up requires him to break free of my concern. I accept that, yet I cannot turn off my fathering mind.

Before leaving for Colorado, I had imagined that he would be able to meet the Rockies with clear eyes, with the freshness of his green age. So long as he was in my company, however, he would see the land through the weather of my moods. And if despair had so darkened my vision that I was casting a shadow over Jesse's world, even here among these magnificent mountains and tumultuous rivers, then I would have to change. I would have to learn to see differently. Since I could not forget the wounds to people and planet, could not unlearn the dismal numbers—the tallies of pollution and population and poverty that foretold catastrophe—I would have to look harder for antidotes, for medicines, for sources of hope.

Tired and throbbing from the river trip, we scarcely spoke during the long drive back to our campground in the national park. This time, though, the silence felt easy, like a fullness rather than a void.

In that tranquility I recalled our morning's hike to Bridal Veil Falls, before the first quarrel of the day. No matter how briskly I walked, Jesse kept pulling ahead. He seemed to be in a race, eyes focused far up the trail, as though testing himself against the rugged terrain. I had come to this high country for a holiday from rushing. A refugee from the tyranny of deadlines and destinations, I wished to linger, squatting over the least flower or fern, reading the braille of bark with my fingers, catching the notes of water and birds and wind. But Jesse was just as intent on covering ground. Although we covered the same ground, most of the time we experienced quite different landscapes, his charged with trials of endurance, mine with trials of perception. Then every once in a while the land brought us together—in the mist of the falls, on the back of the river—and it was as if, for a moment, the same music played in both of us.

Without any quarrel to distract me, I watched the road faithfully as we wound our way up through Big Thompson Canyon. We entered the park at dusk. A rosy light glinted on the frozen peaks of the Front Range.

I was driving slowly, on the lookout for wildlife, when a coyote loped onto the road ahead of us, paused halfway across, then stared back in the direction from which it had come. As we rolled to a stop, a female elk came charging after, head lowered and teeth bared. The coyote bounded away, scooted up a bank on the far side of the road, then paused to peer back over its bony shoulder. Again the elk charged; again the coyote pranced away, halted, stared. Jesse and I watched this ballet of taunting and chasing, taunting and chasing, until the pair vanished over a ridge.

"What was that all about?" he asked when we drove on.

"She was protecting a calf, I expect."

"You mean a coyote can eat an elk?"

"The newborns they can."

When I shut off the engine at the campground and we climbed out of the car, it was as though we had stepped back into the raft, for the sound of rushing water swept over us. The sound lured us downhill to the bank of a stream, and we sat there soaking in the watery music until our bellies growled. We made supper while the full moon chased Jupiter and Mars up the arc of the sky. The flame on our stove flounced in a northerly breeze, promising cool weather for tomorrow's hike into Wild Basin.

We left the flap of our tent open so we could lie on our backs and watch the stars burn fiercely in the mountain air. Our heads were so close together that I could hear Jesse's breath, even above the shoosh of the river, and I could tell he was nowhere near sleep.

"I feel like I'm still on the water," he said after a spell, "and the raft's bobbing under me and the waves are crashing all around."

"I feel it too."

"That's one of the things I wanted to be sure and do before things fall apart."

I rolled onto my side and propped my head on an elbow and looked at his moonlit profile. "Things don't *have* to fall apart, buddy."

"Maybe not." He blinked, and the spark in his eyes went out and relit. "I just get scared."

"So do I. But the earth's a tough old bird. And we should be smart enough to figure out how to live here."

"Let's hope." There was the scritch of a zipper and a thrashing of legs, and Jesse sprawled on top of his new sleeping bag, which was too warm for this fifty-degree night. "I guess things could be scarier," he said. "Imagine being an elk, never knowing what's sneaking up on you."

"Or a coyote," I said, "never knowing where you'll find your next meal."

A great horned owl called. Another answered, setting up a duet across our valley. We listened until they quit.

"You know," said Jesse, "I've been thinking. Maybe we don't need to sleep on snow. Maybe we can pitch camp in the morning at North St. Vrain, where there ought to be some bare ground, then we can snowshoe on up to Thunder Lake in the afternoon."

"You wouldn't be disappointed if we did that? Wouldn't feel we'd wimped out?"

"Naw," he said. "That's cool."

"Then that's the plan, man."

The stars burned on. The moon climbed. Just when I thought he was asleep, Jesse murmured, "How's that knee?"

"Holding up so far," I told him, surprised by the question, and only then did I notice the aching in my knee and foot.

"Glad to hear it. I don't want to be lugging you out of the mountains."

When he was still young enough to ride in a backpack, I had lugged him to the tops of mountains and through dripping woods and along the slate beds of creeks and past glittering windows on city streets, while he burbled and sang over my shoulder; but I knew better than to remind him of that now in his muscular youth. I lay quietly, following the twin currents of the river and my son's breath. Here were two reasons for rejoicing, two sources of hope. For Jesse's sake, and for mine, I would get up the next morning and hunt for more.

22

Bowl of Stones

Chiori Santiago

My earliest memories are of places wild and verdant. First, the banana field behind our house in Singapore, where the sun filtered through the canopy of umbrella-wide leaves and bathed our games of hide-and-seek with emerald light. Later, when my father was posted to Karachi, we lived in a compound surrounded by a garden and a high wall. Within this wall, we were allowed to run at will. My brother and I chased each other across the lawns, trampling the flowerbeds as our butler, Ashraf, watched with boredom and disdain from the shade of the one large tree.

We left that idyllic life behind when we returned to America. I was born in the United States but had no memory of having lived here. What I learned immediately was that living here was frightening. We were no longer upper-class expatriates when my father lost his foreign service job but were reduced to being ordinary Americans. My brothers learned to fist fight. I learned to run, cutting corners, ducking into stairwells, taking short cuts through apartment complexes to escape from other children who chased me home, laughing at my accent.

I missed the abandon conferred by privilege, the servants following us through the banana fields, fending off dogs and strangers so that we could indulge in freedom. I began to rely on hardware—fences and gates with latches, the solidity of buildings and doors—to protect me from the world. In America, I learned to love concrete. My sense of comfort be-came connected to the urban terrain, the tidy logic of city blocks helping me find my way home in this unfamiliar country. Afraid to look up, I looked down, memorizing each square of sidewalk with its burnished dots of dried chewing gum and scribblings of oxalis growing in the cracks. The straight edges of buildings, the warm asphalt in summer on which we staged games of stickball and jacks: these things were beautiful to me and safe.

Our neighborhood was a textbook illustration of the postwar inclination toward order, where any rebellion by natural forces was swiftly contained. Bits of green popped up in measured interstices of the urban grid, mostly in the forms of undernourished trees struggling from holes cut in the sidewalks and in squares of lawn portioned off before each house. Annual layers of white paint and frequent applications of lawn mower and hedge clippers announced that everything was fine, everything was in control.

Our house, on the other hand, reflected my mother's philosophy that everything was out of control and why bullshit about it? After my parents' divorce, she abandoned the neighborhood's landscaping expectations to concentrate on feeding four children. The exterior of our home was a disgrace, a frank confession of the unruly lives within. Patches of yellowing blades interrupted the swath of our front lawn as if it was being overcome by leprosy. A few shrubs squatted around the perimeter. My entire sense of northern California wilderness was represented by the waist-high weeds of our back yard. Not until I grew up did I recognize the defiant expression of our landscaping. Years later, I planted a garden as a kind of apology for the neglect that had settled over our landscaping—as if by watering, trimming, and coaxing, I could achieve balance in the world.

The general disarray in which we lived was even more embarrassing because my mother happened to be Japanese. She wasn't straight-up green-card Japanese (she was born and raised in southern California), but even I expected her to fulfill the mysterious characteristics of her heritage simply because she looked Asian. People were interested in certain Japonesque qualities of design back then, and my non-Asian friends looked forward to seeing the inside of a real Japanese person's house. If they had imagined serenity, emptiness, and order, they were in for a shock.

"All this junk is yours?" they'd marvel. No bonsai, no minimal flower arrangements, no quaint ceramic groupings cohabited with the unwashed dishes, toy shards, and mutilated board games lying around our living room. Perhaps they were relieved when, to distract them, I suggested building secret catacombs using every chair, sofa cushion, and tablecloth we could find. That was the tradeoff. In our house, no one yelled at us to watch out for the bouquet of roses in Grandma's crystal vase. Nothing in my surroundings was valuable, lovely, or worth bothering about until the day one summer my mother declared, "Let's have a picnic at the beach."

The season was winding toward its end, when the angle of sun and a certain melancholy seemed to bake a crust around the edges of each afternoon. I now realize my mother was trying to fend off that devastating sadness that pierces the golden light at that time of the year. She bustled around the kitchen with sudden energy, opening two cans of tuna, stabbing the contents with a fork, mashing it with mayonnaise, and dumping the mixture in mounds on slices of bread. As she wrapped the sandwiches, she yelled for my brothers and sister to come in from the yard.

Our "beach" was a five-minute drive away, a strip of sand just below the frontage road that ran along the Bayshore Freeway. The waves weren't even ocean waves. They were bay waves, just modest ankle-tugging ripples, but they were frisky enough for us. A few feet from roaring traffic, fishers planted their poles in the sand and waited for the lines to twitch, staring out to the grey horizon. My mother parked our turquoise-and-white Buick station wagon on the road's crumbling asphalt shoulder to let the four of us clamber over the tailgate and rush, barefoot, to sink our toes in the gritty sand.

We chased the surging foam and ran around filling our pockets with stones and other sea-washed treasures. We watched the fishers standing, their hands in their pockets, contemplating the lines that never seemed to reward them with fish. Behind us, across the freeway, a steel plant chugged grey clouds into the air. In an adjacent salvage yard, stacks of crushed automobiles rose in jagged mountains as formidable as Yosemite cliffs. I'd never seen Half Dome or El Capitan except in pictures, but those rusty cars were for me an adequate substitute for that famous geology. Years later, I would visit the real mountains of Yosemite. They were certainly glorious but also a little forlorn, as if they passed each day remembering the sights of their youth a million years before, just as the salvage yard cars did with their empty headlight sockets and outdated tail fins.

My mother watched our antics from inside the car. This was one of her few opportunities for serenity, a time when she had nothing in particular to do and could just smoke a cigarette and watch the sun scorch the horizon pink. When the sun was gone and the breeze turned chilly, we rode home and followed my mother up the long flight of stairs home. We emptied the loot from our pockets onto the kitchen table. We could part with none of it—the half rusty bottle caps, bits of wave-polished glass, shells, and pebbles. A small mountain of pebbles as monochrome of the beach, where red, brown, green, and yellow suffused into a grey the color of wet concrete. "Please, please, don't throw them away," my younger siblings pleaded. The oldest brother, Marc, picked out the bottle caps and flipped them at our little brother's head. Our baby sister wailed. My mother reached into the refrigerator for a bottle of Budweiser and, ignoring the chaos rising around her, rummaged in the junk drawer for a bottle opener. She pried off the cap and flung it at Marc.

"Hey!" He rubbed the top of his ear.

"Now you know how it feels," our mother said, closing her eyes to take a long, thoughtful pull on the bottle. I loved the perfection of the diagonal line traced by the bottle and her lifted chin. She was in her forties and tired of kids, a boring job, and a dirty house, but to see her standing there in her black pedal pushers and a black turtleneck sweater, pulling on that bottle of beer for one calm second, I realized she was beautiful.

For that one second, we children were shocked into silence by the unexpected launch of beer-cap retaliation. Recognizing an opportunity, my mother scooped up the pebbles and bits of sea trash and poured them into a soup bowl. She carried the bowl to the kitchen sink and filled it with water, swirling the contents around and around with one hand beneath the running stream in the same gesture she used to wash a pot full of raw Kokuho Rose rice. Satisfied, she carried the bowl back to the table.

"Get rid of that stuff," she commanded, and we scurried to sweep the table clear of old newspapers, stray toys, and encrusted dishes. Then, with an air of ceremony, she set the bowl in the middle of the table.

We stared inside at the evidence of my mother's ability to perform magic. With a sweep of her hand, she had transformed dusty stones into a treasure of glowing roan, jade, aubergine, maple, obsidian, and salt-and-pepper granite. Beneath the window-glass translucency of the water, each pebble had become a planet, each with an individual surface of maroon marbling or facets gleaming with sparks of fool's gold.

The bowl stayed on the table for weeks. Things tended to do that in our household—to move into a spot and never leave. On the kitchen table, yellowing newspapers crept back from their lair to hibernate next to lipstick-stained coffee cups; pink wisps of polyester hair hovered for days above the discarded troll doll from which they'd been clipped. In that archaeology of domestic detritus, the bowl exuded a mystical power, a force field that kept the mess just slightly at bay so that it was never quite overrun by the discards of our daily life. Unlike the stuff around it, which seemed to vanish into our subconscious (we were notorious for our ability to work around clutter rather than clean it up), we noticed the bowl. We stared into it while eating cereal in the morning. At night, while my mother talked story with her friends, I would listen to the cadence of their voices while gazing into the misty galaxy of beautiful stones.

Years later, I outgrew the ugliness of that disorganized house surrounded by dingy plants. As I realized we would not return to Pakistan, I learned to make preemptive strikes from behind the safety of the walls of that house, to go beyond the fence, to adopt the casual aggression of other Americans. I made new friends. I went hiking. I began to look up from the sidewalk to see what I never had been able to see—the silhouettes of Monterey pines against a backdrop of apartment buildings; the hills turning from burnished brass to jade, summer to winter; foxtail, spurge, and mallow that finally turned an abandoned lot into a tough, city-raised version of a meadow.

The neighborhood changed, too. People gradually ripped up the squares of lawn and tangled juniper, and in its place they planted flax and sedge, lupine and poppies. My mother's aesthetic no longer felt so foreign in this newly fashionable wildness. She had simply anticipated a world in which people didn't need to hide behind the facades of their homes to pretend their lives were in order. New neighbors moved in who not only went to therapists but discussed their neuroses while standing in line at the grocery store. And I planted gardens, for myself and for other people who once were frightened of unknown, uncontrollable things hidden in the trees.

Not long ago, our skinny excuse for a beach was declared part of our region's newest public open space. The other day, I listened to an environmental activist laugh at the idea. "What kind of park is that?" he snorted. "A strip of sand between the bay and the freeway!"

He was absolutely right of course. That bit of land is nothing, absolutely nothing worth bothering about. It's not impressive, or restful, or even very pretty. But for us it was everything. My mother made it important because she understood the value of unimportance. She had allowed us to gaze into an ordinary bowl of stones in order to glimpse grandeur, to see limitless possibility hidden within smoke and trash and concrete.

23

Colored Memory

Lauret Savoy

at five

The world and I are present tense. My joy? Sitting on my bedroom porch in late-day Sun. Golden light paints the sky, paints the houses and their yards, and paints me. It makes me. Just look at my veins: sky flows in there! Just look at Sun warm and become my skin—its coppery warmth colors the land, too. I know who I am. Here, now.

at eight

Aren't daffodils yellow? Spring will brighten winter's fade in trees and grass, in corners and shadows. I *know* this. But along the school playground fence, can I be sure what color our garden will grow?

Months before, in October, we knelt along chain-link—ten, eleven, twelve second-graders in dirt. Digging—careless of school clothes. Digging, laughing, squealing—two bulbs each. Digging to Sister Mary Richard Ann's *gently now, children, gently.*

Why then did he have to point at me? Why did he have to sing out *nigger flower nigger flower, ugly dark and dirty flower* . . . ignoring Sister's hush.

I fill each February and March day with *pleases. Please* to the unborn plot, *please* to poking greens, *please* to suspect papery wrappings. *Please.*

Sometimes I awaken at night, disoriented from the same dream. *I breathe, but I'm not alive.* A sense of meaning withheld lingers. *I breathe, but I'm not yet alive.* If there is release, it comes from recalling my beginning in California, the place before race. Then the dream's meaning steps across a threshold between memories of a five-year-old daydreaming in golden light and an eight-year-old praying for yellow. Both remain as vivid as a rainbow ending a storm, and as sharp as a cut on the wrist.

Coastal California was the frame within which my life took distinctive shape. I was born there, near the elastic limit of one of my father's attempts to define his life far from Washington, D.C., his familial home. Because of him, there was frequent movement and change in our lives— from San Francisco to Los Angeles, from bungalow to apartment to second-story flat on Redondo Boulevard. My father envisaged himself a writer and artist but made a living doing other things—marketing, public relations, and jobs I never really knew. We lived by modest means, each place rented, little owned. He and my mother, a surgical nurse, furnished our homes with what was practical and necessary. My father's ceramic handworks and pastel and oil prints are the only adornments I remember.

As the only reliable companions in a neighborhood with few children, southern California's sky and intensely physical landscape imprinted me deeply. Foremost was the quality of light, its depth and brilliance, such that by the time I turned five my self theory was that *colored* meant sunlight and blue sky *in* me. The San Gabriel and Santa Monica mountains formed the rugged northern horizon from our home. To the west lay Santa Monica beaches and Pacific Ocean Park. Any drive to the coast, mountains, or beyond assumed a specialness that embedded it in memory, like the day we crossed the San Gabriel Mountains to visit the Devil's Punchbowl at the edge of the Mojave Desert. All of these elements, along with countless city fountains, Griffith Park, and the "dicker-lights" illuminating night-time Los Angeles, composed the shape and largeness of my known world.

But my father decided to return to Washington, D.C., in another search for employment. Because a seven-year-old has little choice in such matters short of running away, the only possible option was to bring home with me. I tried—but how does anyone gather sunlight or keep Pacific water from spilling or evaporating? In the end I collected postcards and stones on the cross-country drive. As the distance separating California from us grew, so did my vision of home. Postcards of Pacific beaches, the Mojave Desert, the Sierra Nevada, Zion, Bryce, and Grand canyons, the Kaibab Plateau, Colorado River, Rocky Mountains, and other places became sunlit textured *home-cards*. At least I could hold immense landscapes and their stony pieces in my hands.

Then sometime between April and June 1968, between the shootings of Martin Luther King Jr. and Bobby Kennedy, a time of evening news reports of riots and Vietnam casualties, a second-grade classmate taught me another meaning of *colored*. We had not been in Washington long. It was a gray day—after The Move, most days were gray. The city's decay and a sky faded by humidity matched the ugliness of what had quickly become a dangerous racialized world. Although I was too young to feel any impact from the 1965 Watts riots when we lived in California, three years later at the age of eight I feared words spat on me because of my skin color. I feared the power of hatred and that cancer-word *nigger*.

Only a few memories remain of exploring the mysteries of a more-than-human world with my mother or father after we moved to Washington, D.C. Still, my parents quietly lit a path to possibility with cookouts by Rock Creek or a gift of Rachel Carson's *The Sense of Wonder*. The old hardbound copy lies open on my desk as I write these words. I like to think the pages still contain the breath of that moment my parents gave the book to eight-year-old me before I boarded an American Airlines flight, alone, to California to visit Aunt Bootsie for part of the summer. I like to think I can still trace the fingerprints left by my father and mother as they chose, purchased, and wrapped the book. The long-dried, fading blue ink at least traces memory: *For a very precious little daughter, Mommie & Daddy*.

I drew security from Carson's book, along with a tentative feeling of self-acceptance in an otherwise nonsensical world. I had a sweater just like the child in the book's cover photograph. I also delighted in looking up at the Sun, tall flowers, and trees. I, too, had stones and shells and leaves, cones and feathers. And I, like Rachel and her great-nephew and adopted son Roger, marveled at the mystery of water.

The Chesapeake coastal plain, Piedmont, and Blue Ridge were the accessible landscapes after The Move. Unknown to me then, at least five generations of my father's ancestors had lived within tangled dynamics as the indentured, enslaved, and enslaver in this tidewater landscape. My mother was of the second generation to be born in the North, her once-enslaved ancestors having left rural Alabama and Virginia at the close of the nineteenth century. But I've only come to know these things as an adult. As a child, I heard no stories of family history or of connection to any place as home. Neither people nor places were named, and without names they remained elusive, fictive shadows.

Large numbers of African Americans—many of whom, like my parents, were of mixed indigenous and/or European ancestry—lived on and worked the land over a century ago, primarily in the agrarian South. Whether enslaved or "free," these people knew that land with an intimacy born of generations working the soil, and they formed community landscapes distinct from imposed bondage. In the years following the Civil War, millions of these people in the South invested themselves in the land, in its health and productivity, as sharecroppers, tenant farmers, and small farm owners. But they still could not claim the land, their relationships to it, or its harvest as theirs. Like slavery and earlier land removals, enforced Jim Crow laws and practices excluded these people physically and symbolically, such that the turn-of-century migrations that dispersed millions north and west occurred by pushing force as well as pulling choice.

A segregation of ideas and not just of people continues in this country. For example, key metanarratives of the environmental movement and of nature writing seem to have atrophied to a frame primarily defined and limited by Anglo-America. Still not commonly included in either are the experiences of place that are migrant or immigrant, exiled or toxic, urban or indentured. A presumed lack of voices beyond a mainstream context, or a supposed lack of interest in nature by people of color over America's history, reflects more an exclusive sense of what and who count based on color, culture, and class.[1] What's needed instead is a capacity to ask significant questions about our lives in a larger world and about lives not our own.

If one purpose of story is to maintain a vital connection between generations such that children know in the broadest sense who they are, from whom and whence they came, and what place is home, then the loss or silencing of story even in part leaves a gap in generational memory. I can only speculate the reasons behind the absence of handed-down story now that most family elders are dead. Was silence some protection or self-defense from what was considered best left unexposed? Or, perhaps, an erosion of knowledge of ancestors and kinship relationships to each other and to the land quickly followed loss of home. I believe the inability to define a life on the land under one's own terms leaves a deep psychic wound. I know that familial silences about origins, this unvoiced past, both allowed and required the child-me to create my own stories.

I have lived most of my life in the East and have only begun to feel something other than a stranger here. I still don't know how to answer the question *Who are you?* No imagined response ever comes close to feeling right or being enough. To say that I'm a geologist misses the point. To say that I'm a Black woman who enjoys hiking alone in the backcountry also falls short. Maybe I should say I'm the only child of older parents of mixed heritage who were born and lived labeled as "Negroes" in a country long segregated by law and attitude. A child of the 1960s and 1970s, I came of age witnessing acts of hatred unchanged by legislation, and I am still trying to learn as I enter middle age how to balance invisible tensions between absence and presence, between how I would define myself and how the American majority labels me.

California was my origin, both a *place* before race and a *time* when impressions of land and sky took deep formative hold. That western landscapes still pull is a manifestation of and response to not only an early-formed love of light on Earth and sky, made more intense by my family's disruptive move East, but also another child-formed belief that the land itself could be an emotional, spiritual, and intellectual refuge. Love and belief grew from a palpable need for rootedness, for grounding, in the absence of familial placement or direction.

I still have the home-cards from The Move. Top right drawer of my writing table in a bag nearly as old as they.

grizzly creek falls roaring river falls kings canyon zumwalt meadows fawn in meadow sequoia general grant tree middle fork south fork kings river mojave desert amboy crater cronise mountain soda lake joshua tree oasis of mara towers of the virgin zion canyon bryce canyon kaibab forest north rim grand canyon bright angel point colorado river lake powell gunsight butte painted desert

They are all images without people. Smaller than I remember, and fewer—now twenty-eight total—with edges frayed over more than two-score years, but the worn cards still show *it*. Light. Texture. Integrity—a vital "I am" without question or limit.

A child's wish remains, intact. I have yet to look at the cards without the sting of tears. Yes, land was a refuge—as my own sense of wonder came more from a young, tender heart seeking safety, and realizing that rock did not spit, that ocean, sky, and mountains did not hate. Neither did a city creek or daffodils in mid-March.

Note

1. For example, as African American abolitionists fought and wrote against slavery in the early and mid-nineteenth century, they also fought and wrote against the use of arsenic in tobacco fields. Zitkala-Sa (Lakota-Dakota) and Sarah Winnemucca (Paiute) noted more than a century ago in their writings the close links between Euro-American racism and environmental attitudes that led to the degradation of what once was indigenous land. And W. E. B. Du Bois's essay on the African roots of World War I, in the May 1915 issue of *Atlantic Monthly*, is as much an environmental essay as is any piece written that year on the need for a national park system.

24

We Are Distracted

Michael Shay

I. We Are Distracted

We are distracted by the agility of my eight-year-old son Kevin as he clambers up the slick granite rock formation near Rocky Mountain National Park. He is fifty feet above us; we are a bit frightened by the risks he takes, the way he clings like a human fly to the sides of the rock. We all look up and watch one of Kevin's handholds become a fingerhold and just when it's about to become a no-hold, he pushes off the rock with his feet, leaps a three-foot gap between spires and wraps his arms tightly around the precious purchase he has made with this part of the Rockies.

We are like three slugs on a slab—Kevin's classmate Freeman, his father, Randy, and I. We lean against the cool rock surface of this six-million-year-old mountain and watch Kevin. We look up and Kevin never looks down. It would break his concentration, interrupt his communion with the rock, I think. To concentrate is everything for Kevin. He can't do it for extended periods of time unless he is under the influence of Ritalin, a drug that helps him control his hyperactivity-inspired impulsiveness. Right now, as he climbs toward the sharp blue Colorado sky, the Ritalin, a central nervous system stimulant, is working on my son's brain stem arousal system causing it to *not* be aroused. Medical researchers are not sure why a stimulant has the opposite effect on hyperactive kids. Says the 1994 *Physicians' Desk Reference*: There is no "specific evidence which clearly establishes the mechanism whereby Ritalin produces its mental and behavioral effects on children, nor conclusive evidence regarding how these effects relate to the condition of the central nervous system."

II. Hyper/active

When Kevin is in a classroom and a bird flies to a branch on a tree across the street, he will stop everything and look at the bird. A whispered comment at the opposite end of the classroom might as well be a sonic boom. If he is surrounded by too much energy in his orbit, he absorbs that energy. It sometimes causes him to twist and whirl and slam into his playmates; not so much now as when he was a toddler and his way of play was FULL BODY CONTACT. Slam, bam—and there was a kid crying, one nonplussed Kevin and usually a very pissed-off parent, who soon would be in my face, asking me why I didn't control my son on the playground because he was really going to hurt somebody somehow someday.

III.   Names, Alphabets, Names

Physicians have been prescribing Ritalin (a.k.a. methylphenidate) for more than thirty years for a condition that has been known as minimal brain damage (MBD), minimal brain dysfunction in children (MBDC), attention deficit disorder (ADD) and ADD with hyperactivity (ADHD). If some progressive therapists and groups such as ChADD (Children with Attention Deficit Disorder) have their way, the official designation will be changed to attention deficit *syndrome* with hyperactivity (ADHS). This alphabet soup can be confusing. Once, on his first day at a new school, my son announced in front of the class that he had ADHD. The next day, several very nervous parents called the school, concerned about the new student that had AIDS. Being a "hyper" kid turns you into one type of pariah; AIDS carriers get special mistreatment. It was weeks before the confusion was straightened out. But the impression had been made. Kevin was different; different is bad.

IV.   Some Theories

There are those, notably psychiatrist Peter R. Breggin, who regard ADD as a chimera, a noncondition, a conspiracy by the entrenched psychiatric establishment to dose our children with drugs. "Just say no to Ritalin!" could be their battle cry.

Thom Hartmann runs the attention deficit disorder (ADD) bulletin board on Compuserve. In 1993 he published *Attention Deficit Disorder: A Different Perspective*. Writing on the Prodigy BBS, he summed up his book: "If you lived 10,000 years ago, before the agricultural revolution, and were part of a hunting society, then the 'ability' to have an 'open, highly distractible' state of mind would be an *asset*. Walking through the woods/jungle, if you didn't notice that flash of light out of the corner of your eye, you may miss either the bunny which is lunch, or get eaten by a tiger."

Hartmann surmises that the ADD hunters were survivors and their DNA went into the gene pool. "Modern people with ADD are those with leftover 'hunter' genes."

There are a few problems with this theory. Since impulsiveness is one of the hallmarks of ADD and ADHD, isn't it likely that the hunter with hyperactivity might charge headlong into a herd of charging mastodons without considering the consequences? Maybe he would neglect to tread carefully in saber-tooth tiger country?

V.   Contraindications

The pharmacy clerk always gives me a yellow sheet with Kevin's Ritalin prescription. Under "Side Effects" it reads: "Decreased appetite; stomach ache; difficulty falling asleep; headache." Under "Cautions": "DO NOT DRIVE, OPERATE MACHINERY, OR DO ANYTHING ELSE that might be dangerous until you know how you react to this medicine." It says nothing about rock climbing, although you might infer that comes under "dangerous," or at least, risky.

VI.   To Fall . . .

Kevin never has fallen. When he was two, he climbed the highest trees in the park near our Denver home. Fifty-foot-tall pines and spruces. The first time he did this, he looked down at me and yelled, "You worried, Daddy?"

"Yes!" I said, which seemed to please him.

So what if he falls? Randy, Freeman, and I watch him climb, and it occurs to them because Randy says, "Does this worry you?"

"Yes," I say, "It worries me." And it thrills me too. I've seen him all alone in the playground because the mothers won't let their kids near him. I've seen him mark time in his room, usually because he's been restricted in some way because he's had trouble at home or on the school bus or in the playground.

VII.   To Fly . . .

Do rock climbers dream of falling or of flying? Do hyperactive kids dream of solitude on a granite mountain? Or do they dream of this: dancing and laughing, surrounded by friends, the mountains a distant mirage?

25

The Big Talk

Sandra Steingraber

I was Googling myself recently (in an attempt, if you must know, to locate an essay that I had published somewhere), and I managed to misspell my own name. So I was directed to the one source that had mangled my name in the same way. And that is how I was confronted, in an obscure blog, with the question, "Why isn't Sandra Steingraber [with dyslexic spelling] talking about climate change?"

It was unsettling. As the days went by, I began an imaginary argument.

Look, I first wrote about receding glaciers in 1988. I was assigning Al Gore to college students in 1992. Not long ago, I made climate instability the centerpiece of a commencement address I gave at a rural college in coal-is-king Pennsylvania. And if you think all the trustees were pleased with that theme, I invite you to give it a try. So the question is not "Why is S.S. not talking about climate change?" The question is "Why is S.S. not talking about it AT HOME?"

Okay. Why don't you talk about it at home?

Because I have young children and because I believe that frightening problems need to be solved by adults who should just shut up and get to work.

So, how long are you going to keep hiding the truth from your kids?

That's as far as I got before three other notable things happened. First, Elijah asked to be a polar bear for Halloween. As I pinned the chenille fabric, it occurred to me that his costume might well outlast the species. I decided not to tell him that.

A month later, Elijah asked his sister for a weather report. Faith walked out onto the porch, spread out her arms in the manner of Saint Francis, and came back in. "It's global warmingish," she said and went back to her cereal. No comment from me.

And then I overheard a conversation on the playground. One child said, "I know why it's hot. Do you?"

Another said, "It's because the Earth is *sick.*" They all nodded. I said nothing.

It's time to sit down with my kids and have the Global Warming Talk. I carried off the Sex Talk—and its many sequels—with grace and good biology. Surely, I can rise to this new occasion.

On the surface, procreation and climate change seem opposite narratives. Sex knits molecules of air, food, and water into living organisms. Climate change unravels all that. The ending of the sex story is the birth of a family. The climate change story ends with what biologist E. O. Wilson calls the Eremozoic Era—the Era of Loneliness.

But then I realized that the two stories share a common epidemiological challenge. Both are counterintuitive. In the former case, you have to accept that your ordinary existence began with an extraordinary, unthinkable act (namely, your parents having intercourse). In the latter case, you have to accept that the collective acts of ordinary objects—cars, planes, dishwashers, iPods—are ushering in things extraordinary and unthinkable (dissolving coral reefs, daffodils in January). So, I reasoned, perhaps the same pedagogical lessons apply: during the Big Talk, keep it simple, leave the door open for further conversation, offer reading material as follow-up.

Of which there is no shortage. In fact, a veritable cottage industry of children's books on climate change has sprung up almost overnight. These range from the primer, *Why Are the Ice Caps Melting?* (Let's Read and Find Out!), in which lessons on the ravaging of ecosystems also offer plenty of opportunities to practice silent *e*, to the ultra-sophisticated *How We Know What We Know about Our Changing Climate: Scientists and Kids Explore Global Warming*, by foremost environmental author Lynne Cherry, in which middle-school readers are cast as coprincipal investigators. This new literary subgenre is impressive. Reading its various offerings, I found myself admiring the respectful tones and clear explanations. These books describe global warming as a reality that no longer lingers in the realm of debate. And yet, they are not, for the most part, scary. Indeed, the first sentence in the inside flap of *How We Know What We Know* is "This is not a scary book."

And here is where the pediatric versions of the climate change story depart from their adult counterparts. The recent crop of books on global warming intended for grown-ups focuses on the surreal disconnect between the evidence for rapidly approaching, irreversible planetary tipping points (overwhelming) and the political response to that evidence (mostly zilch). The children's books profile heroic individuals fighting to save the planet—in ways that kids can get involved in. To read the children's literature is to see the world's people working ardently and in concert with each other to solve a big problem . . . and enjoying a grand adventure while they're at it.

Is this the fiction we all should be laboring under? I don't know. I do know that a fatalistic mindset, which afflicts many adults but almost no children, is a big part of what's preventing us from derailing the global warming train that has now left the station. On this, I wholly agree with sociologist Eileen Crist, who argues that fatalism, masquerading as realism, is a form of capitulation that strengthens the very trends that generate it. I do know that we grown-ups need visions of effective challenges and radical actions that can turn into self-fulfilling prophecies.

I also know that I needed something to say to my six-year-old when we walked home from the library in April—no leaves to offer shade, the bank's LED sign reading eighty-four degrees—and he turned his ingenuous face to mine to ask, "Mama, is it supposed to be so hot?"

So I am working on my talk. For inspiration, I have arranged on my desk three documents. One is an essay that Rachel Carson published in *Popular Science* in 1951—eight years before my birth. It's entitled "Why Our Winters Are Getting Warmer," and it includes a drawing of Manhattan deluged by seawater. Another is Carson's essay "Help Your Child to Wonder," published five years later. The third is a book by poet Audre Lorde that includes the sentence: *Your silence will not protect you.*

My talk features a story about a boat in which we all live—people, butterflies, polar bears. A storm starts to rock the boat. The waves are chemical pollution, habitat destruction, industrial fishing, and warfare. Now along comes a really big wave. Global warming. The already-rocking boat is in danger of flipping over.

Then what happens? I don't know. For the first time in my life, I have writer's block. Somebody help me out here.

26

On Being "Indian," Unsilent, and Contaminated along the U.S.-Mexico Border

Margo Tamez

Chemical Cocktails, Caste, and Class

I am a young girl chasing grasshoppers down at soil level, where the five-foot-high Johnson grass and the Indian gum plants grow behind our tiny house on Glendora Street in San Antonio, Texas. The house is not big enough to fit all seven of us—dad, mom, Carmelita, Diamantina, José Luis, Maria Rebeca, and me—or the spirits of thousands of Ndé peoples detained between checkpoints, no-Constitution zones, and toxic dumps between southside San Antonio and the Rio Grande River. They visit me in my dreams. They are specters in the dreams of my children as well. Colonialism weaves destruction through our communities, intergenerationally.

My fingers move up and down the rough and shiny, three-foot-long leaves, sharp as blades on the edges. These slice the skin on my fingers when I'm careless, slipping on the greasy residues of pesticide sprays from a program of weed and mosquito control along the Southern Pacific Railroad tracks just past the alleyway.

This is our low-income neighborhood, off the entry ramp to I-35 going south to Corpus Christi or north to Austin, all the way up to the Dakotas and Canada. The tall, blade-sharp weeds challenge me to navigate them. I find my way beyond what my clan can comprehend, and I ask for no companions in my daily jaunts through the weeds. They provide an eerie but somehow habitable hiding place for someone like me who likes being alone most of the time, apt to follow the paths of weeds, snakes, and grasshoppers in lieu of the paths of people.

South Texas and Southern Arizona: Interlocking Indigenous Borders

Another time, I walk on the levee in El Calaboz, our land-grant ranchería—an indigenous community situated near Brownsville and a

few yards from the Mexican border. Here the world views of Lipan
Apaches, Tlaxcalteca farmers, Nahuatl laborers, indigenous mining refu-
gees, and Basque colonists from Spain clashed. I walk on the levee, thinking I see seagull teeth and the skeletons of my Lipan grandmothers
chomping at the soil wall. They are hungry for fresh souls.

The air is dank steam. The scent of sand, roots, and something alive
beneath the soil—deeper and older than memory. When I immerse my
hand in the cloudy water, my hand's shape becomes a fluid form—
something soft becoming something ancient, the ancient informing the
present.

The air today, in this same spot, still breathes heavy with heat and
damp but smells like diesel and herbicides—the NAFTA legacy, "new
invaders ... carpetbaggers," my mother says. The scent reminds me of
failed gestations. My reproduction, the plants', and the water's struggle in
the same web of survival. This water and this land are the places where
my people sprang forth at the time of our creation. From the land, we
hunted to support our families, and we farmed, fished, and wild-crafted
edible plants. We made sacred relationships with other tribal peoples and
with the animal nations with whom we shared these sacred elements. We
entered into sacred agreements with *Shash hastin*—Old Man Bear—and
the *diyin*, who are the medicine people. Our ancestors taught us to keep
our relationships with the animal and plant nations balanced, respectful,
and in dignity. This is the sacred ground of the Lipan. We are the Ndé
Hada'didla', Lightning Clan people, the Tuntsa' Ndé, Big Water Clan
people, and the Cúelcahén Ndé, the Tall Grass Clan people. These lands—
on both sides of this sacred river—are the customary lands and sacred
sites of my ancestors. The places where the Lipan prayed and continue to
pray to this day are contoured by sacred burial grounds as well as sites
that are holy to our people and that give us our identity as aboriginal
peoples. These things are especially important in light of the fact that the
Lipan are a people who have suffered persecution by four governments—
Spain, Mexico, Texas, and the United States. We have been pushed into
the margins of mainstream society and pushed into wage labor, migra-
tion, and in some cases diaspora across the continent.

I maintain my connection to my Lipan community ways and ties where
I live in Pinal County, Arizona, in a rural farming community near three
O'odham reservations and the Mexico border. In these lands, like South
Texas, the industrial agricultural complex overwhelms the ecology. The
radical modification of the soils, water, air, and landscape resulted from a
settler mindset. I connect the burial sites and histories of many indigenous peoples in southern Arizona to the places where four of my own

children are buried on ancient Huhugam and O'odham land. Those unborn died as a result of the toxics I ingested from the food, air, and water
that overwhelm the natural environment in Arizona. Thus, it is important
to understand that indigenous peoples—families, mothers, elders, and
children—are in many cases deeply affected by the industrial pollution of
the ecosystems. Indigenous peoples often equate the destruction of the
environment to persistent colonialism, dispossession, militarism, and violent death. This is an indigenous cultural landscape of memory, resistance, and resilience.

There is a silence in the rural lands here in Arizona that sustains an
arrogance about people, culture, memory, and place. Through and
through, down five hundred feet and going deeper daily, the ancient
underground river flows beneath the prey of the green revolution and
cattle feedlots, a legacy of environmental catastrophe we inherited from
John Wayne and corporate beef—Red River Ltd. My children's graves
signify the grim disparity of the heavier environmental burdens that communities of indigenous peoples and peoples of color shoulder.

I think about the language of wars and the war chemicals that I eat
and drink. I think about what war silences. All this crosses the spongy
walls of the placenta, and the tensions between the old world and the
modern reverberate and quiver within the uterine walls, vibrating the
fetus I now carry close to delivery, close to passage across the ocean of
the womb. All this roots from one moment when my grandfather, José
Emiliano Cavazos Garcia, a beautiful, Southern Lipan Apache, asked
me to eat a small clump of soil from the levee where he irrigated his
sugarcane, back in 1968—his way of showing my connection to our
place, the tenderness he felt for the only place he ever knew or wanted
to be, the faith he had in the earth's curative powers. His knowledge
of the soil was sacred with humility he felt for the land. The belief was
that when we ate this soil, we reentered the sacred space of all time, a
universal field of being and belonging to her—our ancient mother.

I opened my mouth anticipating the sandiness, the clay taste, the minerals, and precious moisture. He couldn't talk anymore by that time, his
throat shredding and peeling away, inside out, from cancer. He was in
good shape otherwise, lean and handsome, with a bright smile and a
bright mind. He was only forty-seven—smiling a large toothless smile,
grunting, motioning me to take a little more, chuckling as he watched me
knit my brows as I tried to do so earnestly. I loved him so.

Through the years, I continued to eat, breathe, touch, and inhale the
soil he loved, a soil irrigated with Gulf backwash contaminated by industrial pollutants. We ate the oil spills, pharmaceuticals, and industrial

chemicals of the world's capitalist fleets. He didn't know. He was an Indian, a farmer, a devoted family man, a member of a stateless indigenous people living in their aboriginal lands, bifurcated by the militarized border of two nation-states.

My body ingested toxins. Invisible chemical cocktails within the soil's microminerals invaded my body and the bodies of my fetuses. Poisons seeped through the fibrous layers of placenta and into the lagoon of birthwater. I filled their tiny bodies with mother's milk heavy with chemicals, pesticides, herbicides, and fungicides in every fat cell.

This invisible text within the body and the negated context of environmental racism and colonialism maintain the normalcy of oppression against our indigenous communities. This normalcy of racism poured into me when I was a child. I feared there was no power beyond muteness and no way to call out.

Growing up as an Indian on the U.S.-Mexico international border, a war zone, I struggled with knowing and having an identity that stemmed from being other to the violent power of white authority and mainstreaming of hate. After numerous clashes with Anglo kids in our ethnically mixed, low-income, urban neighborhood, my obsession with learning the arguments of Eurocentric archaeology and Eurocentric anthropology came as no surprise to me later at the University of Texas. I wanted to know about motivations. I wanted to get to the root causes of the inter-ethnic and racial conflict between European Americans and our indigenous peoples.

As a child, I asked my mother many *Whys?*, especially *Why do we still persist?* and *How do we stay safe?* There were times I feared to ask. I don't remember feeling safe.

My mother once told me—in a this-purse-is-snapped-shut gesture—never to ask. The answers would unravel a tightly woven story of survival, revenge, anguish, heartbreak, disasters, and wanting.

Breaking away from her request makes me a marked woman.

The Living Talk

When my mother finally speaks, she roars. A panther spirit of the river—her usual guide.

On yellow progress reports, my teachers complained that I spoke out and asked impertinent questions. My mother wrote them essays crammed onto the back of the small yellow forms, her elegant cursive script flowing into the margins, spilling in between the lines of the teachers' writing and filling in places on the sheet that said "Administration Only." Her words laid out maps for those who didn't recognize us as first peoples. I came to understand that these were merely snarls, hints of roars much deeper, greater, and far too powerful to fit onto a five- by six-inch piece of paper.

Like some new-spawned, all-powerful, frightening yet necessary creature, she showed me where to look for the repressed unknowable. Her growls posed a promise, a frightening and desirable one, from which I could retrieve who we used to be back in south Texas—before the land, race, and class wars; the barbed-wire fences; the fumes of pesticides and diesel fuels; the ravages of the natural world on which our peoples depended for millennia; the disappearance of hundreds of species; the clogged, chemically imbibed, sluggish halt of the once mighty flow of the Rio Grande River. It was before scientists and conservationists appropriated the now unfit water and land as theirs to research and corral off into privately held preserves, where science experts fret over the damage inflicted and proclaim Scientific Truth as doctrine. This world view disregards the knowledge, insight, and agency of locals to steward this once glittering, tropical paradise. It excludes the story of the people, the water, and the land, recolonizing in the name of science, protection, and preservation.

I explain to my young students on the reservation that I've been handed some precious keys that were forged by the skill and pain of my mother and foremothers. I take them with me everywhere I travel. This process is a sacred exploration. I must facilitate living talk and validate the saying, the orality of knowing passed down by the story keepers. There is no allowing science or the mainstream culture to power over the meaning of our knowing. Meaningful language and powerful story are rendered from our very life force. I invoke the joy as well as the struggle—and most important, the ongoing inquiry, the *Why?*

My life offers unexpected stones, divots, and sometimes sinkholes. These afford me spaces to explore the hidden and buried, to nudge me to take on my beasts and demons, to fly, to huddle, and to take shelter within the cavern of my own history of oppression and dispossession. Recovering our community's experiences of violence is critical to changing the future for all of us.

As a young girl, I wanted change. I remember not feeling that I could make change. I remember muteness. Inside my dark brain and my dark mind of secret upheavals and rebellions, I gathered in my pockets the insidious, daily, small trespasses authored by the funk of human society in my neighborhood. These I've held onto, building a mountain of despair, resistance, and inquiry, desperately hungry for change.

I connect my *Whys?* to my mother's and my ancestors' in many ways and list the ingredients of witnessing and identity expressed to me as in a recipe: needed—ample soul secrets, wild soul desires, the reverence of soul disappointments, the freedom of soul dreams. This is what I can cook for the young. To provide nutrition and nurturing, I need specific instructions about the work laid down by my mother and the work of the ancestors who laid it down to her. I go to the memories, stories, and rituals. I take deep breaths and pray before I stir in my own secrets, my own desires, my own darkness, and my embraceable light.

Earth Talks

In the Rio Grande River flows my ancestors' life force. This essence is connected to the elements of water, air, soils, minerals, fire, and creation. Today, we are entangled in a web that is destroying the life forces of the body and spirit, and indigenous knowledge systems are critical to recovering the wisdom of balanced and sustainable life ways with Mother Earth. This philosophy has not been abandoned by indigenous peoples, whose knowledge systems are resilient through enduring kinship relationships throughout the continent that know no borders. Due to anti-indigenous sentiment by the settler societies (the dominant Eurocentric American system), we find ourselves in a global struggle to regenerate indigenous culture, thought, languages, economies, and kinship. These are crucial systems to both educate and to challenge settler ecologies and the industries stemming from these that are poisoning the Gulf of Mexico, the Rio Grande River, and the larger watersheds and ecological integrity of our Lipan Apache customary domains.

My clan mothers say that they are out there unable to hear or see the songs of the moon. The border-wall security zones are lit up at night by stadium-size lights, dimming the starlight in the night sky required by many creatures for mating, nesting, and feeding. At night, the moon radiates the places to find food; however, the animals do not know how to walk along the wall to the few militarized checkpoints, where movement to the south side of the wall is a slim possibility. The border wall prevents the deer, javelina, oceolots, and turtles from reaching their primary source of water—the Rio Grande River.

In southern Arizona, beneath the land where I have lived for fifteen years, some elders say an ancient river used to run hundreds of feet deep into the earth. This aquifer holds knowledge tightly between slabs of stones, deep inside ancient caverns, in the dark crevices of our mother. The small lakes that once lay above are now sucked dry by the effects of the green revolution and beef-addicted Americans, risks and damages accrued on the desert floor. All this toxicity—from raising cattle in forced and fearful conditions and growing cotton and water-greedy alfalfa plants—in one of the most fragile ecosystems on the planet steams and bubbles into the water, air, and food chain that we humans depend on for life. An altered terrain and scale of oppression contaminates our bodies, our minds, and our fetuses and silences the future.

Knowledge

I grind up our condiments in the four-hundred-year-old *molcajete* handed down to me from a wise, old Tarahumara woman. I cook up strength and courage to face struggle and to share a radical vision to transform and change ourselves. My hunger to answer the *Whys?* demands of me to carve, shape, name, place, say, speak, want, dare, desire, invoke, and actualize change. The rivers above and the rivers below course through my veins and my children's. This flow of the river, the river's song, the river's life is not abstract. Yet the damage remains officially sanctioned as indecipherable to the silent majority. The river, though struggling for her very life, still peels back our shut eyelids and softens the hardened flesh around our hearts.

"Because the river is still alive. Are you *listening*? Listen with your heart, before your pen. Listen and remember," was my mother's eventual exasperated response to my *Whys?* She says it without English words. She says it with her face, the way she pounds harder on the wall she's patching. She says it through her knitted disapproving eyebrows when I'm not reading her traditional way of sharing knowledge—through allegory, rituals, speech patterns, her stomping feet, her body.

I want to assure my mother that her exasperation and emphatic memory of intertwining stories and rituals are integral—that they *center* the most obvious answer to my question, flowing her rough-rock wilderness into the swirling current of all my questions, all answers, all the all of me.

27

The Prophets of Place

Stephen Trimble

Dreams lie under the hardpan surface of the desert West, hidden beneath an alkali-white crust. Stories underlie meadows; visions sleep in mountains; every place name carries lives within it. And from these dreams and places emerge the stories of generations of my family.

My father was born in Westhope, North Dakota. *West* and *hope*—the destinies and desires of thousands of dreamers caught up by the frontier distilled in two words. The town had existed for just thirteen years when "Doc Charley" Durnin delivered tiny, premature Donald Eldon Trimble and kept him alive by incubating him in a shoebox placed in the office oven. March 6, 1916. Baby Don's parents, my grandparents, were authentic pioneer offspring. I heard their stories as a child, and they brought the opening of the West close.

My grandmother Ruby Seiffert was one of the first white children—as the family stories always put it—born in that part of North Dakota in 1892. The Seifferts, Alsatian and Scotch immigrants, had made their way west through Canada, from Ontario to Manitoba, finally crossing south over the line to North Dakota in the 1880s.

One of the family homesteads lay along the curl of Antler Creek within sight of the international boundary, a little stream that ambled between the two countries through box elder, elm, and ash thickets—past a rock farmhouse, a plank bridge, a springhouse smelling of butter and cream. Another branch of the Seiffert family chose a spot along Antler Creek in 1883 when they spooked a remnant herd of buffalo. The guard bull roused his herd when he spotted their carriage from his lookout post on a hint of a hill—and on that rise they built their house.

My grandfather's Trimble forebears followed the American frontier westward from Alleghany County, Maryland, in pre-Revolutionary days—to Ohio, Iowa, and North Dakota. Branches of that clan reach back to the early Europeans' voyages to New England.

My great-grandfather Grant Trimble was the star of many of the family stories, a terrific character—the flawed patriarch. He came west when he drove horses from Iowa to North Dakota, made a profit, and decided to stay. He platted and built the town of Richburg, North Dakota, in 1898, and an old family photograph shows his center of operations, a storefront for Trimble's Dry Goods Department and Trimble's State Bank. Promotional signboards completely covered the building: "The Greatest Sale of Modern Times." "The Wonder of the Age." "They Kan't Ketch Up." "Fat Bargains." "A Happy Shopping Place."

When the railroad bypassed him five years later he platted his brother's farm, which happened to lie next to the railhead, and competed for sales by offering land at a fraction of the price of the railroad's lots. The Great Northern succumbed to his bluff, lowered their prices, and gave him a major portion of the lots in the new town. Great-grandfather Trimble gleefully put Richburg on wagons, building by building, and moved his frontier minidevelopment to the new railhead town of Westhope a mile and a half away. His oldest son, my grandfather Donald Enoch Trimble, was the first graduate of Westhope High School. (There were only two graduates that spring day in 1909, Trimble and Warner, and commencement was alphabetical.)

In Wallace Stegner's pithy words, the families who came west at this time were "boomers" or "stickers." The boomers followed their dreams, booming and busting but always refusing to knuckle under to the reality of the dry West, always refusing to stay put and "stick." Grant Trimble was a boomer.

This was the homestead era as well, and the Trimbles and the Seifferts claimed land for their own. Public land was simply unhomesteaded land, and that's where the men went duck hunting in the marshes, where young Don Trimble and Ruby Seiffert courted by hooking up the sidecar to my Grandpa's Indian motorcycle and bumping over the Turtle Mountains to Lake Metigoshe for picnics.

For a time, Grant Trimble avoided the bust; he even served as a state senator. The bust came in 1912, when he lost all his money in the wheat futures market. While cleaning out his office, Grant found the deed to an apple orchard in Washington that he'd won in one of his business deals and forgotten. It was all he had left. And so the Trimbles moved to Toppenish, a small town in the Yakima Valley.

Unlike the tragic arcs of the boomers dramatized in Wallace Stegner's books, Grant Trimble put down roots in Toppenish. Giving up his wilder dreams, he transformed the Trimbles into settlers—"stickers"—for the remainder of the twentieth century.

In my childhood my paternal grandparents lived at the far west of our family space in the Yakima Valley in Washington. Here, in Toppenish, where my father had grown up, my father's parents and my grandfather's two brothers and three sisters all lived within a few blocks of each other.

The Trimbles had brought their stories with them when they moved from North Dakota. They were townspeople now, but they stayed close, interdependent, with the special affinity of those with a shared past—in their case the boom times back in Dakota. They would spread their Adirondack chairs in a backyard circle and sip iced tea, reliving life on the farms and surrounding prairie as an adventure, reliving the golden memories of their youth.

Those Toppenish backyards contained some of my first wild places. The great evergreen tree that sheltered my grandfather's fishing boat, where I would hide in sharp-needled shade. A cement-lined fishpond. A dusty alley with hollyhocks and bumblebees. These are my elemental, fundamental memories, from a time almost beyond memory. I can tell just how primal because when I recall those explorations, diving deep into that ancient lizard brain where awareness begins with scent, I smell that dust and those pine needles as much as see them.

The Trimbles' experience of moving with the frontier was classically western. They may not have trapped beaver with the mountain men, but my great-uncles' stories of hunting and fishing in North Dakota, the photographs of the family farm that freeze moments of my father's earliest childhood, all tied me to The West, as home and myth, and to the nineteenth-century colonization of the frontier and the great dividing of the continent into private and public realms.

From Toppenish, the Trimbles looked up to the western horizon every day to see if their mountains were visible—the sublime glacier-covered half rounds of Mount Adams and Mount Rainier. These were ever-present, hovering presences in their lives. My father climbed these mountains as a boy with the Boy Scouts and the Mountaineers Climbing Club.

He took road trips with his pals, saving his money for gas so that he could see the saguaros in the Sonoran Desert, the Grand Canyon, the Great Southwest. When his family visited North Dakota, they detoured to Glacier National Park and to Yellowstone. He loved mountains, he loved the outdoors, and he studied geology in college so that he could work outside—putting himself through school with stints as a hard-rock miner.

After World War II deprived him of his home landscape during a three-year exile in the South Pacific theater, my father was delighted to be back on the road in the West. He had heard that the United States Geological Survey was hiring in Denver. At thirty, footloose and in need of a job, this sounded good to him. He moved, within two years married the office clerk-typist—my mother—and spent more than thirty years as a USGS field geologist.

Dad and his fellow geologists and their wives were my primary childhood circle. These scientists did field work in summer in wild country all over the West, then returned home to Denver in winter to work out the meaning of their notes and maps, publishing their theories as monographs. Their work verged on exploration, less than fifty years after John Wesley Powell had worked in some of the same places.

When I read Wallace Stegner's biography of John Wesley Powell, *Beyond the Hundredth Meridian,* I realized that Powell and his protégés Clarence Dutton and Grove Karl Gilbert were icons for my father and his friends. And that, in turn, my father's cohort of government scientists were my models, the men I would choose to emulate.

The landscape where Powell and Dutton and Gilbert made their mark was the Colorado Plateau, that great maze of canyons carved by the Colorado River. My father introduced me to these places on family trips. Later I worked in the canyon country as a park ranger. Today my retreat—my Eden—rises on a sandstone mesa with views across public land to a national park in the heart of the plateau. My imagination travels far but always comes home to these canyons.

The anti-intellectual stereotype of masculinity in the West veers in another direction entirely—that of the cowboy who turned up in western movies and television series of the 1950s, a man of the land but one who is driven to possess, own, and dominate—quick to take up arms to defend his property. Americans fancy this stereotype. We imagine these mythic heroes as our leaders—and we keep electing to the presidency men who play to that myth.

My father and his friends, by contrast, were men who drank and swore but treasured clear thinking and well-spoken ideas. They socialized as couples, women and men together. With plenty of World War II footage on the black-and-white television screen of our living room, I knew what they had done in the war a few short years before. Now "going out with the boys," for them, meant getting together with their sack lunches at the office to talk politics, argue theories, and banter. They saved their extra energy for climbing mountains and anonymous ridges, intent on deciphering the story of the landscape. Mostly irreligious, geologic time was their scripture.

Their fieldwork mixed the physical and the cerebral. They drove Jeeps and forded rivers and sweat-stained their hatbands. They mused in grand scale, comfortable with the millions and billions of geologic time, but they spent their days in physical contact with the earth, picking up rocks warmed by the sun, collecting rough horn coral fossils and knife-sharp chunks of obsidian, kneeling to measure grain size and the angles of rocks jutting from the surface of the planet. Mapping and photographing and drawing in their journals, these men made art while doing science.

In my childhood, I chose my father's lineage for my connections. Geology was the bedrock underlying patriarchy. Science was our religion, western history and natural history our tribal lore, the public domain of the West our Holy Land. Like my father, I took as my prophets the pioneers and mountain men, the explorer-scientists and writers journeying and journaling across the continent, and paid due respect to Lewis and Clark and to my grandfather's pioneer energy.

A subliminal message ran through this history: that government was good. From Lewis and Clark themselves to Powell and the nineteenth-century surveys, Aldo Leopold, and Bob Marshall's invention of the modern concept of wilderness while working for the Forest Service—the stories that nourished me featured federal bureaucrats as heroes. I grew up with the assumption that civil servants did visionary work.

The visionaries' disciples were the men of my father's generation, not long back from the war, returned alive to family, to good work, and to the canyons and deserts and rivers and mountains of the West. These were the places that gave them their stories. These were the places that make us who we are.

28

Huckleberry Country

Michael Umphrey

All my life I have made annual trips to Montana's huckleberry country, first with my parents, later with my own children. Occasionally, I've had people along who do not quite understand the culture of huckleberrying. One year I went with a college friend who was majoring in business. Randy swore at the endless flies and mosquitoes that assailed him whenever he stopped moving to pick, then he started in fiddling with numbers, the tanks of gas to drive to the woods, the hours we spent on the hillside, the total gallons of berries we finished with, and several other pieces of data, which he added and divided and arranged until he knew for certain that we had been fools. He proved it to me.

And then there was Daniel, the two-year-old son of Ken and Sarah Reeve who came with us one summer. He had little experience of deep woods, and he found something ominous and frightening about the dense tangle. Or maybe it was the drizzly rain. At any rate, like Randy, he fussed and fussed all day, wanting something other than this world.

Of course, the infant just needed time and help to find his way to be with us. My oldest daughter, Christa, held him on one hip and moved slowly through the woods, putting delight in her voice as she pointed things out so that he would understand he was in a good place. She was home from college for the summer, and I remembered her, even younger than two, peeking out from a tent at the rain, needing to be told which things in the endlessly complicated world around her were worth wanting. But the business student probably just needed to get out of Montana. He lives in Seattle now, where the whole world has been improved beyond help by his way of thinking.

Randy also couldn't understand one of the minor art forms among Montana newspaper columnists—the comic tale of woe they encounter each year as they head out to save money by hunting for free meat or gathering free firewood. We like to laugh at our irrationality, at our justifying $20,000 four-wheel-drive trucks so we can get into the hills in November to bring home a carcass or two. We like to be amused at the wood-gathering trip where we puncture a $250 tire, put a $750 dent in the truck, and back over a $450 saw before safely making it home in a mood of enterprise and thrift with our $75 cord of wood.

We have to laugh, because laughing is our way of shoving economic reckoning back against the wall so we feel free to do the things we want to do. Randy misses the point. The columnists have no intention of changing their ways. They aren't making fun of financial foolishness so much as they are making fun of the abstract emptiness we are left with when we apply economic methods to anything so fundamental and irrational as joy.

When my oldest boy, Eldon, was nine, he came down the hill with about a pint of berries in his can. He'd seen a buyer's sign in Hungry Horse, and he was beginning to understand the uses of money. "How much does a trampoline cost?" he asked.

"About three hundred dollars."

"How many gallons of huckleberries is that?"

"About twenty."

He looked at the berries in the bottom of his can, hesitating on the brink between the two worlds. The moment ended when he poured out a whole handful and put them all into his mouth at once. "Enough," he laughed, making it true.

Fortunately, it isn't even necessary to love the luxury of a mouth over-full of berries to understand. As I remember it, my father never did pick or taste a huckleberry. Still, every summer he took us back to the huckleberry place, a small parking spot beside a small creek in the vast and heavily logged ridges of the Flathead National Forest south of Hungry Horse Reservoir. The people's woods. While Mom and we six kids fanned out from camp in eager search of a magical patch, Dad sat in the shade beside his car, listening to the radio, content to be away from the maddening round of work days that began at five and ran on till midnight, of things breaking, bills arriving, people making messes or bustling to clean them up. He wasn't there to participate in the economy, through saving money or utilizing a resource or any other forsaken business.

Just before lunchtime, he made us a pile of baloney sandwiches, in his neat and impeccable way. My mother tended to throw things together, whether a sandwich or a conversation, and Dad was characteristically in retreat from the commotion of her presence. She had buckets and Styrofoam coolers and canning pots into which we poured gallon after gallon of berries, and she measured the success of our trip by the quantities we collected. She had always been poor, and this left her with a frantic habit of accumulating and storing.

Dad, of course, had never been poor, lacking the knack for it. He trusted that what he needed would come or could be found, and he didn't like cluttering his house and his head with either worries or stuff. He could always afford time to enjoy leisure and peace. She was always noisily engaged in the moment's crisis.

For a few years, their contrary temperaments were amplified by Earl Dunn and Missus Dunn. They began going to the woods with us. I never really knew why. Huckleberrying was the only time of year we ever saw them, and their own children were long grown. Earl was a thin, whiskey-drinking man dressed like a cowboy. He liked to sit and laugh at things, always near a cup of coffee in the mornings and a cup of whiskey in the evenings. Missus Dunn was a huge woman who moved through a swirl of activity. She always wore pants, her hair was cut short, and she had a tough, aggressive way of talking. She didn't think things or wonder about things; she knew things, and she told you so.

She wagged her finger at you and nodded her head in firm agreement with whatever she said. It would take a braver person than any of us were to disagree with her. Earl said little, sitting at the edge of her whirlwind presence with his cup, grinning now and then and mumbling quips that she pretended not to hear. "What's that?" she accused.

"Nothing. Nothing," he mumbled, flashing a conspiratorial glance at us.

Missus Dunn lived the culture of huckleberries. She had a special bucket, which she slung on her hip from an oversize belt adjusted to keep the rim at just the right height. She also had a berry picker, fashioned from a coffee can with its open edge cut into fingers, which she could theoretically sweep over a bush, plucking dozens of berries in a single swoop. She could talk about berry patches she had found over the years, master pickers and their methods, recipes, and she remembered how many gallons she had gotten on trips going back to years before I was born.

I never did find out why once each year the Dunns suddenly appeared as though they were close friends. I thought for a while that they came berrying with us because Mom wanted Missus Dunn's reinforcement and Dad wanted Earl's helpless company. But now that I'm of the age where I understand berrying better, I think it's more likely that my parents simply understood that Earl and Missus Dunn had to go berrying and that what they needed they couldn't get on their own. They needed to join, to share some work with others. It helped to believe the task was important, but in truth the work mattered less than the sharing.

So while Earl and Dad hung around camp, Mom and Missus Dunn and we kids barged through the woods, hollering for others to come share our good luck when we stumbled or tumbled into an especially good patch. We'd meet at odd intervals as our meandering searches led us to cross paths. "The berries this year are as big as your thumb," Missus Dunn would say every year, thrusting her thumb at us with an emphatic nod of her head.

All day we would go, seeing places we would never see unless some mission drew us out of our routines, out of our dailiness, and we had such a mission. We filled cottage cheese containers and old ice cream buckets and coffee cans, and we poured them into the bigger containers stored in the back of the red 1965 Volkswagen that we all crammed into for the trip. We drank water straight from cold streams. We stopped dropping berries into our buckets and ate them by the handful. We studied squirrels and chipmunks. Ran into deer.

It was wilderness to us, though we parked our car in the middle of it. Occasionally another car would drive by, but for the most part we stayed there beside the road without seeing or being seen. The first elk I ever saw in the wild came out of the woods into a clearcut above our camp. The bull and two cows walked with regal slowness across the open ground, pausing to browse and to look around as they picked their way, unafraid, through our vision and back into the forest. I knew I belonged there.

I take my own children to the general place, though ten years passed between the last time I was there with my parents and the first time I went with my children, and I've never been able to find the precise spot where we camped. I'm sure I would still recognize it—the huge rock, higher than a house, leaning over a ring of melon-sized stones where we built fires. Fingerling trout darting at tossed scraps of baloney in the two-foot-deep pool at the bottom of the small waterfall where the creek leveled for a few yards before passing through the four-foot culvert under the road and falling down the steep bank toward the dark ravine. But it was a place made by the road, and the roads have been remade.

So we choose another place, better in many ways than the one my dad settled for. Ours has a bigger, wilder creek. It is farther from a main road. The woods are less obviously logged. We go there every year, layering the scene with our pasts, picking huckleberries though not enough so that it feels like work or so that we can tell ourselves we are on the trip to save money. We all know, without needing to say so, that the trip is pure and simple celebration.

When my five children fan out, no longer needing my encouragement or my help, I tend not to go far before sitting down, listening to the sounds of younger voices finding what they want. It isn't the berries, exactly, though without the berries they might never know it was there. A few years ago, I took our three foster boys there along with our five birth children. During the day, they whined and complained and picked almost no berries. But as evening came, they became nearly frantic with a sense of freedom and possibility they were inexperienced at feeling. They ran up and down the mountain as they dared to get farther and farther from the fire. They could almost see, almost hear.

A bit later an enormous full moon rose over the nearby mountains, and the night was light enough to see colors at thirty yards. We ran up the road, throwing wild shadows through the trees, intoxicated by the sheer exuberance of the earth. The world was in order, even the night blessed with a portion of light. The foster boys didn't know their own father. I have no illusions that a night in huckleberry country will give them what they need.

But I find it easy to believe that it might let them at least taste a little of what they need, so that when other chances come they will recognize the taste, and follow it.

29

Scorched Earth

Rick Van Noy

"We are leaving in twenty minutes," I announce, making clear our intentions to get out this winter Saturday on a hike. I must declare our time of departure early so as not to spring it on the children or surprise them, even though they know this moment is coming. Earlier in the morning I had asked if they wanted to go on a hike today, and the kids agreed but didn't want to leave anytime soon. They first wanted to play and have the morning to themselves. I try to justify why leaving early is a good idea, but my argument has no effect.

"I want to play," Sam says.

"But you can play later," I say back. "And besides, I don't want to get bogged down here all morning." Our mornings sometimes follow the pattern of one of our favorite books, *If You Give a Pig a Pancake*. In the story, if you give a pig a pancake, he'll want some syrup. Syrup will make him sticky, so he'll want a bath. Pretty soon you're writing letters and packing for a trip and wallpapering a tree house, and then the sticky paste takes you back to syrupy pancakes.

Sam doesn't like the first warning and is silent at the rest. As he hears it, or perhaps just after, he gets out paper and markers and starts in on a picture. I warn him just after he gets this project out because he will bring to it a laserlike focus and will not be easy to interrupt. He's drawing a picture of squirrels in trees that say, "Do not kill my friends," to be used for rain forests or even local oaks—some early political art. Elliot grabs markers and paper too and starts in on her own artist's statement. Because I like the kids to play and draw, they're not making this easy.

But I am anxious to leave and have prepared the sandwiches, my wife's winter outing favorite, Underwood Deviled Ham with yellow mustard. The hike is my idea, so Catherine leaves me to do the packing. I have filled the water bottles and packed the fruit. While Sam is drawing, I start to clean the house, but where to start? I make the beds first and then start picking up the books left scattered on the floor. Would I rather have them read or be neat, I have to ask, because certainly there's creativity in this clutter. Eventually, it's on to the Legos, spilling out of their containers, and the Barbie clothes that jumped out of their baskets. Appalachian poet Jim Wayne Miller writes that children are "sorcerers" for the way they turn houses upside down, and in his "Saturday Morning" he too finds "books, bats, balls, dolls and teddy bears / with idiot smiles—the contents of every bedroom / spilled like puzzle pieces over floors."

I pick up a half-empty container of animal crackers and a juice box and am starting to curse under my breath. It's also a winter day, a day we were going to go skiing, my favorite winter pastime, but the weather hovered around 60 degrees all week and there's no snow left. I have to readjust my time clock, programmed for winter sports. Plus, I didn't sleep well last night, slumber-party night, when I get kicked out of bed and the kids join Mom in my place.

I am mad for the mess and mad that I've had to say something to Sam to get us out the door today. Like Miller, I want to nurture the imagination and relish in this sorcery of the ordinary, and Sam's intonation, "but we're playing," is hard to argue with. But soon the beds will be stripped of their blankets to make pirate ships, the couch cushions will form parts of alligator habitat, and all the animals, stuffed and plastic alike, will all play roles in the theater, and I might end up picking it up. I understand Miller's teddy bears to have "idiot smiles" because they have no reaction to the room. Perfect parents must smile all the time, as should their perfect little children.

I take to the outside in part to save the house from being further ransacked and often to replenish or let off steam. Anyone who has raised young kids has at some time or another wanted to scream, and I've had my share of inappropriate responses. Nearly every time I reach in to buckle kids in a car seat and am welcomed with sticky hands or a furry, fuzzy animal to the face—then bump my head on the door frame—I've wanted to unleash a chain of expletives. It's not found in any of the parenting books, but getting mad can be a very effective tool, more simple than the carrot, not quite as harsh as the stick. And I must admit to being frustrated at how raising kids can be an incredible drain on time. Before children, I used to ride and run, heck, I used to read, and I would hike, and that's why we're going out today, goshdarnit, whether rain or shine, foul mood or perky idiot smile. Since you can't beat them, have them join you.

I leave for the local whole-foods store, Annie Kay's, to get a few "carrots" for the trip, some espresso beans for the adults and some cocoa-covered almonds for the kids. I also pick up several gold-covered chocolate coins, treasure for those who make it to the end of the trail. I will tell them about this treasure and hide it under a log when we get to the top. They're on to me, but we keep doing it anyway. When I return from the store, we're still not ready. My tension has rubbed off on my wife, and she has yelled at Sam for tracking mud from his sneakers through the kitchen. I had to put them back on while he colored. He lies on his stomach and gives me a foot, heel up. He comes out crying and sulks in his car seat. But we have finally crossed that most important stile a hiker with children must cross—just getting out the door.

We pick up Rob, our doctor, and his son, Noah, who is in Sam's first-grade class. Rob is a kind, humble man who loves to spend time with his kids and is open to alternative forms of medicine. "Americans think there is a pill for everything," he says in the car, when talking about his recent trip to China and the healing art of massage. In the middle of the conversation, the kids have gotten into a fight over a toy and Noah says, "God damn."

"Noah!" Rob yells, though he's not particularly religious. It's more that he's worried over the impression he makes.

"He picks that up from his older sister," he assures me. "Sorry about that."

The hike we are going on is named Scorched Earth Gap because, our guidebook says, a woman came to the steep part of the long hike and yelled such profanity that she "scorched the earth." I tell Rob he need not worry about the cursing, and I relate to him our own story. When Sam was three and home with his mother, he asked her permission to do something, like watch a favorite show. Sticking to our policy of limited TV, she told him no, that he'd have to find something else to do. He stayed there for a few minutes, holding back what we call a "shibba," where the lower lip sticks out in a pout. "Fuck," he blurted out.

The tiny preemie she first held in her womb, whose glass incubator she stood over in the NICU, whose regular breathing she willed out of him so we could go home, had used the language of a foul-mouthed sailor, defiling the room. With a word he rendered her speechless, until she called me.

We don't know the precise origins of Sam's use of the phrase, but it probably came from me. I am, after all, from New Jersey, where the governor joked that the middle finger is the state bird. My accent comes out,

I'm told, when I'm talking to plumbers and hardware store salespeople. And having spent some time in the trades, let's just say I've learned to express myself when angry. Probably, he heard it in the car when someone cut in front of me.

Sam uttered the word several more times before he stopped. Sometimes, he would hold back but not quite: "I almost said *fuck*, but I didn't say *fuck*. What? I didn't say *fuck*? I'm only saying it now." Each time it came out, it was like glass breaking. We tried not to react too strongly lest he sense how powerful the word could be. Kids discover the power and play of language through the potty variety, but the F-word crossed the line.

In guidance class in school, the kids have learned more effective means for expressing frustration or anger. They have learned to scream into a pillow or hit it, to run around the house a few times, or to draw pictures of the thing that makes them angry. In our house, we have drawings of a parent saying, "No, no, no" with an X marked over the drawee. These papers are then sometimes crumpled or ripped to pieces, their subjects X-ed out, as we say in New Jersey.

As bad as the F-word in our house is the W-word—*whatever*. I hear it much from the college students I teach, but we don't allow it. It means "I don't care, I refuse to become engaged or exert effort, and I will show no passion or exuberance. My primary duty is to fit in, and since we all have our own opinions, and I am not curious about anything, whatever." Even worse is the B-word, as in "I am bored," as if the child must be constantly entertained. For use of the B-word, my wife and I might not wash the mouth out with soap, but we offer this standard advice: go outside. Get out of the house and get outside of yourself.

Catherine, Rob, and I hike through a woodland and then into a pasture and along Catawba Creek and a tributary. As the road and parking lot fade into the background, the morning's anger has dissipated too. Noah, Sam, and Elliot take off out in front. Eventually we can no longer hear their shouts and cheers as they skip on ahead. Occasionally, at a crucial junction, like the one that says "No Trespassing" (an old sign, we tell them), they wait. They hike like dogs, running forward and then doubling back to check on our progress, then bounding forward all over again.

For the first hour, the hike goes well. We find our rhythm. We see a scooped-out trunk and remember the beginning to our Richard Scarry: "My name is Nicholas and I live in a hollow tree." We point out a bird species, a kinglet, and almost hear the burble of the nearby stream over the shouts of the children. When hiking by myself, I drink in the silent woods, and I might stop and look. But kids are constantly moving, jumping, talking, although they may just stay in the creek that crosses the trail and look for salamanders, in which case we won't get very far. For John Muir, the hills and groves of the Yosemite Valley were temples, the mountains cathedrals, and everywhere in nature he saw God's grandeur. When I hike with kids, I tend to look at nature less as sacred but more as playground. I am constantly looking for a rock we might turn over, a log we might walk across, or a tree we might climb. And everywhere there could be fossils or wild things or caves to hide in. Before nature can become sacred, it must be accessible. It must be lain in and walked on, climbed up and run down. It must ooze between fingers and toes. It must be eaten, whole, and again.

But our energy eventually fades. Elliot is the first to go. There's a *New Yorker* cartoon that shows a set of parents in the woods with their kids. "This is hiking," they say. "It's walking you don't like." Though two years younger, she keeps up with the older boys, but when she gets close, they pick up their pace so as not to be passed. My wife, middle child of seven, relates to always having to be fourth on such outings.

A third of the way up, we are so warm that we shed some clothing, a choice we regret near the top. After two hours of huffing and puffing up switchbacks, we are feeling tired. Elliot and Catherine have turned back. Noah, Rob, Sam, and I are pushing on. At lunch, we had asked another passing hiker how far to the top, but he didn't know, and with kids, we are better off taking things as they come anyway. It's most often when we deviate from some plan that either one of us gets mad. After another half hour, we also turn back before the summit, an act unthinkable before I had children, but it is the right thing to do. The kids would rather play anyway. Noah and Sam are acting like dinosaurs or cavemen. They grunt words and use hand gestures. Neither Rob nor I know what they are saying, but the kids are clear to each other, and the message is simple: "Follow us. We know the way."

And while the kids surge ahead, neither Rob nor I, an M.D. and a Ph.D., can remember exactly the physics of why it gets colder at higher altitudes (because you are farther from the heat absorbed by the earth's surface). "Though I'm freezing," Noah says—we are all a little slaphappy now—"I remember my manners." And though we are tired, cold, and stupid, we skip along and do not curse at all. On the way back, I slip down the steep part, the scorched earth part, falling on my tail, and everyone laughs. No one has cut me off in these woods.

When we get to the lower elevation, where the forest meets the more level pastureland, our fatigue dissolves, and we feel a resurgence of energy. We meet up with the girls and read the plaque dedicated to "trail-builder and friend" Andy Layne: "May he lighten your step. If he sensed you were tired, he would say he was and would request a rest, and then he'd tell a story so you'd forget how tired you were." We've been trying this diversion tactic all day, asking the kids what they might like to have for a snack later. "If I were to fall over, don't any of you SOBs put your mouth to mine and bring me back to life. Let me die right here," Layne was known to say, perhaps the closest he got to swearing.

Rob, mild-mannered Rob from a good Jewish home, looks back over where we've come: "Holy hell," the good doctor says, "that was a long-ass hike." Our step is a little lighter, and we are unburdened of the social taboos of vulgarity, even in the presence of first-graders. Smelling the end of the trail, the kids' pace seems to slow some for a moment as if they don't want to hike to the end, but soon the games have resumed—follow the leader, Daddy's the vampire, everyone hide! "In the woods," Emerson says, "is perpetual youth." For poet Jim Wayne Miller, "you must be born again / and again / and again." These are ecstatic moments—the kids lost in the woods, all of us returned to our senses.

On the way home, Elliot asks, "Do those purple flowers grow up to be trees?" And Sam: "What is the second highest peak in the world?" The very purpose of this hike has been to awaken them to potential.

I see Rob a couple of weeks later at Annie Kay's. It is our night to cook at home. He tells me he was worn out after the hike but woke up refreshed, like his senses had been invigorated. "Me too," I say. "Like I had a whole new perspective on things." We talk of our next hike, to Angel's Rest. This time we will keep the jackets and hats. And we will warn the kids about not getting their feet wet too early. And though there may be words profane on the way up or down or to get out the door, I cherish the sacredness of these outings. They return me to the father I want to be rather than the one I sometimes am.

30

Children in the River

Gretel Van Wieren

Steelhead Spawning, April 2009

Little Manistee River, Irons, Michigan

It's early, 7 a.m., and the girls and I are trying to make a fishing plan. I'll go downstream past the Fairmans' cabin to Rainbow Run first and fish the beds I know are active right now, and then the girls will leave the cabin around 9 a.m., hike the path along the river by themselves, and meet me at the Fairmans'. If I am not there, they will "hoot-e-oot," our family call since my father invented it for woods-calling when my three sisters and I were young. The Fairmans have a trampoline, which makes it easy to convince the girls to hike the half mile of river path alone. The trampoline is at least forty years old, decrepit, rusty, moldy in the middle, superspringy, and terribly dangerous. The girls love it, and so do I— because it means I can fish.

In last spring's steelhead season, while I was down the hill in front of the cabin fishing a deep, dark hole full of steelhead, my middle, mystical daughter, Clara, did a sky-high, circuslike jump, landing with both legs straddled through the rusty red springs. She howled like I have never heard a child, wolf, or coyote call. I sprang out of the river with such abandon I almost lost my rod. I thought for sure she had catapulted herself into a full-on head dive and broken her neck. But no, she had two scraped calves with a slight chance of tetanus. I held her on the mossy ground, kissed her again and again, quickly calculated when her last tetanus shot was, asked her not to jump so high, and then told her not to worry. I would be in the same spot at the bottom of the bank. Just hoot-e-oot if you need me.

This year, however, the fish are not yet on beds, and fishing is slow. I begin walking the path back to the cabin. About halfway back, I hear the girls talking and laughing, anticipation ripe in their voices. They hear me coming and yell, "Did you hear all those turkeys across the river?" I ask where they thought they were coming from. Simultaneously, they shout, "That way," pointing in polar opposite directions like a clip from a Laurel and Hardy film.

We decide to track down the gobblers. Because we will need to cross the river to reach them, we run back to the cabin so the girls can put on their waders. I take my rod, just in case. Then we hike back downstream, up the hill, past the high bank and the Fairmans'. When we get to Rainbow Run, our other family cabin, we scout the river for a good place to cross. Even though we see no fish on beds,

I do not want to tromp across the river where the stones look lightened as if fish may have at least begun to build their gravel nests.

We find a darker sandy area, step into river's edge, grab hands, and begin wading slowly across the river. The current is strong on the east side of the river and becomes even stronger ten feet in. Then it happens. A giant silvery-pink crash, thrash, LEAP, not once but twice, three, four, five times, right in front of us. Steelhead, a female, at least ten pounds and two feet long. The first of the season. The spectacle is one I have witnessed several hundred times in my life, in the same river, at the same time of year. I look over at my daughters, their mouths widening a notch with each jump. I am silent, a huge grin on my face, staring and smiling at my beholden, fish-struck girls.

The art and experience of children and adults fishing together have long been mythologized in the American environmental imagination. Norman Maclean's *A River Runs through It* perhaps best narrates this phenomenon, yet there are numerous other examples—Huckleberry Finn and Jim fishing on the Mississippi River; Laura Ingalls and her Pa pond and creek fishing in Wisconsin, Kansas, and Minnesota; and Hemingway's Nick Adams angling in Michigan's Upper Peninsula with his father, figuratively and literally, always nearby. Even today, taking one's children fishing remains an American cultural rite of passage. Posted on the refrigerator door at my family's cabin, for instance, is a recent magazine advertisement that pictures a seven- or eight-year-old girl in a boat holding a fishing rod. It reads: "Take me fishing. . . . Because bouncing in a boat gives me the giggles."

My own fishing experiences began when my father took me to rivers in Michigan and Utah, hoisted in a bright blue baby backpack. As soon as I could sit up on my own, I would fish with my mother, grandmother, grandfather, and later with my three younger sisters. We lived on Lake Michigan, retreated to a cabin on a river in northern Michigan, and frequented family places in Lake of the Woods, south Florida, and the Rocky Mountains. My father was a college professor and my mother a homemaker, so summers and breaks our family was off in search of water. Anywhere, everywhere, and in all seasons, we fished. Winter was ice fishing for perch; spring brought brown and rainbow trout, Great Lakes steelhead and Gulf of Mexico sea trout; summer was filled with walleye, northern pike, and small and large mouth bass; fall ushered in the chinook salmon and browns again.

One river in particular, the Little Manistee, and its fish—rainbow and brown trout, steelhead, and salmon—had the most profound effect on my childhood. Of all the places I have fished since, it remains my favorite. Relatively small, especially in comparison to its larger cousin, the Big

Manistee River (the "Little Man" and "Big Man," as the rivers are referred to by locals), its character is large. In front of the family cabin, it stretches thirty feet across and four feet deep at the most. There are few holes in the entire river that would reach over my head, but there are plenty that were dark, deep, and ominous enough to frighten us as children.

My father "discovered" it for us. Growing up, he was a boy in obsessive and steady search for fish. As a high school student, he and a friend would make the more than two-hour drive from the southwestern part of the state to stalk the salmon and steelhead that returned from Lake Michigan to the Little Manistee River every year. And he came for the big, beautiful brown trout that haunted the holes in this clear, cold, spring creek.

There he fell in love. Shortly after Dad graduated from college, his father helped him buy a large parcel of land along the river, an inholding within the Manistee National Forest. When he and my mother married, they began building a cabin from the cedar trees that line the river's banks. From the first, they called it "The Cedar Shack," posting a small hand-painted sign by the front door made from barn siding. Ever since, this has been home. This is where my father, my sisters and I, and now my own children have been steeped in water; this is where we have come to love to fish.

The Ojibwe called the land where the cabin now sits *ministigweyaa*— "river with islands at its mouth" or "spirit of the woods." Birch, maple, oak, northern white cedar, balsam fir, and basswood trees close in along the banks, making the river almost impenetrable at many points. We never knew what might emerge from the thicket when we were hacking through it. Once, making my way to a favorite salmon hole, I nearly stepped on a brightly spotted newborn fawn hidden by low-lying brush and tall grass. Another time, I snuck up on a ruffed grouse, barely discernible in the surrounding brown branches, sitting on a full nest of eggs.

Trees have fallen across and along the river, making it particularly challenging to paddle and wade. Occasional grassy islands growing on rotting wood are dotted with jack-in-the-pulpit, white and lavender asters, and oxeye daisies. Beaver, mink, and otter slide in and out of holes dug under banks. Kingfishers, swallows, bluebirds, warblers, tanagers, grosbeaks, and cedar waxwings dart in swoops and bows. Bald eagles and red-tailed hawks keep watch from tall trees at river's edge. And then there are the fish. Most plentiful are the smallish rainbow trout, six to eight inches in length. They can be caught on virtually every cast with any fly from a caddis to a Madam X to a fuzzy, grey-and-white shrimplike pattern one of my daughters inventively tied last spring. At times, I have caught these little lively creatures one after another standing on the edge of the bank, inviting my then three- and four-year-old daughters and one-year-old son to strip them in on a fly line.

The brown trout are another story. They are far less numerous and much more wily. They hide in the deepest, scariest holes covered with layers of criss-crossing logs and thick bank-hugging brush, making them especially difficult to get to with a fly. If you are able to hook one, they run for the spots they know will free them—the logjams and branch masses. My most desperate fishing losses have been big browns, lost in the end by their innate ability to find the places that will pop the hook or break the line.

If the rainbows and browns are the staples of the river, though, the salmon and steelhead are the candy. Without them, the river remains charming and feral and beautiful. With them, this unassuming trout stream is transformed into an exquisite, exceptional jewel. Most years, over ten thousand salmon and three thousand steelhead find their way back from Lake Michigan to their river home.

The steelhead are my favorite, in large part because they are simply beautiful. Steel-grey with a bright pink-red swath down the middle of the females' sides, they are smooth, fierce, and graceful metallic firebirds when they leap out of the water. Nicknamed "steelies" by anglers, they are the regal queens and kings of the river.

The Little Manistee is the mother river for virtually all Great Lakes steelhead. Each spring, five million steelhead eggs are collected at the Little Manistee weir by the Michigan Department of Natural Resources and sent off to hatcheries around the Midwest. It makes me feel proud and protective. The steelhead that migrate here are maintained by natural reproduction. In fisheries lingo, they are "wild," not "planted." The flies are teeny-tiny natural-looking imitations. Size six to ten hooks (about the length of your ring fingernail) with patterns of stonefly and caddis variations tied in blacks and browns are the norm. If you manage to hook one of these giants, a feat in such a small river on such a tiny hook, the fish rips the line out so fast and with such force that it is as if you have been struck by lightening.

Last season, on a bright spring day, standing knee-deep at river's edge, I cast to an active bed in a fast run halfway across the river, hooked up on a steelie, and then handed the rod over to either of my daughters to fight the fish for as long as she could hold on. The rod, twice their height, doubled over, and their tiny bodies bent and contorted from the fish's ten to fifteen pounds. Usually, I ended up landing the fish, and then one or both girls somehow managed to net it. Together we flailed, yelled, cheered, and then gawked silently at the huge, mysterious creature that found its way into our clumsy hands.

I find myself asking many questions now that I have children: Why has fishing in my home river profoundly shaped the person I have become? What is it about wading and fishing in cold running rivers that makes many people fall in love with the rivers of our childhoods, and why do I feel it is important for my children to have that experience? What is this river-love thing all about anyway?

Numerous fishing writers have catalogued the ways in which rivers, especially the rivers that we fish in, can wind their way into and through the deepest parts of the human heart. The first person known to have penned an essay on fishing ("A Treatyse of Fysshynge wyth an Angle," 1496) was Julian Berners, abbess of a Benedictine nunnery in England. Some two centuries later, Izaak Walton wrote *The Compleat Angler: Or The Contemplative Man's Recreation*, which ranks third (behind the Bible and *Pilgrim's Progress*) as the most printed volume in the English language. Since then, various authors have written about the deep spiritual values that fishing can help form in its adherents. There is "no clear line between religion and fly-fishing," as Maclean's narrator famously states. For the avid angler, the river becomes a cathedral, and casting a fly-line, a devotional practice.

Fishing in rivers can foster deeper, spiritual, moral values within children too. This point is important to me, for in today's culture, practical outdoor arts like fly-fishing have become rare jewels. There is not only an extinction of outdoor experience among children, as Robert Michael Pyle has suggested. There is an extinction of particular types of experiences, particularly those that connect children practically and spiritually to the whole life-death-life process, including its consumptive aspects. Fishing, similar to canoe and pack travel as Aldo Leopold pointed out, is a primitive art that still makes sense for children to learn. Practically, it gives them a skill critical for human survival (catching their own food); spiritually, it is an act poised to create deep meaning and fulfillment.

When I began thinking about what gives fishing its distinctive capacity for wonder formation, I asked my older daughter, Inga, what she thought. Initially, she wondered what kind of fishing I meant. Was I talking about fishing from the bank, a dock, out of a boat, or with waders? I said, "With waders, in the middle of the river." Her face lit up. Immediately she retorted, "Well, you feel like you are *in* the river when you are wading. You're not just looking at it but actually part of it." "Don't you feel like this, like you are in nature, when you are hiking a trail in the middle of the woods or even canoeing?" I probed further. Her response: "No." Pause. "When you are wading in the river, you feel everything around you so much more. When you are hiking and canoeing, you're mostly watching and looking all around and thinking."

Standing in waders in a cold running river *is* a full-bodied, sensual experience. It connects the child angler with the natural world in ways that are nearly overpowering. Myriad other life forms continually "bump into" her sense of smell, sight, touch, and hearing. Her whole body is enlivened by the river.

This heightened sense of feeling is accentuated by the fact that the angler is actively participating in the life and ways of a wild, living system. As my daughter's comments suggest, the angler actively participates *in* the biological ways of the river by engaging in a wild act herself. In attempting to catch a fish, she is becoming a sensing, hunting, extra-aware animal. She is, for a moment, an otter, an eagle, a muskrat, a fish.

But most children do not think of fishing in these literal or symbolic terms. My children love to play in the river simply for the feeling of the water sucking around their legs, bellies, and chests. My daughter Clara peed in her waders the first time she walked into the river when she was six, and she begged to just keep on wading (I let her, too). A child's experience of the world is different from an adult's. It is unfiltered. Much is new, fresh, "right there." Bioregional writer Freeman House says he wants to learn to trust his senses as a path to reality. Children just do it, following their senses intuitively to find their way in the world.

Fly-fishing literature has tended to focus on either angling's outer dimensions, related to details of the "catch," or its inner aspects, related to personal experiences of transformation and renewal. Yet one of fishing's most poignant contributions to growing up human in the modern world may be its capacity for tactilely and vernacularly connecting children's bodies and spirits to the bodies and spirit of a particular place, a certain river, or a special fish. Not many activities today have the capacity to match the contours of our senses with those of the land.

This is no small matter, for most of us living in highly urbanized contexts are hard pressed to find activities that can map our species intimately into land and water. As adults, fishing with children inspires us to feel our bodies, once again and anew within the river. Children talk incessantly while wading, demanding we feel the water around our waders, the cork in our hands, the fuzziness of the fly, the sweat under our vest and shirt, the cool air, light rain, hot sun, freezing wind, dry mouth, tired feet, bug bite. "What is that smell?" they ask. "Do you hear that? Sssh-hhh. Ahhhhh, something hit me. A fish. It's a fish!" "No," I say, "it's just a log." "Feel it, Mama. Make sure it's not a big, dead fish."

I touch it first with my boot, then with my hand, reaching clear down into the dark water. I find the log with my fingers. It is covered with algae, river grass, and bunched up decaying leaves. It is smooth, soft, and silky, fishlike from being submerged for a long time. I stand up. My arm is soaking wet; my shirt thoroughly drenched and dripping with water. "Definitely, a log," I tell them. "Put your foot right here. I don't think you can reach it with your hand." "No way," they shriek. "We believe you! Let's go up to the shallower water, Mama. Come on, hurry! Hurry!"

For just a moment, even with their hollering and near-panic clutching, my children have reminded me that I am matter touching matter, water touching water, skin touching skin. There are feet with the gravel, a log with the fish, leaves with the larvae. My arm is wet, my fingers get cold, rivers can be dangerous. I can feel fear and confidence, weariness and happiness, uncertainty and shame, delight and giddiness. Maybe I really can trust my senses as a path to the heart of reality. Anglers fish, in part, as a way to escape daily, modern, cultured life by vicariously returning to a more primitive, biological state. "When you are fed up with the troublesome present, with being 'very twentieth century,'" writes Spanish philosopher Ortega y Gasset in his classic *Meditations on Hunting*, "you take your gun, whistle for your dog, go out to the mountain, and, without further ado, give yourself the pleasure during a few hours or a few days of being 'Paleolithic.'" When the angler is fed up with the troublesome present, she grabs her rod, slips into her waders, and heads for the river. She gives herself the pleasure for a few hours or, if she's lucky, a few days of being integrally, bodily connected to her ecology, of being an active, participating member of a river community.

Even as fishing thrusts the angler back in historical time, it simultaneously focuses him on the moment and context at hand. To become Paleolithic, for the fisher-hunter, means to become sensitized to, aware of, and engaged with one's immediate circumstances—the nymphs under the rocks, the flow of the water, the flies hatching, the wind's direction, the branch's position, the fly rod's angle, the fish's rise. Even when your mind and body are entirely consumed by the act, not a moment passes without heightened attentiveness.

Fly-fishing has tended to represent a certain romantic quality in American culture—wide-open landscapes, grand rivers, scotch and cigars, the effortless wading of Brad Pitt in the Hollywood version of *A River Runs through It*. Harmony and fly-fishing seem to go hand-in-hand. Yet fishing with children also involves more difficult emotions. On a practical level, it is rarely a romantic or tranquil experience. In fact, it is often tainted with annoyance, boredom, even anger, for both child and adult. This is especially the case for fly-fishing, where the river (the smaller the worse) is lined with trees. Nothing can inspire more frustration in children and adults than attempting to learn to cast while routinely getting caught in overhanging branches. Casting for hours, days, weeks, years without a single rising fish runs a close second.

There are also the mixed emotions that arise for the avid angler when she is fishing with children instead of fishing alone. Often there is nothing I would rather be doing than untangling line, tying on flies or baiting hooks, and (best-case scenario) taking off fish. But there are also times, actually more than I would like to admit, that I long for solitary, childless fishing. Fishing with children is an exhausting endeavor.

The element of tragedy in the fishing experience, however, reaches beyond its practical challenges. As hunting, moral animals, we address creaturely death and not just any death, but death caused by us and for our own benefit. Because of its primitive nature, hunting provides an opportunity for participating in evolutionary biological life in ways other modern outdoor activities do not. We encounter the necessary underside of our evolved existence in the suffering that has to be.

The child angler is thrust into the painful, brute realities of biological existence—of killing and eating, reproducing and dying—encountering them head on. "It is so mean, Mama, to pierce a worm on a hook." "Why do the salmon have to die after just one time laying their eggs?" "It's so unfair." "It is so sad, that dead moldy fish, lying over there." "What will happen to it? Will it be eaten or just go back into the earth?"

The death involved with fishing makes me, as a parent, wonder if it is good to subject children to it at a young age. Maybe it would be better to wait until they are older before they watch the cleaning of a fish or learn to remove one from the hook. Perhaps children should not begin fishing until middle childhood, when their capacities for critical reflection and evaluation are better formed. Or maybe catch-and-release is the answer—avoiding the final act of killing and eating what one has hunted and captured. Yet even with no-kill fishing, situations inevitably arise where the fish does not survive. More important, catch-and-release does not solve the fundamental human predicament of simultaneously being an eating, killing, growing, reproducing animal and a self-conscious, reflective, critically evaluative one. It does not solve the dilemma of death.

But can anything, really? Perhaps death is something we need to help children learn to handle. "Deal with it," we should tell our little girls and boys about the cycle of life. "You've got to toughen up, grow up." "Learn to be pragmatic, hard-hearted ecologists." "It's just part of the system." "Eagles eat fish, fish eat mice, mice eat grain." "It's red in tooth and claw." "That's life."

This seems callous, however, and callousness and curiosity do not go together well. If we think that developing a deep sense of wonder in relation to nature is an important part of being fully human, then we will need to figure out how to help children deal with nature's surprisingly horrendous parts. There are "natural evils" in this worldly biological life, writes philosopher Holmes Rolston III, and somehow we must learn to see them as inherently part of this prolific, generative life.

We may be "surprised by joy," as writer C. S. Lewis poignantly noted, or we may be surprised by death. We might not know when or where it is coming from. There is an "empty-minded awe," an "uneasiness," a "looming existential dread that sometimes attains the physicality of a lump in the throat," House writes, when he stands in the river with king salmon. Children often experience these emotions in ways that can be acute. When they do, they tend to verbalize them directly, to the point of crassness. Children know that there are things beyond them—death, decay, moldly, stinking, rotting salmon, for instance—that they ought to reflect on if they want to learn about life's deepest mysteries.

My younger daughter frequently wonders out loud why we are trying to "trick the fish" with bait on a hook or an artificial fly. She does not like the idea. And part of me does not either. Last summer, while fishing Hyalite Creek just outside Bozeman, my older daughter cried because her sister wanted to keep the six-inch rainbow trout she had caught, her first all alone, on a cinnamon caddis. "It is just a baby!" Inga wailed. "You have to let it go!" She didn't stop for an hour while we were hiking through a glorious canyon dotted with late summer wildflowers. My son insists on letting the fish go back to their mothers and fathers because "they are just so cute, Mama. And their Mamas and Daddies would be so sad without them."

In part, these childhood reactions to the capturing or killing of another living being stem from the relative newness of confronting creaturely death and, on top of that, death that they impose. A constellation of complex and often conflicting emotions accompany the hunting, catching, killing, cleaning, and eating of a fish or other animal. Fishing allows us as humans to enter into and participate actively in the wild side of life, including its more troublesome aspects.

A sense of wonder in relation to the world around us should not necessarily be equated with naïve delight. Children are not always innocent when it comes to experiencing the natural world. Often they feel emotions more deeply and expansively than many adults, which is one reason they tend to be better wonderers. Children are open to being amazed, uncertain, uncomfortable, and mystified by the admixture of this tragic and beautiful life. When it comes to fishing, they can see and feel it for what it is—not just a pragmatic act of humans killing to eat but a serious engagement with the sacramental aspect inherent in life.

One of the things I find myself doing frequently is attempting to help my children express the emotions they may be feeling. Rather than just saying, for example, "Well, that's life," to my daughter when she cried and cried over that small rainbow trout that her sister wanted to keep, I tried to listen to her wails, even though they become old very quickly. Then I asked her what exactly made her so sad and what we could do about it. I tried to get her to hold the fish, to turn it over in her hand, to really look at it, recount its colors, touch its skin. She wouldn't. So I asked her to breathe and walk in the shallow edges of the river. I rubbed her back under her waders. We looked for mushrooms and wildflowers along stream's edge. After a good long while, she calmed down, only to get all whipped up again when we returned to camp and her sister pulled the fish out of her pocket, grinning from ear to ear.

It is not always easy or fun to attempt to draw out children's deep feelings when they fish. Like therapists or ministers, we often wonder how much to say, attempt to explain, or resolve for the child emotionally. When do we listen, and when do we talk? Most of us do not engage in the hunting rituals of traditional cultures that have historically served to educate children in the ways of productively confronting the inherently difficult dimensions of biological and social life. But many anglers do engage in practices that are demarcated, even made sacred, by virtue of their distinction from ordinary activities. Going fishing in a cold running river is different from going grocery shopping or checking email. Cleaning fly-line, putting on waders, tying on tippet, stepping into the water are simple acts made glorious by their distinction from more conventional ones.

At my family's cabin, we always clean the fish immediately when we return, still in our waders, down at the old dock, on a cutting board made of a loose board stashed haphazardly under the deck. It is a quotidian activity, though one that has come to mean much more than just the necessary act that it is. I recall sitting on the deck as a child, watching and talking with my father as he cleaned fish. He stood in waist-deep water, concentrating and chatting, cutting and filleting one side of a trout and then the other. He dipped their flesh in the water, laid them back on the dock, picked up the carcass, and flung it clear across the river for the eagles, otters, or perhaps even bear to feed on. It was ordinary, and it was significant. My father had walked out into the morning or evening and had returned with fish. We would eat them for dinner. They were bright pink. Their spots would glow when they were fried, skin on, in half oil and half butter. They had come from our river. We ate them only when we were at the cabin. "Kings and queens of all the land are not eating better than we are tonight," my father would proclaim ceremoniously as we tasted our first bite of rainbow or brown trout at dinner. He said it every night.

Nature writer Gretel Ehrlich writes that "to trace the history of a river or a raindrop, as John Muir would have done, is also to trace the history of the soul, the history of the mind descending and arising in the body. In both, we constantly seek and stumble on divinity." To trace the history of a river by fishing with children is to be led into hearts bursting with feeling and bodies growing fast into expanding minds and worlds. Children in a river have a nose for the miraculous, a hunch for the amazing, a penchant for being awed. They are conduits for seeking and stumbling on divinity for their adult angling companions. Water, gravel, insects, fish: child anglers feel their river worlds "so much," to quote my daughter again. They are like divine guides. They lead us into sacred territory.

Afterword

It seems inevitable that readers of the often challenging, always insightful essays in this book will ask: What should I do? How can I, my friends and family, and the organizations we support help get children outside and revive our youths' and our cultures' connections with the natural world? How can we counteract the innumerable forces conspiring, as Carson puts it, to isolate people—each generation more than the last—"from the realities of earth and water and the growing seed"?[1]

Parents, grandparents, and other family members, sometimes called "first responders" in the movement to reconnect kids and nature, often feel acute responsibilities to shape their young relatives' futures.[2] Well-meaning advice abounds, yet the profusion of parenting books, articles, Web sites, other media, courses, workshops, nature center outings, and anecdote-based personal suggestions can obscure the path ahead. For these caring individuals, we can make several recommendations that are consistent with current research and often connect directly with the stories and reflections of Barry Lopez, Sandra Steingraber, Robert Michael Pyle, Carolyn Finney, our other contributors, and even Rachel Carson:

- *Make time a few days a week.* Children need frequent outdoor experiences to conquer fears, discover new abilities, and attach to special places. Be willing to take conflicting activities off the family to-do list and begin viewing nature time as an essential, healthful release from other pressures.

- *Start with enthusiasm.* There is no need to master ecology or geology before leading your family's first hike. Modeling a positive attitude will encourage children to stop worrying about ticks or thorns and step off-trail for the first time.

- *Resist overinvolvement.* Share some of your knowledge, memories, and ideas, but let children discover, observe, and invent their own games and fantasies. Try to become another "loose part" that your kids can respond to and with outside. And rather than warning of dangers, teach commonsense safety skills as part of your role as outdoor mentor.

- *Foster boredom indoors.* Nothing draws kids outside like a long weekend with the computer games, Internet, and television turned off. Banning iPods and cell phones from camping trips can be as important as packing the tent, though a digital camera safari or other electronics-facilitated activity can sometimes stimulate kids' interest.

- *Keep trying.* Do not expect your first outing to kindle interest, much less wonder. Experiment with different activities in various natural settings, different seasons, and different times of day. And despite protests by reluctant teens, keep leading the family outside throughout childhood.

The village that is rearing our children includes nonrelatives, too—often professional educators devoted to our schools, nature centers, museums, child care centers, and other formal and informal learning environments. Research in these diverse settings presents particular challenges both in execution and in application to the wider world, but we feel confident in making the following general recommendations to teachers, park and nature center staff, camp counselors, scout leaders, and other environmental educators:

- *Encourage biophilia.* If nothing else, avoid fanning disproportionate fears of outdoor risks such as snakebites, and minimize lessons about human-caused ecological disasters, especially for young students. Children will feel closer to nature simply by not learning that it is threatening or doomed.

- *Respect developmental levels.* Teachers of children who are under age seven should offer stories, make-believe games, and other activities that foster empathy with familiar creatures and natural settings, while children from about seven to eleven need the challenges of exploring, mapping, and shaping a wider natural community. Teachers of adolescents can introduce more remote, abstract issues such as the effects of climate change on coral reefs and investigate empowering ways students can affect the problem locally.

- *Involve the senses.* At all grade levels, children learn best when their eyes, ears, nose, and body are engaged in an experience. When studying trees, feel the bark, smell crushed leaves, listen to birds high in the canopy, and climb up and feel the breeze.

- *Teach across the curriculum.* There is no need to confine a caterpillar study to science class. Measure larval instar growth in math class, interview local farmers for social studies, and paint a butterfly mural in art.
- *Limit homework.* With fewer hours required at the computer after school, students have more time to spend outdoors. Suggest that students take their families outdoors to earn extra credit.
- *Restore the school grounds.* Whether you're surrounded by asphalt or wilderness, engage students in hands-on, direct efforts to enrich habitat, reduce energy use, and increase recycling. Designing safety into the setting will reduce the need for teachers to direct and protect children during learning and play. Outdoor classrooms and play spaces will encourage creative nature connections now and in the future.

A wealth of adult-child activities, projects, and outing ideas can be found in many books, some that were published in direct response to *Last Child in the Woods* and others that are classics well known to educators and experienced parents. Some of our favorites for caregivers and educators include *The Bumper Book of Nature* (Stephen Moss, 2010), *Childhood and Nature* (David Sobel, 2008), *Handbook of Nature Study* (Anna Botsford Comstock, 1911), *Keeping a Nature Journal: Discover a Whole New Way of Seeing the World around You* (Claire Walker Leslie and Charles Roth, 2003), *Mapmaking with Children: Sense of Place Education for the Elementary Years* (David Sobel, 1998), *Sharing Nature with Children* (Joseph Cornell, 1998), *Toad Cottages and Shooting Stars: Grandma's Bag of Tricks* (Sharon Lovejoy, 2010), and *Treehouses and Playhouses You Can Build* (David Stiles and Jeanie Stiles, 2006). Outstanding books written for children include *Crinkleroot's Guide to Walking in Wild Places* (Jim Arnosky, 1993), *Ecoart! Earth-Friendly Art and Craft Experiences for 3-to 9-Year-Olds* (Laurie Carlson, 1992), *The Kids Book of the Night Sky* (Ann Love and Jane Drake, 2004), *The Kids' Nature Book: 365 Indoor/Outdoor Activities and Experiences* (Susan Milord, 1996), *Kids' Easy-to-Create Wildlife Habitats: For Small Spaces in City-Suburbs-Countryside* (Emily Stetson, 2004), and *Planet Patrol: A Kids' Action Guide to Earth Care* (Marybeth Lorbiecki, 2005). The most useful books may be field guides—whether to birds, bugs, clouds, or rocks—that, ideally, are small enough to stash in your daypack and leave your hands free to hold a child's.

Despite our concerns about children's overexposure to electronic media, we also recommend judicious use of appropriate Web sites, podcasts, blogs, and cell phone applications that aim to draw families and others outdoors. A parent who visits the Nature Rocks Web site, for example, can enter her zip code to view an annotated map of nearby parks, farms, camps, and trails while planning an accessible adventure. A new family in a neighborhood can check the Kaboom! site to locate the closest playground—or learn how to improve or create place spaces if choices are few. To join a worldwide game of hide-and-seek, caregivers can learn about the necessary technology and techniques on geocaching sites. Interactive sites such as Project Budburst and National Wildlife Federation's "Wildlife Watch" invite adults and children to observe nature, share their discoveries, and connect with people pursuing similar interests. Innovative educators will also want to visit the North American Association for Environmental Education's Web site and state and local environmental education Web sites, where they can learn about conferences, initiatives, resources, and funding to support their latest ideas.

By far the most comprehensive and dynamic resource in the field, however, is the Children & Nature Network Web site. The site lives up to the organization's lofty mission: "to give every child in every community a wide range of opportunities to experience nature directly, reconnecting our children with nature's joys and lessons, its profound physical and mental bounty."[3] Practical assistance to parents and educators includes downloadable toolkits and action guides, frequent national and international news updates, policy analysis, and annual reports on the state of the movement. C&NN founders and advisers include leading social researchers, resulting in a site that is dedicated to reporting the latest original research and committed to applying the most promising findings to the task at hand.

More research and deeper reflection on the vital questions of why, how, when, and where to reconnect children and nature are urgently needed. Some of the approaches to which we now earnestly adhere may prove to be ineffectual or even to distance us from our goals. Carson, frustrated by contemporary educators' overemphasis on knowledge acquisition, once asserted, "It is not half so important to *know* as to *feel*."[4] Today's children suffer from no shortage of emotional stimulation, at least from Xboxes, Wii consoles, and similar virtual sources. In our culture, too many children are not just sedentary but tethered to an unnatural world. We argue that what our youth need most, more than to know or to feel, is to do. As we read and reread the selections in this volume, our conviction grew that the mere act of spending time with a child in the wind and sun, beside a quiet stream or ankle-deep in pounding surf, has inestimable value. We trust that you will heed these writers' calls, whether voiced in the form of an admonition, plea, or benediction: get outside.

Notes

1. Rachel Carson, "Design for Nature Writing," in Linda Lear, ed., *Lost Woods: The Discovered Writings of Rachel Carson* (Boston: Beacon Press, 1998), 94.

2. Richard Louv, *Last Child in the Woods: Saving Our Children from Nature-Deficit Disorder* (Chapel Hill, NC: Algonquin Books, 2008), 359.

3. Available online at http://www.childrenandnature.org/about/contact.

4. Rachel Carson, *The Sense of Wonder* (New York: HarperCollins, 1998), 56.

Credits

Awiakta, Marilou. "Motheroot." *Selu: Seeking the Corn-Mother's Wisdom*. Golden, CO: Fulcrum, 1993. Copyright © Marilou Awiakta. Used with permission of Fulcrum Publishing.

Bass, Rick. "The Farm." From Scott Slovic, ed., *Getting Over the Color Green: Contemporary Environmental Literature of the Southwest*. Tucson: University of Arizona Press, 2001. Copyright © 1999 Rick Bass. Used with permission of the author.

Branch, Michael P. "My Child's First Garden." *Hawk and Handsaw: The Journal of Creative Sustainability* (2008). Copyright © Michael Branch. Used with permission of the author.

Cramer, Jeffrey S. "The Toad Not Taken." Excerpted and adapted from "Praying for Mantises," *Boston Parents Paper* (1995); "The Twenty-Dollar Starling," *Snowy Egret* (1997); "The Toad Not Taken," *Endangerspeak* (2000); "A Different Education," *Paths of Learning*. Copyright © Jeffrey Cramer. Used with permission of the author and the publishers.

DeBaise, Janine. "Of the Fittest." *Hawk and Handsaw: The Journal of Creative Sustainability* (2010). Copyright © Janine DeBaise. Used with permission of the author.

Lopez, Barry. "Children in the Woods." *Crossing Open Ground*. New York: Scribner's, 1988. Copyright © 1982 Barry Holstun Lopez. Used with permission of the author.

Louv, Richard. "Fathers and Sons." Excerpted and adapted from two of his earlier books: *Childhood's Future* (New York: Anchor Books, 1993), and *Fatherlove* (New York: Pocket Books, 1994). Copyright © 2010 Richard Louv. Used with permission of the author.

Lyons, Stephen J. "Moving through the Landscape of Healing." *Landscape of the Heart: Writings on Daughters and Journeys*. Pullman:

Washington State University Press, 1996. Copyright © Stephen Lyons. Used with permission of Washington State University Press.

Masumoto, David Mas. "Belonging on the Land." In Alison Deming and Lauret Savoy, eds., *Colors of Nature: Culture, Identity, and the Natural World*. Minneapolis: Milkweed, 2002. Copyright © David Mas Masumoto. Used with permission of the author.

Moore, Kathleen Dean. "A Field Guide to Western Birds." *Holdfast*. New York: Lyons Press, 1999. Copyright © Kathleen Dean Moore. Used with permission of the Lyons Press.

Peterson, Brenda. "Animal Allies." *Orion* (1993) and *Singing to the Sound: Visions of Nature, Animals, and Spirit*. Troutdale, OR: NewSage Press, 2000. Copyright © Brenda Peterson. Used with permission of the author.

Peterson, Brenda. "Grandmother, Grizzlies, and God." *Build Me an Ark: A Life with Animals*. New York: Norton, 2001. Copyright © Brenda Peterson. Used with permission of W. W. Norton & Company.

Pyle, Robert Michael. "Parents without Children: Confessions of a Favorite Uncle." Revised from "Parents without Children," *Orion* (1995). Copyright © Robert Michael Pyle. Used with permission of the author.

Ray, Janisse. "Raising Silas." *Wild Card Quilt: Taking a Chance on Home*. Minneapolis: Milkweed, 2003. Copyright © Janisse Ray. Used with permission of the author and Milkweed Editions.

Sanders, Scott Russell. "Mountain Music I." *Hunting for Hope: A Father's Journeys*. Boston: Beacon, 1998. Copyright © Scott Russell Sanders. Used with permission of Beacon Press.

Shay, Michael. "We Are Distracted." In Judith and Mary Paumier Jones, eds., *In Short: A Collection of Brief Creative Nonfiction*. New York: Norton, 1996. Copyright © Michael Shay. Used with permission of the author.

Steingraber, Sandra. "The Big Talk." *Orion*. (2008). Copyright © Sandra Steingraber. Used with permission of the author.

Tamez-Hrabovsky, Margo. "On Being 'Indian,' Unsilent, and Contaminated along the U.S.-Mexico Border." Revised from "Toxic Talk and a Living Language: Being Indian, Unsilent and Contaminated." *The Los Angeles Review* (2004). Copyright © Margo Tamez. Used with permission of the author.

Trimble, Stephen. 2008. "The Prophets of Place." *Bargaining for Eden: The Fight for the Last Open Spaces in America*. Berkeley: University of

About the Contributors

Rick Bass is a writer and activist living in the Yaak Valley of northwest Montana. He is the acclaimed author of poetry, fiction, and nonfiction, including *Brown Dog of the Yaak: Essays on Art and Activism* (1999), *The Ninemile Wolves* (2003), and *The Wild Marsh: Four Seasons at Home in Montana* (2009).

Michael P. Branch is Professor of Literature and Environment at the University of Nevada, Reno, where he teaches American literature and environmental studies. He is a cofounder and past president of the Association for the Study of Literature and Environment (ASLE), and his books include *John Muir's Last Journey: South to the Amazon and East to Africa* and *Reading the Roots: American Nature Writing before Walden*.

James Bruchac is a storyteller, wilderness skills instructor, animal tracker, and founder and director of the Ndakinna Education Center in Greenfield Center, New York. He has written celebrated picture books with his father, Joseph Bruchac III, including *Raccoon's Last Race* (2004) and *The Girl Who Helped Thunder and Other Native American Tales* (2008).

Joseph Bruchac III is a poet, storyteller, naturalist, and author of over 70 books for children and adults, including a picture book, *Rachel Carson: Preserving a Sense of Wonder* (2004) and an autobiography, *Bowman's Store: A Journey to Myself* (2001). Bruchac often writes about his Abenaki ancestors and the Adirondack foothills where he grew up and still lives.

Susan A. Cohen is the editor of a major anthology of women's nature writing, *Shorewords: A Collection of American Women's Coastal Writings* (2003), and coeditor of *Wildbranch: An Anthology of Nature, Environmental, and Place-Based Writing* (2010). She teaches literature and writing at Anne Arundel Community College in Maryland.

Jeffrey S. Cramer is curator of collections at the Thoreau Institute at Walden Woods. He is the editor of the definitive *Walden: A Fully Annotated Edition* (2004), *I to Myself: An Annotated Selection from Journal of Henry D. Thoreau* (2007), and *The Maine Woods: A Fully Annotated Edition* (2009).

Janine DeBaise's poems and creative nonfiction have appeared in numerous journals, including *13th Moon, Minnesota Review,* and *Phoebe.* Her collection of poetry, *Of a Feather,* was published by Finishing Line Press. She teaches in the department of environmental studies at SUNY-College of Environmental Science and Forestry in Syracuse, New York.

Alison Hawthorne Deming is renowned for her lyrical poetry and prose. She finds inspiration in the sciences and the arts, as reflected in such works as *Science and Other Poems* (1994), *Temporary Homelands* (1994), *Writing the Sacred into the Real* (2001), and *Rope* (2009). She is coeditor, with Lauret Savoy, of *The Colors of Nature: Culture, Identity and the Natural World* (2002). Deming teaches creative writing at the University of Arizona.

Carolyn Finney, a professor at University of California, Berkeley, explores how difference, identity, representation, and power play significant roles in determining how people negotiate their daily lives in relation to the environment. Although Carolyn pursed an acting career for eleven years, a backpacking trip around the world changed her life. She earned a PhD in geography in 2006 and recently was selected to serve on the National Parks Advisory Board. Carolyn's first book, *Black Faces, White Spaces: African Americans and the Great Outdoors,* is forthcoming from the University of North Carolina Press.

Stephen R. Kellert is a pioneering researcher in the field of human relationships with wildlife and the environment. His empirical and theoretical investigations have led to groundbreaking publications such as *Children and Nature: Psychological, Sociocultural, and Evolutionary Investigations* (2002), and *Building for Life: Understanding and Designing the Human-Nature Connection* (2005). Kellert is Tweedy Ordway Professor of Social Ecology at the Yale School of Forestry and Environmental Studies.

Barry Lopez, winner of the 1996 National Book Award for *Arctic Dreams,* is the author of *Crossing Open Ground* (1988), *About This Life: Journeys on the Threshold of Memory* (1999), *Resistance* (2004), and other esteemed works of fiction and nonfiction. He is the coeditor of *Home Ground: Language for an American Landscape* (2010). Lopez lives and writes in the temperate rainforests of western Oregon.

Richard Louv was the 2008 recipient of the Audubon Medal for his writing and activism on behalf of reconnecting children with nature. His best-selling book, *Last Child in the Woods: Saving Our Children from Nature-Deficit Disorder*, sparked an international movement that Louv continues to lead through writing, speaking, and chairing the Children & Nature Network. An award-winning journalist, his many books include *The Nature Principle* (2011) and *Childhood's Future* (1992).

Stephen J. Lyons has written two meditative collections about exploring the American West, often with his young daughter—*Landscape of the Heart: Writings on Daughters and Journeys* (1996), and *A View from the Inland Northwest: Everyday Life in America* (2004). A recipient of an Illinois Arts Council fellowship for prose writing, his most recent book is *The 1,000 Year Flood: Destruction, Loss, Rescue, and Redemption along the Mississippi River* (2010).

David Mas Masumoto is a third-generation Japanese-American farmer who grows organic peaches, grapes, and raisins in California's Central Valley. His award-winning books include *Four Seasons in Five Senses: Things Worth Savoring* (2003), *Epitaph for a Peach* (1995), *Heirlooms: Letters from a Peach Farmer* (2007), and *Wisdom of the Last Farmer: Harvesting Legacies from the Land* (2009).

Kathleen Dean Moore is Distinguished Professor of Philosophy and University Writer Laureate at Oregon State University in Corvalis. She is the author or coeditor of ten books, including *Rachel Carson: Legacy and Challenge* (2008), *Holdfast: At Home in the Natural World* (2004), and *Wild Comfort: The Solace of Nature* (2010). Her writing accolades include the Sigurd Olson Writing Award and the Oregon Book Award.

Danyelle O'Hara is a consultant to foundations and nonprofit organizations working on community development, environmental conservation, land retention, and various other issues. She has worked for a range of international and U.S.-based nonprofit organizations, including Catholic Relief Services, the World Wildlife Fund, and the Conservation Fund. O'Hara is the author of numerous reports and publications on organizational effectiveness and learning; this is her first published essay. She lives in Oklahoma with her partner, Marc, and their children, Jonah and Marjanne.

Brenda Peterson is a novelist, poet, and essayist who teaches writing in Seattle, Washington. She is the author of *Build Me an Ark: A Life with Animals* (2002) and *Sightings: The Gray Whales' Mysterious Journey* (2003, with Linda Hogan). Her memoir, *I Want to Be Left Behind:*

Finding Rapture Here on Earth (2010), was named a "Top-Ten Best Non-Fiction Book of 2010" by the *Christian Science Monitor*.

Robert Michael Pyle is an ecologist, a founder of the Xerces Society for invertebrate conservation, and the author of esteemed books including *National Audubon Society Field Guide to North American Butterflies* (1981) and *Mariposa Road: The First Butterfly Big Year* (2010). *Sky Time in Gray's River: Living for Keeps in a Forgotten Place* (2008) was a finalist for the 2009 Orion Book Award.

Janisse Ray's first book, *Ecology of a Cracker Childhood* (2000), won the Southern Book Critic's Circle Award. It was followed by a second memoir about nature, community, and family in south Georgia, *Wild Card Quilt: Taking a Chance on Home* (2003), and by *Pinhook* (2005), an impassioned account of an imperiled Georgia swamp. Ray teaches writing at Chatham University and campaigns for the protection of the Altamaha River and other wild places.

Enrique Salmon is an anthropologist and ethnobiologist, studying his family's own Rarámuri culture and the role of plants in Rarámuri medicine and religion. He has published many essays and academic articles on his ethnobotany research and is completing a book on indigenous farmers' roles in maintaining biocultural diversity. Salmon is an assistant professor in ethnic studies at San Francisco State University.

Scott Russell Sanders is Distinguished Professor Emeritus at Indiana University and the author of celebrated essays, novels, and children's stories including *Meeting Trees*, a picture book about a father and son's walk in the woods. His essay collections include *Staying Put: Making a Home in the Restless World* (1994), *Hunting for Hope: A Father's Journeys* (1998), and *A Conservationist Manifest* (2009). He is the first writer to twice win the John Burroughs Award for Outstanding Nature Essay.

Chiori Santiago was a beloved writer who explored music, arts, culture, travel, nature, and the Japanese and Hispanic communities around San Francisco. A Japanese American, she was an editor of *Nikkei Heritage*, the magazine of the National Japanese American Historical Society, and of the membership magazine of the Oakland Museum of California, and she wrote the sensitive picture book, *Home to Medicine Mountain* (2002). She lived in Berkeley, California.

Lauret Savoy writes across threads of cultural identity to explore their shaping by relationship with and dislocation from the land. Of African American, European American, and Native American heritage, she is a professor of environmental studies and geology at Mount Holyoke College. Her books include *The Colors of Nature: Culture, Identity and the Natural World* (2002, coedited with Alison Hawthorne Deming), *Living with the Changing California Coast* (2005), and *Bedrock: Writers on the Wonders of Geology* (2006).

Michael Shay is a poet, creative writing teacher, and literary and performing arts specialist for the Wyoming Arts Council. His fiction and essays have appeared in *Northern Lights*, *High Plains Literary Review*, and other prominent periodicals, and he is coeditor of the anthology *Deep West: A Literary Tour of Wyoming* (2003).

Sandra Steingraber has been heralded as "the new Rachel Carson" for her poetic writing, incisive research, and tireless activism against environmental toxins. An ecologist as well as a poet and nonfiction writer, her exemplary works include *Having Faith: A Ecologist's Journey to Motherhood* (2001) and *Living Downstream: An Ecologist Looks at Cancer and the Environment* (1997). Steingraber currently is Scholar in Residence at Ithaca College.

Margo Tamez (Lipan Apache, Jumano Apache) is the author of *Naked Wanting* (2003) and *Raven Eye* (2007). Her current project focuses on the environmental, political, economic, and social history of Lipan Apaches, Tlaxcaltecas, Nahuatl, and Basque kinship networks of the indigenous borderlands of the U.S. Southwest and Mexican northern highlands.

Stephen Trimble, a writer, editor, and photographer, has published twenty-two books during thirty-five years of work with western landscapes and peoples. With Gary Paul Nabhan, he cowrote a seminal book about children's need for outdoor experiences, *The Geography of Childhood* (1995). Trimble's *Bargaining for Eden* won the 2008 Utah Book Award for nonfiction. He makes his home in Salt Lake City and in the red rock country of Torrey, Utah.

Michael Umphrey is a journalist, teacher, poet, photographer, director of Montana's Heritage Project, and author of *The Power of Community-Centered Education: Teaching as a Craft of Place* (2007). Umphrey writes and speaks often about civic engagement, writing, and place-based education.

Rick Van Noy teaches American and environmental literature and writing at Radford College in Virginia. He is the respected author of scholarly works such as *Surveying the Interior: Literary Cartographers and the Sense of Place* (2003) and personal reflections such as *A Natural Sense of Wonder: Connecting Kids with Nature through the Seasons* (2008).

Gretel Van Wieren teaches in the Department of Religious Studies at Michigan State University. Her interests lie at the intersection of religion, nature, and ethics. Van Wieren's work has appeared in *Worldviews*, *The Spirit of Sustainability*, *Perspectives*, and *Earth Letter*. She is an avid fly tyer and fly fisher, particularly on her home river, the Little Manistee, in northern Michigan. She has a PhD in religious studies from Yale University.